# Abstracts of Philadelphia County Pennsylvania Wills

## 1748-1763

F. Edward Wright

HERITAGE BOOKS
2007

**HERITAGE BOOKS**
*AN IMPRINT OF HERITAGE BOOKS, INC.*

**Books, CDs, and more—Worldwide**

For our listing of thousands of titles see our website
at
www.HeritageBooks.com

Published 2007 by
HERITAGE BOOKS, INC.
Publishing Division
65 East Main Street
Westminster, Maryland 21157-5026

Originally published 1997



International Standard Book Number: 978-1-58549-057-8

# INTRODUCTION

These wills were abstracted under the auspices of the Historical Society of Pennsylvania in the early 1900s. Copies of these abstracts were made available to various libraries in Pennsylvania and microfilm copies made by the Genealogical Society of Utah (LDS). Recently bound photostat copies of the abstracts were offered for sale by the Genealogical Society of Pennsylvania.

We extend our appreciation to the staffs of the Historical Society of Pennsylvania (1300 Locust Street, Philadelphia, PA 19107) and encourage use and support of its facilities and to the Genealogical Society of Pennsylvania whose collections are housed in the Historical Society Library. We also encourage membership in the Genealogical Society of Pennsylvania (address same as HSP).

F. Edward Wright
Westminster, Maryland
1995

# ABSTRACTS OF PHILADELPHIA COUNTY WILLS, 1748-1763

LANG, ALEXANDER. City of Philadelphia. Merchant. Nov. 21, 1748. Dec. 4, 1748. J.1.
Brothers: James, Hugh. Nephew: John Maxwell Nesbit. Exec: Conyham[?] & Gardner.
Witnesses: Peacock Bigger, Walter Shee.

EDGE, ANDREW. Northern Liberties, City of Philadelphia. Tanner. Proved Dec. 7, 1748. J.1.
Children: Susannah, Mary, Andrew. Son-in-Law: Richard Hall. Exec: Richard Hall, Robert Shewell.
Witnesses: Eben. Kinnersley, Jo. Beddome, Lewis Evans.

DUBREY, JOSEPH. Northern Liberties, City of Philadelphia. Yeoman. Nov. 11, 1748/9. Dec. 8, 1748. J.3.
Wife: Hannah. Child: William. Kinsmen: Jacob Dubrey, Junr., Samuel, John and William Bissal. Exec: Jacob Dubrey, Samuel Bissal, Oswald Peel.
Witnesses: George Dorland, Samuel Bissal.

GOATSCHALK, FREDRICK. Franconia, Co. of Philadelphia. Husbandman. Nov. 7, 1748/9. Dec. 8, 1748. J.4.
Wife: Ann Mary. Children: Agnes, Andrew, Elizabeth, Mary Ann. Son-in-Law: Johan Crout. Exec: Ann Mary Godtschalk, Youst Panncak.
Witnesses: William Tennes, William Nash.

SHUTE, THOMAS. City of Philadelphia. Yeoman. 8 mo. 4, 1748. Dec. 10, 1748. J.5.
Children: Christian, Joseph, William, Jacob, Isaac. Grandchildren: Elizabeth Hood, Elizabeth Milner, Martha Renshaw, Rebecca Mitchell. Sons-in-Law: Children of Samson Davis, William Davis. Great-Grandchildren: Rebecca Milener, Thomas Mitchell. Exec: Edward Warner, Joseph Fox, William Davis.
Witnesses: Samuel Jones, Benjamin Hooton, Alexander Seaton.

PENSILL, DOROTHY. Northern Liberties, City of Philadelphia. Widow. Sept. 9, 1748/9. Dec. 10, 1748. J.9.
Children: John Adam Galer. Exec: John Adam Galer.
Witnesses: Jacob Dubre, Thos. Hood, Junr., Andrew Walker.

LEDDRAFF, JOHANES. Salford, Co. of Philadelphia. Yeoman. Aug. 17, 1748/9. 12 xbris 1748. J.10.
Children: John, Modlin, Margaret, Jacob, Christian, Mary, Barbara. Son-in-Law: Jacob Graff. Exec: John Leadraff, Jacob Graff. Guardians: Andrew Zeigler, Jacob Shoomaker.
Witnesses: Robert Jones, Elizabeth Jones, Grace Jones (her mark).

WILLS, MICHAEL. Lower Merion, Co. of Philadelphia. Nov. 28, 1748/9. Dec. 13, 1748. J.11.
Children: Michael, Stephen, Rebecca, Thomas, Mary, Enomon, Joanna, Sarah, Sophia. Grandchild: Joanna Caldwell. Cousin: John Cuthbert. Son-in-Law: Owen Thomas. Exec: John Cuthbert, Michael Wills.
Witnesses: John Jordon, Nathan Thomas, James Much (his mark).

POOLE, LAWRENCE. White Marsh, Province of Penna. Malster. Nov. 5, 1748/9. Dec. 17, 1748. J.13.
Sarah, daughter of Mary Lewis of Nether Stowey, Great Britain. Exec: Anthony Morris [Brewer].
Witnesses: Joseph Crellins, Christopher Robins, Wilhelm Addheit.

COATS, SAMUEL. City of Philadelphia. Merchant. Sept. 1, 1748/9. Dec. 20, 1748. J.14.
Wife: Mary. Children: Thomas, Josiah, Margaret, Mary, Beulah, Alice. Brother-in-Law: John Langdale. Exec: Mary Coats.
Witnesses: Thomas Campbell, Jno. Reily.

NANNE, MARGARET. Germantown, Co. of Philadelphia. Widow. Nov 26, 1748/9. Dec. 20, 1748. J.16.
Nephews and Nieces: David and Thomas Owens, Margaret Thomas, Thamer Dunn. Friends: Henry Jones - four children, Edward, William, Thomas and Rees Peters [sons of Thomas Peters, decd.]. Exec: Thomas and Rees Peters.
Witnesses: Sarah Ashmead, John Ashmead, Edw. William.

RICHARD, JOHN FREDERICK. Hanover, Co. of Philadelphia. Feb. 26, 1747/8. Dec. 22, 1748. J.17.
Wife: Anna Maria. Children: Casper, Mathias. Grandchildren: Rebecca and George Sheyner. Exec: Anna Maria Richards, Mathias Richard.
Witnesses: Andrew Kepler, Jno. Campbell.

BRANSON, SARAH. City of Philadelphia. March 7, 1747. Dec. 23, 1748. J.18.
Husband: William Branson, merchant. Nephew and Niece: Wilcox Phillips, Rebecca Phillips. Cousin: Samuel Rhoads. Exec: Samuel Rhoads. Guardian: William Branson.
Witnesses: Samuel Kirke, Barnaby Barnes, Wm. Parsons.

EMLIN, CALEB. City of Philadelphia. Chair maker. 1 mo. 11, 1747/8. Dec. 23, 1748. J.20.
Brothers: George, Samuel, Joshua. Sisters: Mary Armut, Ann Miller, Sarah Creson. Nephews and Nieces: Samuel, George, Joseph and Hudson Emlin, Caleb and Joshua Creson, John and Hannah Miller, Hannah Logan, Sarah Emlin. Brother-in-Law: John Armit. Friends: Randal, Thomas and Sarah Crockson, Jos. Chatham. Exec: Samuel and Joshua Emlin, John Armit.
Witnesses: Obadiah Eldridge, William Attmore, Alexr. Seaton.

MORRIS, JOHN. Hilltown, Co. of Bucks, Penna. Dec. 1, 1748/9. Dec. 24, 1748. J.22.
Wife: Jean. Children: Mary, Elizabeth, Margaret, Juan, John. Grandchild: Lewis Morris. Exec: John Morris.
Witnesses: Moses Aron (his mark), Richard Williams, Benjamin Davis.

MAROLFF, RUDOLPH. City of Philadelphia. Proved Dec. 28, 1748. J.26.
Wife: Willhelmina. Children: ---. Exec. and Trustees: George Georges, Bernard Dotterer.
Witnesses: Johannes Werstler, Kasper Bowman.

CHRISTLER, LENARD. Franconia, Co. of Philadelphia. Husbandman. Dec. 8, 1748/9. Dec. 29, 1748. J.27.
Wife: Elissamaera. Child: Mary Barber. Exec: Johannes Haines, Frederick Zillener.
Witnesses: George Cressman, William Nash.

CAREY, HENRY. Abington, Co. of Philadelphia. Yeoman. 9 mo. 30, 1748/9. Dec. 31, 1748. J.29.
Children: Martha and others. Brother-in-Law: John Mac Micken. Exec: John Mac Micken, Robert McKee.
Witnesses: Thomas Fletcher, Elinor Fulton (her mark).

HOWARD, THOMAS. City of Philadelphia. Joyner. Dec. 24, 1748/9. Dec. 28, 1748. J.30.
Wife: Susanna. Children: John, Mary, Joanna. Exec: John Howard. Witnesses: Edmond Skinner, Jno. Reily.

KNIGHT, THOMAS. Cheltenham, Co. of Philadelphia. Husbandman. Feb. 7, 1746/7. Jan. 4, 1748. J.33.
William, heir of Thomas. Child: William. Grandson: Thomas Knight. Trustees and Exec: Richard Mathers, Anthony Williams, Isaac Clever. Witnesses: Hans Wolfaker, Sarah Knight, Thos. Rose.

AUSBACH, BALTHASER. Tulpehocken, Co. of Lancaster, Penna. Sept. 5, 1744/5. Jan. 3, 1748. J.34.
Wife: Anna Maria. Children: Peter, John, Maria Barbara, Catrina and Leonard. Grandchildren: John Jacob, John, George, Anna Margrad Ausbach. Exec: Anna Maria Ausbach. Witnesses: Peter Klob, Adam Liverbach, Hermanus Walborn, Adam Lifenback.

EACKER, ANDREW. Whitpain, Co. of Philadelphia. Mason. Dec. 28, 1748/9. Jan. 9, 1748. J.36.
Children: Cathrin, Baltest and Margaret. Exec: Sebastian Miller, John Moch.
Witnesses: Jacob Levering, Andrew Hissler, Garrett Levering.

MILLER, GEORGE. City of Philadelphia. Vintner. Dec. 29, 1748/9. Jan. 16, 1748. J.37.
Child: Thomas. Housekeeper: Mary Lokey. Friends: Mrs. Dollison, wife of Captain Dollison, Patrick Brennon, Sarah Reily, Richard Crane. Exec: William Blair.
Witnesses: Mary Bell (her mark), Jno. Reily.

CARTER, MARY. City of Philadelphia. Widow. June 22, 1746/7. Jan. 16, 1748. J.39.
Children: Howell Sutton and Mary, wife of John Morris.
Grandchildren: William, Mary and John Morris. Son-in-Law: John Morris. Friends: James and Israel Pemberton, Junr., William Logan, Michael Lightfoot, Daniel Stanton. Exec: John Morris and wife Mary. Witnesses: Peter Stretch, C. Brockden, Owen Jones.
Codicil: Nov. 28, 1746/7.
Heirs of Howell Sutton Carter. Grandchild: Joseph Morris. Son-in-Law: John Morris. Friends: Israel Pemberton, Senr., Israel

Pemberton, Junr., James Pemberton, John and Charles Pemberton, William, Hannah and James Logan, Junior.
Witnesses: C. Brockden, Owen Jones.
Codicil: Nov. 20, 1747/8.
Mary Carter.
Witnesses: Owen Jones, Joseph King.

EMERSON, CALEB. City of Philadelphia. July 16, 1748/9. Jan. 16, 1748. J.43.
Child: Joshua. Son-in-Law: William McIlvaine. Exec: William McIlvaine.
Witnesses: Tho. Coombe, David McIlvaine, Roby. Greenway.

UNGER, JOHN. City of Philadelphia. Labourer. Jan. 6, 1748/9. Jan. 18, 1748. J.45.
Wife: Margaret. Children: Jacob, Philip, Christian, Mary and Barbara. Exec: David Clark.
Witnesses: John Freeman, Katey Harteen (her mark), John Green.

WILSON, GEORGE. City of Philadelphia. Joyner. Jan. 10, 1748/9. Jan. 20, 1748. J.46.
Wife: Mary. Children: James, Mary, Ann, William, Joseph, Hannah and George. Exec: Mary Wilson, Edward Catherel, Jonathan Zane.
Witnesses: Sol. Fussell, Arthur Forster, Benj. Dawson.

WILLIAMS, CATHARINE. Montgomery, Co. of Philadelphia. Widow. 10 mo. 7, 1745/6. Jan. 21, 1748. J. 48.
Daughter-in-Law [daughter?]: Anne Foulke. Sons-in-Law [sons?]: William Williams, Theopholous Williams. Grandchildren: Edward, David, Morris, and William Morris, Catherine Eaton and Alce Clark. Nieces and Nephews: Margaret, Sarah, Catherine and Mary Morgan, Jane and Margaret George, Jane and John Jones, Evan Robert, Griffith Hugh. Cousins: David Hugh and wife Jane, David, Obadiah and Zachariah Edwards, Mary wife of Peter Evans, Jesse George, Arden Davis and his sisters - Mary, Catharine and Hannah, Evan, John, Cadwalader, Rowland and Margaret Evans, children of John Jones. Great Grandchild: Catherine Case. Friends Meeting at Gwynedd, poor of Gwynedd. Friends: John Davis and wife, Arne Roberts, Elizabeth and Catherine Ellis, William Hart, Thomas David, Elizabeth William. Exec: John Jones. Overseers: Owen Evan, John Jones.

Witnesses: Garret Peters, John Roberts, Awbry Roberts.

FISHER, JOHN. Heidleberg, Co. of Lancaster, Penna. Jan. 15, 1749/50. Jan. 23, 1748. J.51.
Child: Elizabeth. Exec: William Fisher, Philip Fillsmeyer, William Reasor.
Witnesses: Adam Spone, Frederick Gerhard.

BRODGATE, THOMAS. City of Philadelphia. Dec. 20, 1748/9. Feb. 2, 1748. J.52.
Daughters: Sarah Green and Mary Snow. Grandchildren: Sarah Garrigues, John and Elizabeth Snow, William and Elizabeth Green.
Exec: Sarah Green, Mary Snow.
Witnesses: Edw. Shippen, Owen Jones, Joseph Shippen, Junr.

GRAY, GEORGE. Lower Ferry Kingsess, Co. of Philadelphia. Yeoman. June 29, 1748. Feb. 2, 1748/9. J.54.
Wife: Mary. Brothers: Samuel and Joseph. Son George. Daughter: Mary James. Sons-in-Law: James Couttas [Coultas?] and Elizabeth [his wife], Thomas James. Exec: Mary and George Gray.
Witnesses: Sarah James, Neels Jonason, Roby Greenway.

SADLER, CONRAD. Exeter, Co. of Philadelphia. Jan. 7, 1748/9. Feb. 3, 1748. J.56.
Wife: Mary. Children: Philip and others. Exec: Mary Sadler, Robert Partison.
Witnesses: William Boone, Michael Waren, George Lotz.

DAVIES, BADAM, Merian, Co. of Philadelphia. Sawer. Aug. 18, 1747/8. Feb. 6, 1748. J.57.
Brothers: Roger, Walter, Joseph and his children. Cousins: Hugh, John, Ruth and Envets Hughes. St. Davids Church, Radnor. Friends: Ann, Martha and Mary Bevan, Richard Bevan, Junr., William Owen.
Exec: Richard Bevan, John Hughes.
Witnesses: Peter Jones, Richard Sutton, Richard Boran, Jo. Hughes, Robert Jones, David Harry, Junr.

LLOYD, ELIZABETH. City of Philadelphia. Widow. Dec. 2, 1748/9. Feb. 6, 1748. J.59.
Children: Evan, Elizabeth and Jane. Daughter-in-Law: Elen.
Grandchild: Sarah Lloyd. Exec: Evan Lloyd.

Witnesses: G. Lewellen, Wm. Thomas, David Harry, Junr.

HUNTSBERGER, JACOB. Francony, Co. of Philadelphia. Jan. 9, 1748/9. Feb. 10, 1748. J.60.
Wife: Susanna. Children: Abraham, Isaac, Barbara and two other daughters. Exec: Susanna and Abraham Huntsberger.
Witnesses: Jacob Funck, Henry Klemmer (his mark).

WATKINS, HESTER. City of Philadelphia. Spinster. Proved Feb. 14, 1748. J.62.
Children: Joseph and June Loxley. Exec: Benjamin Loxley.
Witnesses: William Henderson, Richard Bailey, David Evans (his mark).

BAMBERGER, ARNOLD. Northern Liberties, Co. of Philadelphia. Yeoman. Jan. 17, 1748/9. Feb. 15, 1748. J.63.
Children: Rudolph, Martin and Elizabeth Knerr. Exec: Rudolph Bamberger.
Witnesses: William Shute, John Adam Galer, Chrisn. Lehman.

FREYER, JOHN JOST. Hannover, Co. of Philadelphia. Farmer. Feb. 6, 1749/50. Feb. 20, 1748. J.65.
Wife: Anna Mary. Children: Hanry, Elizabeth, Houchen, Cathain and Schmiden. Exec: Philip Hahn, George PflatzGraff.
Witnesses: Zacharias Zeickler, Henry Grobb.

MOSS, ABRAHAM. City of Philadelphia. Yeoman. 11 mo. 20, 1748/9. Feb. 14, 1748. J.66.
Children: Richard, Isaac, Rebecca and Hope. Exec: John Stuart of Alloways Creek, North Jersey, Isaac Moss.
Witnesses: Benjamin Kendall, Joseph Ogden, Alexr. Seaton [witnessed in Salem, New Jersey].

FECK, PETER. Heidleberg, Co. of Lancaster, Penna. Feb. 4, 1741/2. Feb. 20, 1748. J.68.
Wife: Anna Maria. Children: John Linhard, Peter, Anna Catrina Ruth, Ann Eve Weisor, Evely, Elizabeth Sheffer and Maria. Exec: Anna Maria and John Linhard Feck.
Witnesses: George Meintzer, John Peter Krieger.

PASTORIES, SAMUEL. Horsham, Co. of Philadelphia. Feb. 5, 1748/9. Feb. 22, 1748. J.70.
Wife: Leagh. Father: William. Mother: Sara. Child: William. Uncle: John Boutcher. Exec: Samuel and John Boutcher. Trustees: Enoch Morgane, John Williams.
Witnesses: David Jones, John Benson, Samuel Meanon (his mark), William McDowell.

CARPENTER, SAMUEL. City of Philadelphia. Gentleman. 9 mo. 11, 1748/9. March 1, 1748. J.72.
Wife: Hannah. Children: Preston, Thomas, Rachel and Hannah. Grandchildren: Samuel and Thomas Carpenter. Exec: Hannah Carpenter.
Witnesses: Samuel Preston, --- Moore, Joseph Coleman, Jno. Reily.

JOHNSON, FRANCIS. City of Philadelphia. Sept. 26, 1748/9. March 1, 1748. J.74.
Wife: Ann. Friend and Exec: Henry Sparks.
Witnesses: John Fleming, Jno. Reily.

CHAPMAN, WILLIAM. City of Philadelphia. April 14, 1746/7. March 3, 1748. J.75.
Exec. and Friend: Lavinia Greenman.
Witnesses: John Fullerton, Randall Dicas, John Long.

WRIGHT, RICHARD JUNR. Kensington, Co. of Philadelphia. Shipwright. Jan. 9, 1748/9. March 8, 1748. J.75.
Wife: Mary. Children: George, Mary, Lydia and Sarah. Father: Richard Wright of Burlington. Brothers-in-Law: Warwick and Abram Coats. Exec: Mary Wright, Warwick and Abram Coats. Trustees: Richard Wright, John Coats, Thomas Penrose.
Witnesses: John Coats, Junr., Sarah Coats, Roby. Greenway.

BOWER, HANS. Colebrookdale, Co. of Philadelphia. Yeoman. Oct. 27, 1748/9. March 9, 1748. J.77.
Wife: Anne. Children: Michael, Abraham, Samuel, Barbara and Susannah. Grandchildren: Children of son Hans dec'd. and his widow. Exec: Samuel Bower, George Shultze.
Witnesses: John Conrad, Bob George Shultze, Christopher Sholtze.

HAYSER, JOHN. Shoeppak, Co. of Philadelphia. Weaver. Jan. 12, 1748/9. March 8, 1748. J.79.
Wife: Doroty. Children: Andreas, Valentine, Anna Mary, Christena, Mary Sallinas, Elizabeth and Barbara. Exec: Dorrity and Valentine Hayser.
Witnesses: Lodwig Horning, Richard Jacob, Leonard Vanfeaissen.

BENNET, WILLIAM. City of Philadelphia. Taylor. Jan. 31, 1749/50. March 13, 1748. J.81.
Wife: Mary. Exec: Mary Bennet.
Witnesses: Lawrence Anderson, Samuel Stevenson, Alexr. Seaton.

COX, JOHN. City of Philadelphia. Brickmaker. Feb. 10, 1748/9. March 14, 1748. J.82.
Wife: Sarah. Exec: Sarah Cox.
Witnesses: Thos. Williams, Daniel Duprey, Arthur Foster.

DAVIS, JAMES. City of Philadelphia. House carpenter. March 10, 1748/9. March 15, 1748. J.83.
Wife: Rachel. Children: James and Sarah. Exec: Rachel Davis, Isaac Zane.
Witnesses: William Davis, Nehemiah Allen, Jno. Reily.

MAYER, JACOB. New Hannover, Co. of Philadelphia. Husbandman. Feb. 25, 1749/50. March 18, 1748. J.85.
Wife: Elizabeda. Children: Jacob and others. Exec: Elizabeda Mayer, Henry Krabs.
Witnesses: Jacob Meyer, Conrad Dudderar.

KENARD, JOHN. Moreland, Co. of Philadelphia. Yeoman. Feb. 20, 1748/9. March 22, 1748. J.86.
Wife: Margaret. Children: Samuel, Joseph, Thomas, Mary Fry, John and Anthony. Exec: John and Anthony Kenard.
Witnesses: Sarah Mullen (her mark), Mary Hart (her mark), Steph. Jenkins.

KNAUS, PETER. Worcester, Co. of Philadelphia. Cooper. March 5, 1747/8. March 25, 1748. J.88.
Wife: Margaret. Children: William, Peter, Jacob, Joseph, Benjamin, Margarett, Christian, Henry and Philip. Exec: Margaret Knaus, Alick McCormick.

Witnesses: Leonard Spert (his mark), Henry Dewees, Peter Spycker.

DUBOY, ABRAHAM. City of Philadelphia. March 20, 1748/9. March 29, 1748. J.89.
Brother-in-Law: Henrick Reinhart. Poor of the Congregation.
Friends: Alexander Mackshall, Peter Baker, John Frick. Exec: Peter Grauling.
Witnesses: Christopher Saur, George Baltzer Gantz.

JONES, JOHN. City of Philadelphia. Innholder. March 25, 1748/9. March 30, 1748. J.90.
Wife: Sarah. Sons-in-Law: John Price and William Price. Daughter-in-Law: Jane Price. Friend: Richard Ellis. Exec: Sarah Jones, John Thomas.
Witnesses: Evan Jones, Amos Evans, George Owen.

THOMAS, ABEL. Merion, Co. of Philadelphia. Yeoman. 11 mo. 19, 1748/9. April 1, 1749. J.91.
Children: John, Richard, Sarah Moore, Moses, Jane Owen, Margaret Rhoades and Ellen Shoemaker. Grandchildren: John and Elizabeth Thomas. Exec: John Thomas. Trustees: Robert Evans, Hugh Evans, Robert Roberts, Edw. Williams.
Witnesses: John Kite, John Roberts, Edw. Williams.

NAYLOR, RICHARD. Mountgomery, Co. of Philadelphia. Yeoman. 1 mo. 7, 1748/9. April 1, 1749. J.93.
Mother: Jane. Brothers: Joseph, John Foreman and John Williams. Sisters: Mary Priscilla, Hannah and Margaret. Brother-in-Law: John Williams. Nephew: John Naylor. Friend: Sarah Shoemaker. Exec: John Williams, Mary Naylor. Trustees: John Roberts, Isaac Jones.
Witnesses: Joseph Ambler, Jno. Sulivan, Samuel Thomas.

CHANNEL, SAMUEL. Germantown, Co. of Philadelphia. Cooper. Dec. 27, 1748/9. April 3, 1749. J.95.
Wife: Catherine. Exec: Catherine Channel, Peter Evans.
Witnesses: Thos. Yorke, John Shepherd, Sarah Shepherd.

CAPLER, MARTIN. Bathel, Co. of Lancaster, Pa. Yeoman. March 1, 1748/9. April 3, 1749. J.96.
Wife: Marialis. Children: Abraham, Cretle, Esely [and four others by first wife]. Exec: Casper Schnebly, Henry Dubs.

Witnesses: Harman Miller (his mark), Nicholas Youngblood, Barnard Rough, Jacob Meily, young Martin Capler (his mark), Leonard Capler (his mark).

BAILERD, VINCENTS. Germantown, Co. of Philadelphia. Husbandman. March 27, 1749/50. April 4, 1749. J.97.
Wife: Anne Barbara. Child: Anne Katherine [in Switserland, Europe]. Exec: Anne Barbara and Anne Katherine Bailerd.
Witnesses: Gottfried Lehman, Jacob Sneider, Christ. Lehman.

HOVEY [Houey?'], JOSEPH. Abington, Co. of Philadelphia. Feb. 13, 1748/9. April 5, 1749. J.98.
Wife: Eleanor. Children: Rachel, Morgan, Samuel, Agnes and Margaret. Brother: John. Exec: Eleanor and John Hovey.
Witnesses: Richard Treat, William Gibb, Simon Thomas.

LEAMAN, CHRISTIAN. Salford, Co. of Philadelphia. Husbandman. Oct. 11, 1748/9. April 29, 1749. J.100.
Wife: Ann Margaret. Children: John, Susannah, Anne, George, Han Adam, Dority, Jacob and Ludwig. Exec: Daniel Hester, Jacob Husse.
Witnesses: Jacob Arnt, Philip Gable, William Nash.

COATS, WILLIAM JUNR. City of Philadelphia. Brickmaker. Feb. 26, 1746/7. April 7, 1749. J.101.
Wife: Mary. Father: William Coats. Children: William and Mary. Exec: Thomas Say, John Coats, Junr.
Witnesses: William Wallace, Stephen Wooley.

SHIERS, GEORGE. City of Philadelphia. Merchant. 9 mo. 21, 1748/9. April 10, 1749. J.103.
Wife: Hannah. Child: Deborah. Kinsman. Daniel Durborow. Exec: Hannah Shires, Daniel Durborow.
Witnesses: Joseph Trotter, William Trotter, Jno. Reily.

PHILPOTT, WILLIAM. Bristol, Co. of Philadelphia. Currier. Aug. 25, 1740/1. April 21, 1749. J.104.
Wife: Mary. Children: Rachel Forster, Sarah Blackledge, William, John and Phebe. Granddaughter: Mary Forster. Exec: Mary, John and William Philpott.
Witnesses: Hannah Street, John Aikine, M. Davies.

BROWN, PETER. City of Philadelphia. Shipwright. 2 mo. 17, 1749/50. April 24, 1749. J.107.
Wife: Sarah. Children: Nathaniel, William, John and Mary. Exec: Sarah Brown, Thomas Say.
Witnesses: Thomas Clifford, George Bradley, Alexr. Seaton.

KEPLINGER, MARTIN. McCalls Manor, Co. of Philadelphia. Nov. 22, 1748/9. April 27, 1749. J. 109.
Wife: Catharine. Children: John George, and five other sons and one daughter. Exec: Peter Conradt, Mathias Hollenback.
Witnesses: Adam Wartman, Johan Jacob Loeser.

KRUNZEN, MICHAEL. New Hanover, Co. of Philadelphia. Jan. 15, 1749/50. April 27, 1749. J.111.
Wife: Barbara. Children: Stephanus and three daughters. Exec: Michael Swinhart, Mathias Fonebach.
Witnesses: Mattes Nuger, Peter Specht, William Reiffschneyder.

KAPP, FREDERICK. Heidleberg, Co. of Lancaster, Penna. March 27, 1749/50. April 28, 1749. J.112.
Wife: Eva Maria. Children: John Frederick, John George and George Michael. Exec: Leonhard Hallstein, Nicholas Swingle. Guardians: Adam Lesh, Andrew Saltsgerer.
Witnesses: Adam Lesh (his mark), John Nichles Schwingle.

SWINTON, ISAAC. City of Philadelphia. Mariner. Feb. 19, 1745/6. April 29, 1749. J.113.
Friend and Exec: Elizabeth Murphy.
Witnesses: John Ellis, John Morgan.

WOODS, ANN. City of Philadelphia. Widow. Sept. 13, 1748/9. May 1, 1749. J.114.
Children: Elizabeth, Ann and Abram Hooper. Grandchildren: Ann Snowks and John Saunders. Exec: Elizabeth Tomlinson, Ann Saunders.
Witnesses: Hannah Pricket, John Fleming, Paul Isaac Voto.

EATON, JOSEPH Mount Gomezy, Co. of Philadelphia. Yeoman. April 3, 1747/8. May 3, 1749. J.116.
Wife: Uriah. Children: John, Mary Williams, Joseph, Joan Goodwin, Edward, Sarah Jones, David, Jacob, Isaac and Hannah. Friends:

Thomas and Charles Humphrey. Exec: Uriah [wife] and Isaac Eaton. Trustees: Thomas Gill, Simon Butler.
Witnesses: Isaac James, Daniel Jones, Rebecca Butler.

PUGH, HUGH. Vincent, Co. of Chester, Penna. Yeoman. Feb. 16, 1748/9. May 10, 1749. J.119.
Wife: Mary. Children: Anne Rogers, Evan, Mary, Daniel, Margaret, Elizabeth, Hannah and Rachel. Exec: Mary and Evan Pugh.
Witnesses: John, James and Mordecai Roberts, John Thomas.

KERN, NICHOLAS. Bucks Co., near Lehigh. Dec. 28, 1748/9. May 11, 1749. J.120.
Wife: Maria Margaretha. Children: Lorents, Henry, Frederick, Cornelia, William, Nicholas, John, George and Maria Barbara. Exec. and Guardians: Maria Margaretha Kern, Jacob Fozber.
Witnesses: J. Ch. Seybert, Jacob Hefelfinger (his mark), Jacob Ferbez, Joh Nicholas Sneider.

CRISPIN, THOMAS. Lower Dublin, Co. of Philadelphia. Yeoman. April 30, 1749/50. May 13, 1749. J.121.
Father-in-Law: Joseph Ashton. Children: Silas, Thomas and Joseph. Exec: Joseph Ashton, Silas Crispin.
Witnesses: Jacob Hall, John Crows, Nicholas Randel (his mark).

LEWIS, FRANCIS. Rockhill, Co. of Bucks, Penna. Yeoman. April 13, 1749/50. May 16, 1749. J.123.
Wife: Abigal. Children: Elizabeth, Jacob and Francis. Friend: Andrew Jugler. Exec: Walter McCool, Isaak Colp.
Witnesses: John Finley, Thomas Bountin, Richard Graham.

GEORGE, EDWARD. Blockley, Co. of Philadelphia. Yeoman. 3 mo. 5, 1747/8. May 17, 1749. J.124.
Mother: ---. Brothers: David, George, Richard and Evan. Sisters: Jane Owens, Katherine Eveson. Cousin: Mary Hutton. Exec: David, George and Richard George.
Witnesses: Thomas Winne, Ed. William.

HERPIN, ABRAHAM. Olyin, Co. of Philadelphia. Yeoman. Nov. 4, 1747/8. May 24, 1748. J.126.
Children: Mary Elizabeth Reser and Philip. Brother and Exec: Jonathan Herpin.

Witnesses: Jacob Yonker, Jacob Sedzer, Samuel Guldin.

PARREY, THOMAS. Mooreland, Co. of Philadelphia. Yeoman. 7 mo. 22, 1748/9. May 29, 1749. J.127.
Wife: Jane. Children: Stephen, Edward, David, Mary, Jacob, Isaac, Thomas, Philip and John. Exec: Jane, John and Stephen Parrey.
Witnesses: Elizabeth Walton, Grace Michener, Steph. Jenkins.

BUTTERFOSS, MATTHIAS. Germantown, Co. of Philadelphia. Weaver. May 17, 1749/50. June 3, 1749. J.128.
Wife: Magdalene. Children: Frederick, Barbara, Magdalene and Michael. Exec: Magdalene Butterfuss, Jacob Swank.
Witnesses: George Rex, John Tibbin, John Barge.

KRESMAN, HENRY. Upper Sancan, Co. of Bucks. Yeoman. Dec. 24, 1748/9. June 10, 1749. J.130.
Wife: Catherine. Nephews: Peter Kresman, Nicholas Kresman and Peter Wilhalm. Exec: Catherine Kresman, William Morry.
Witnesses: Thomas Owen, Anthony Become.

PALMER, ANTHONY. Kensington, Co. of Philadelphia. May 29, 1749/50. June 10, 1749. J.131.
Wife: Katharine. Daughters: Thomasine Keith and Elizabeth. Grandchildren: Samuel Palmer and Eliner Berkeley. Exec: Thomasine Keith, Elizabeth Palmer, Charles West.
Witnesses: Edward Pare, Margaret Edwards.

KINSING, CHRISTIAN. Bristol, Co. of Philadelphia. May 7, 1749/50. June 14, 1749. J.133.
Children: Christina Ruchen and Peter. Exec: Christina Ruchen, John Zachary, Immanuel Kaleglesser.
Witnesses: Adam Haas, Casper Meyer.

ROBERTS, THOMAS. Abington, Co. of Philadelphia. Yeoman. March 6, 1748/9. July 7, 1749. J.134.
Wife: Elizabeth. Child: Prissilla. Grandchildren: Children of Evan Roberts. Father-in-Law: John Tyson. Brother: Evan. Exec: Elizabeth Roberts, John Tyson.
Witnesses: Steph. Jenkins, William Jenkins, Robert Nuftin.

KNOODLE, FREDERICK. Gwynedd, Co. of Philadelphia. July 2, 1749/50. July 8, 1749. J.135.
Wife: Anna Maria. Children: George, Jacob, John Frederick, Anna Maria, Michael and Cunrad. Exec: Anna Maria Knoodle, Michael Kline. Trustees: William and Edward Foulke.
Witnesses: Yost Dever, William Foulke, Rowd. Evans.

SHARP, JUDETH. Bristol, Co. of Philadelphia. Widow. 2 mo. 6, 1748/9. July 8, 1749. J.137.
Child: Thomas Potts. Daughter-in-Law: Susanna Potts. Grandchildren: Hannah, John, Rachel, Lydia, Rebecca and Jasper Potts. Exec: Thomas Potts, Thomas, Junr. and John Roberts.
Witnesses: John Rose, Thos. Rose, Marget Rose (her mark).
Codicil.
Witnesses: Mary Hellings, Thos. Rose.

POSTETHWAITE, JOHN. Conestogoe, Co. of Lancaster, Penna. Feb. 22, 1748/9. July 10, 1749. J.139.
Wife: Mary. Children: Susanna, John, Samuel, Catherine, William, Edmund, Richard. Son-in-Law: Isaac Baker. Friend: Sarah Cartlidge. Exec: Thomas Cookson, George Smith.
Witnesses: Edward Taylor, Jacob Shonk, Jno. Love.

BICKLEY, SAMUEL. City of Philadelphia. May 15, 1749/50. June 17, 1749. J.143.
Signed and proved at New Castle, Delaware. Wife: Margret. Children: Abraham, William and Mary. Exec: James Polegreen, Margret and Abraham Bickley.
Witnesses: Jno. Finney, Gideon Griffith, David Finney.

HANNIS, JOHN. Passyunk, Co. of Philadelphia. Merchant. May 23, 1744/5. July 16, 1749. J.145.
Brother: Andrew and wife Sarah. Nephews and Nieces: Andrew and John Hannis, Barholomew Penrose, Elizabeth, Dorothy, Rebecca, Rachel, Sarah and Margret Hannis, Mary Penrose and her children, Joseph, Sarah, Margret and Mary Hannis. Housekeeper: Hannah Garrison. Friends: Huldah Garrison, John Peel, Rev. Mr. Grayton, Catholic priest. Child: Jervis. Grandchild: Margaret Hannis. Exec: Andrew Hannis.
Witnesses: Peter Cox, Joel Cozens, Jno. Reily.

RODGERS, WILLIAM. City of Philadelphia. June 6, 1749/50. July 18, 1749. J.148.
Brother: Robert. Nephew: John Rodgers. Exec: Robert Rodgers, David McIlvaine.
Witnesses: William Stewart, Alex. Rannald.

ASH, THOMAS. Passyunk, Co. of Philadelphia. Butcher. June 8, 1748/9. July 22, 1749. J.149.
Father: ---. Brothers: Joshua, John and Edward. Sisters: Sarah Council and Elizabeth. Nephews: John, Edward and Thomas Ash. Exec: John Ash, Richard Brockden.
Witnesses: Enoch Bonsell, Thomas Pearson, Isa Pearson.

LEIBGEB, GODFRYD. Germantown, Co. of Philadelphia. Mason. Oct. 19, 1747/8. July 26, 1749. J.150.
Wife: Mary Christina. Children: Agnes, Solomon, Christina, Elizabeth, Matthias and Sophia. Exec: Mary Christina Leibgeb. Battles Resev.
Witnesses: Blasins Daniel Mackinet, Christopher Ming, Christn. Lehman.

NIXON, THOMAS. City of Philadelphia. Yeoman. 4 mo. 8, 1748/9/50. July 26, 1749. J.152.
Wife: Rachel. Child: Jane Waite. Grandchildren: Thomas Nixon Waite, Grace, Rachel, Temperance and Benjamin Waite. Cousins: William Watkins, James Chattin. Exec: Rachel Nixon, Jane Waite.
Witnesses: Thomas Stretch, Joseph Stretch, Alexr. Seaton.
Codicil:
Witnesses: Joseph Parker, Elizabeth Townsend.

BRIGHT, ANTHONY. City of Philadelphia. Silversmith. Proved Aug. 3, 1749. J.156.
Wife: Jane. Children: Thomas and James. Brother-in-Law: Henry Surman [of London]. Exec: Jane Bright, Joseph Richardson.
Witnesses: Wm. Parker, Willm. Lawrence, Junr.

COOPER, EDWARD. City of Philadelphia. Aug. 9, 1744/5. Aug. 7, 1749. J.157.
Wife: Sarah. Exec: Sarah Cooper.
Witnesses: Thomas Broadgate, Charles James, Peter Snow.

MONTGOMERY, ARCHA. City of Philadelphia. July 21, 1744/5. Aug. 12, 1749. J.158.
Wife: Sarah. Brothers: Hugh and Sober. Sisters: ---. Exec: Sarah Montgomery.
Witnesses: Robert Shewell, Alexander Crukshank.

HOLT, ELIZABETH. City of Philadelphia. Widow. July 10, 1749/50. Aug. 21, 1749. J.159.
Son-in-Law: Ryves Holt. Children: Rebecca Cox and Samuel. Grandchildren: John and Samuel Cox. Exec: Samuel Holt.
Witnesses: Alexander Armand, Wm. Biddle, James Read.

DAVIES, DAVID. Charlestown, Co. of Chester, Penna. Feb. 25, 1746/7. Aug. 26, 1749. J.160.
Children: Zephaniah [in England] and Nathaniel. Exec: Nathaniel Davies.
Witnesses: James Glascow, John Jones, David Mathas (his mark).

CHALKLEY, MARTHA. Frankford, Co. of Philadelphia. Widow. 6 mo. 5, 1749/50. Aug. 28, 1749. J.161.
Son-in-Law: Abel James. Children: Rebecca James and Hannah Finney. Grandchildren: Martha James and Martha Chalkey Browne. Exec: Hannah Finney, Abel James.
Witnesses: John Griffen, John Hudson, Henry Drinker.

STONE, JACOB. Springfield, Co. of Bucks, Penna. Yeoman. Aug. 4, 1749/50. Sept. 4, 1749. J.162.
Wife: Mary Sarah. Children: John Jacob, Shurlota, Mary Elizabeth and Ann Margaret. Exec: Mary Sarah Stone, George Overpeck.
Witnesses: Christian Shug, Conrad Feter (his mark), Uriah Humble.

PLEADWELL, EDWARD. City of Philadelphia. Shopkeeper. June 3, 1749/50. Sept. 12, 1749. J.164.
Child: Sarah. Exec: Christopher Marshall, Sarah Pleadwell and John Eastbourne.
Witnesses: Robert Shewell, Allexr. Crukshank, Alexr. Seaton.

HURT [HART], THOMAS. City of Philadelphia. Bricklayer. Aug. 1, 1749/50. Sept. 19, 1749. J.165.

Wife: Mary. Children: John, Susannah, Thomas, Samuel, Martha, Mary, Sarah, Hannah, Margaret and Jane. Exec: Mary and Thomas Hurt [Hart].
Witnesses: Samuel Hurford, Thomas Paschall, Mary Dulles.

KOYLE, MICHAEL. City of Philadelphia. Shipwright. April 7, 1749/50. Feb. 29, 1749. J.167.
Children: Seth and Martha Read. Son-in-Law: John Read. Exec: Thomas Leech, Benjamin Franklin.
Witnesses: W. Bingham, Emanuel Rouse, Lewis Evans.

VONDERWEYD, JACOB. Germantown, Co. of Philadelphia. Carpenter. Sept. 13, 1749/50. Oct. 2, 1749. J.168.
Wife: Mary Salome. Child: Susannah Salome. Exec: Mary Salome Vonderwyed.
Witnesses: John Frederick Ax (his mark), Nicholas Lochman, Christn. Lehman.

REYNER, HENRY. Limerick, Co. of Philadelphia. Farmer. Aug. 11, 1749/50. Oct. 2, 1749. J.170.
Wife: Hannah. Children: Philip, Jacob, Lawrence, David, Henry and Elizabeth. Son-in-Law: Andrew Paul. Exec: Hannah and Philip Reyner.
Witnesses: John Umstead (his mark), John Henry (his mark), George Evans.

LOREMAN, PETER. Upper Dublin, Co. of Philadelphia. Yeoman. March 2, 1748/9. Oct. 2, 1749. J.172.
Wife: Margret. Children: Hannah, Margret, Swarts, Catrine Arnal Wan. Exec: Peter Cleaver, Volentine Puff.
Witnesses: Isaac Cleaver, Jno. Cleaver.

LEWELLIN, MORRIS. Merion, Co. of Philadelphia. Aug. 26, 1749/50. Oct. 3, 1749. J.173.
Wife: Catherine. Children: Cisly, Mary, Elizabeth, Margaret and Catherine. Grandchildren: Morris Cran (Evan) and Lewellin Taylor. Sons-in-Law and Exec: Evan Evans, Alexander Cruickshank, James Truman, Isaac Taylor.
Witnesses: G. Lewellin, John David, Mary Ann Lewellin.

HERBERT, JOHANNES. Germantown, Co. of Philadelphia. Stocking weaver. Nov. 18, 1748/9. Oct. 7, 1749. J.174.
Wife: Amalia. Children: ---. Exec: Amalia Herbert, Cunrad Frick.
Witnesses: Danl. Mucknet, John Shoemaker, Christ. Lehman.

ROBERTS, ROWLAND. Mountgomery, Co. of Philadelphia. Yeoman. 7 mo. 12, 1749/50. Oct. 10, 1749. J.176.
Wife: Anne. Child: Eldad. Daughters-in-Law: Hannah Jones and Mary Davis. Son-in-Law: James Williams. Exec: Eldad Roberts.
Witnesses: George Lewis (his mark), Joseph Ambler, John Evans.

KEITH, THOMASINA. Kensington, Co. of Philadelphia. Widow. Sept. 20, 1749/50. Oct. 13, 1749. J.177.
Sister: Elizabeth Palmer. Brother: Francis Palmer. Mother-in-Law: Catherine Palmer. Brother-in-Law: Samuel Palmer. Sister-in-Law: Elizabeth Palmer. Nephew: Samuel Palmer. Niece: Eliner Berkeley. Exec: Elizabeth and Samuel Palmer.
Witnesses: Alexander Allaire, Hannah Simpson, Lewis Evans.

DILLWORTH, RICHARD. Bristoll, Co. of Philadelphia. Yeoman. 1 mo. 7, 1748/9. Oct. 14, 1749. J.180.
Wife: Ann. Brother: James. Children: Jacob, James and Sarah. Exec: Ann and Jacob Dillworth.
Witnesses: Thos Roberts (his mark), Elinor Roberts, Thos. Rose.

DOD, THOMAS. Kingsess, Co. of Philadelphia. Scrivener. Sept. 20, 1740/1. Oct. 19, 1750. J.182.
Wife: Ann. Children: ---. Exec: Ann Dod, Peter Jones.
Witnesses: Patrick Branun, Wm. Preist, Henry Hodge.

ROBBINS, MARY. Lower Dublin, Co. of Philadelphia. Tailoris. Aug. 9, 1749/50. Oct. 21, 1749. J.183.
Brothers: John and Robert. Sister: Susannah Rummon. Exec: John Robbins.
Witnesses: George Boale, Hugh Barnes (his mark), Jos. Miles.

SUPPLEE, JACOB. City of Philadelphia. Yeoman. Oct. 4, 1749/50. Oct. 28, 1749. J.184.
Children: Jacob and others. Exec: John Moore, Matthias Holstein.
Overseer: Jacob Supplee.
Witnesses: Rees Moore, Matthias Holstein.

PICKERING, CHARLES. City of Philadelphia. Goldsmith. Oct. 1, 1749/50. Oct. 26, 1749. J.184.
Exec: Simon Siron.
Witnesses: John Loak Sprogell, Thomas Say.

RINCKER, HENRY. Lower Milford, Co. of Bucks, Penna. Sept. 13, 1749/50. Oct. 31, 1749. J.186.
Wife: Fronicka. Children: Anne Barbara, Anna Mary, John Jacob, Anne Elizabeth and Henry. Exec: John Breghall, John Rodrock.
Witnesses: Peter Baker, Peter Kreiling.

BULLIGER, FRANCY. Germantown, Co. of Philadelphia. May 24, 1745/6. Nov. 1, 1749. J.188.
Brother: Michael. Nieces and Nephews: Jacob Bulliger, Francy, Susannah Bulliger and Michael Bulliger, Junr. Exec: John Frederick Ax, John Ax.
Witnesses: Daniel Pastorious, Frederick Hesser.

GLASCOW, JAMES. Fredyfryn, Co. of Chester, Pa. Oct. 15, 1749/50. Nov. 8, 1749. J.189.
Wife: Margaret. Children: Nathaniel, Jane, Margaret, James and Robert. Exec: Margaret Glascon. Guardians: Enoch Walker, Isaac Davis.
Witnesses: Enoch Walker, John Rowland, John Griffith.

JUSTIS, MOUNCE. Northern Liberties, City of Philadelphia. Yeoman. Feb. 12, 1743/4. Nov. 8, 1749. J.190.
Wife: Christiana. Children: John, Peter, Mounce, Gunner, Bridget, Ann and Christiana. Son-in-Law: Richard Tyson. Exec: Christiana and Gunner Justis, Richard Tyson.
Witnesses: Samuel Hastings, John Hoster [Koster], Paul Isaac Voto.
Codicil: Sept. 18, 1749.
Grandchildren: Richard, William, Hester and Christiana Tyson.
Witnesses: Edwd. Jones, Francis Garrigues.

GAMBAGH, JOHN. City of Philadelphia. Joyner. Oct. 7, 1749/50. Nov. 10, 1749. J.192.
Wife: Anna Catharina. Children: ---. Exec: Anna Catharina Gambagh.
Witnesses: Samuel Suther, Randolph Goodman, Johannes Heiser, John George Wittener.

SCHLEER, JOHANNES. Northern Liberties, City of Philadelphia. Sept. 3, 1749/50. Nov. 13, 1749. J.193.
Children: Balthazer Schleer and Margaret Ram. Brother: Hans Mathies Schleer. Exec: Leonard Herman, Lorent Bast, Hans Jurg, --- Miteleberger.
Witnesses: Peter Brumholtz, Adam Clampfer.

ASHMAN, ABRAHAM. Oley, Co. of Philadelphia. Jan. 18, 1742/3. Nov. 21, 1749. J.193.
Wife: Elizabeth. Children: Rebecca and Magdalena. Exec: Elizabeth and Rebecca Ashman.
Witnesses: Blasins Daniel Mackinet, Bernard Reser, Christn. Lehman.

FOX, JOHN. Kensington, City of Philadelphia. Shipwright. Sept. 7, 1749/50. Nov. 20, 1749. J.194.
Wife: Elizabeth. Brothers: George and Robert. Mother: Mary Watson. Sisters: Elizabeth Martindale and Ann Chambers, wife of Alexander. Nephew: John Fox. Exec: Elizabeth Fox.
Witnesses: Jos. Oldman, Richard Dennis, Isaac Dutton.

LINTON, JOHN. City of Philadelphia. Harness maker. April 7, 1748/9. Dec. 3, 1749. J.195.
Wife: Martha. Child: Mary Mackey. Exec: Martha Linton.
Witnesses: Benjn. Britton, Mary Holland, Samuel Gifford.

WENTZ, PETER. Worcester, Co. of Philadelphia. Yeoman. June 7, 1745/6. Dec. 5, 1749. J.196.
Children: Jacob, Peter, Philip, Abraham and Catherine Haker. Grandchildren: Elizabeth, Peter, Adam and Jacob Snyder. Exec: Jacob and Abram Wentz. Trustees: Peter Wentz, Henry Snyder.
Witnesses: Jules Cassel, George Mercle, Robert Jones.

BOWES, FRANCIS. City of Philadelphia. Merchant. Jan. 27, 1747/8. Dec. 12, 1749. J.203.
Wife: Rachel. Children: John, Theodosia Reed, Sarah, Mary and Ester. Exec: Thomas Lawrence, John Kinsey, Peter Delage, Andrew Read, Rachel Bowes.
Witnesses: Ann Mullan, Elizh. Griffin, Ann Lindsay.

ANDREWS, RUDOLPH. Upper Milford, Co. of Bucks, Penna. Yeoman. Proved Dec. 12, 1749. J.205.

Wife: Barbara. Children: Anna Barbara, Martin, Michael, Lodwick, Mary, Dorothy and Staffel. Exec: Barbara Andrews. Guardian: David Geesey.
Witnesses: Mich Rishell (his mark), George S---, Thos. Owen.

PARKS, FOSTER. City of Philadelphia. Husbandman. Nov. 29, 1749/50. Dec. 13, 1749. J.206.
Wife: Margaret. Exec: Margaret Parks.
Witnesses: Edward Turner, James Stephens, Jno. Reily.

EDWARDS, JOHN. Horsam, Co. of Philadelphia. Husbandman. 10 mo. 9, 1749/50. Jan. 3, 1749. J.207.
Wife: Gennet. Children: Rebecca Miller and John. Exec: Gennet Edwards.
Witnesses: Ephram Leech, John Williams, Isaac Jones.

COLES, DANIEL. Exeter, Co. of Philadelphia. Nov. 6, 1749/50. Jan. 5, 1749. J.208.
Wife: Dinah. Children: Solomon, Mary and Deborah. Brothers-in-Law and Exec: John Hughes, William Boone.
Witnesses: Josiah Boone, George Moore (his mark), Thomas Embree.

PASTORIOUS, JOHN. Germantown, Co. of Philadelphia. Yeoman. 11 mo. 2, 1749/50. Jan. 17, 1749. J.209.
Sister: Mary Keyser. Step-brothers: Daniel, Mathias, Jacob, William and Samuel Keyser. Father-in-Law: Andrew Keyser. Mother: Hannah Keyser.
Witnesses: Daniel Shaner, Thomas Rose.

OGDEN, JOSEPH. [Barbadoes], late City of Philadelphia. Hatter. July 15, 1749/50. Jan. 24, 1749. J.211.
Mother: Hannah. Brother: William. Exec: Hannah Ogden, William Mode, Hezekiah Williams [of Barbadoes].
Witnesses: Joseph Thomas, Augustine Moller, Sarah Campbell (her mark) [of Barbadoes].

HART, JOHN. City of Philadelphia. Bricklayer. May 4, 1743/4. Jan. 26, 1749. J.213.
Wife: Mary. Children: John, Thomas, Mary Warner and Elizabeth Maddock. Exec: Mary Warner, Elizabeth Maddock.
Witnesses: James Sullivan, Saml. Gray, Jno. Durborow.

SHUTZ, MICHAEL. Germantown, Co. of Philadelphia. Carpenter. Feb. 26, 1747/8. Jan. 29, 1749. J.214.
Wife: Julian. Children: Jacob, Elizabeth and Barbary. Exec: Julian Shutz, George Hoofman.
Witnesses: John Sheppard, Peter Evans, John Barge.

BELL, MARY. City of Philadelphia. Widow. Jan. 12, 1749/50. Feb. 11, 1749. J.215.
Brothers: Thomas, John and Francis Stamper. Child: Mary. Exec: John Stamper.
Witnesses: Rebekah Stamper, Jno. Reily.

HARPER, MARGARET. Widow of John Harper. Northern Liberties, City of Philadelphia. Feb. 1, 1749/50. Feb. 12, 1749. J.215.
Brother: Edward Richey. Sisters: Dorcas, Elizabeth and Martha Richey. Exec: John Richey.
Witnesses: James Richey, Alexander A. McCurdy, Christn. Lehman.

ROBERTS, EDWARD. Gwynedd, Co. of Philadelphia. Oct. 3, 1748/9. Feb. 14, 1749. J.216.
Wife: Ann. Children: Robert and Margred Jones. Grandchildren: Robert, Edward, Jesse and Hugh Evans, Joshua, Ann, Ellen and Margred Foulke. Friend: Sarah Banks. Exec: Robert Roberts.
Overseers: Thomas Evans, Junr., John Jones, Junr.
Witnesses: David Humphrey, Ellis Hughs, Thomas Williams.

JOHN, JAMES. Merrion, Co. of Philadelphia. March 7, 1747/8. Feb. 14, 1749. J.218.
Children: Joyce Jones, Mary Harriss and Thomas. Grandchild: Jabez Jones. Daughter-in-Law: Elizabeth Jones. Friend: Elizabeth, wife of John David. Exec: John David, Griffith Lewellin.

DEXTER, HENRY. City of Philadelphia. Gentleman. Oct. 31, 1749. Feb. 15, 1749. J.219.
Wife: Elinor. Children: James, Henry, George, John, Enos and William. Exec: Elinor Dexter. Grandchild: Letice Dexter.
Witnesses: Jonathan Shoemaker, Wm. Wriggins, Paul Isaac Voto.

STORY, WILLIAM. Mountgomery, Co. of Philadelphia. Husbandman. 12 mo. 7, 1749/50. Feb. 16, 1749. J.222.
Wife: Katherin. Exec: Katherin Story.

Witnesses: James Killpatrick, Agnes Killpatrick (her mark), Isaac Jones.

BURK, HUSE. White Marsh, Co. of Philadelphia. Yeoman. Dec. 14, 1749/50. Feb. 17, 1749. J.222.
Children: Edward, John and William. Exec: Edward, John and William Burk.
Witnesses: Samuel Morris, Abraham Dawes, Samuel Gilhesey.

NASH, JAMES. Horsham, Co. of Philadelphia. Yeoman. 11 mo. 26, 1749/50. Feb. 20, 1749. J.224.
Wife: Katherine. Child: John. Brothers: William and Joseph. Exec: William and Joseph Nash.
Witnesses: Esther Shea, John Smith, Samuel Mannan (his mark).

WILLIAMS, EDWARD. Blockley, Co. of Philadelphia. Yeoman. Sept. 3, 1749/50. Feb. 21, 1749. J.225.
Wife: Eleanor. Children: Joseph, Edward Loome, Jane, Sarah and Daniel. Grandchildren: Clement, Elm, ---. Friends: Elizabeth, widow of Joseph Morgan, Evan Lloyd. Exec: Daniel and Joseph Williams.
Witnesses: Hugh Evans, James Jones, Richard George.

BELL, RICHARD. Hannover, Co. of Philadelphia. Aug. 14, 1749/50. Feb. 24, 1749. J.227.
Children: William, Thomas and Mary. Grandchildren: William, Mary and Richard Bell and Mary and Richard Bell. Exec: Mary Bell.
Witnesses: Jeremiah Jordon, John Linderman.

TROTTER, WILLIAM. Plymouth, Co. of Philadelphia. 2 mo. 5, 1748/9. Feb. 24, 1749. J.228.
Wife: Hannah. Children: Rebecca, Esther, Lydia, Margaret and Joseph. Son-in-Law: William Jones. Brother-in-Law: John Jones. Friends: Elizabeth and Catherine Ellis. Exec: Hannah and Joseph Trotter. Guardians: Joseph and John Jones.
Witnesses: John Davis, Griffith Thomas, Joseph Tucker.

GRIFFITTS, MARY. City of Philadelphia. Widow of Thomas Griffitts. 6 mo. -- 1749/50. March 1, 1749. J.230.
Children: Isaac, Mary and Hannah. Exec: Mary and Hannah Griffitts.
Witnesses: Joseph Warner, William Griffitts.

POWELL, SAMUEL. City of Philadelphia. Cooper. Feb. 15, 1743/4. March 5, 1749. J.231.
Wife: Sarah. Children: Ann, John, Thomas, Joseph and Martha.
Exec: Sarah Powell. Trustee: Jacob Dueberry.
Witnesses: William Bissell, Jos. Rakestraw, John Stephen.

MAURICE [MORRIS], SAMUEL. Vincent, Co. of Chester, Penna. Yeoman. Jan. 7, 1746/7. March 7, 1749. J.232.
Wife: Lettice. Children: David, Martha and Mary. Brothers: Thomas and Philip. Exec: Lettice, Thomas and Philip Maurice.
Witnesses: John Meredith, John Thomas, Jno. Thomas.

STARR, JAMES. Charles Town, Co. of Chester, Pa. 12 mo. 2, 1749. March 7, 1749. J.234.
Wife: ---. Children: Samuel, Joseph, John, James, Moses, Richard Richardson and wife Mary, Rees Williams and wife Rachel. Grandchild: Rachel Starr. Exec: Wife --- and Joseph Starr.
Witnesses: Jacob Hildebrand, Bryan Keegan, Jer. Starr.

SMITH, HENRY. Co. of Lancaster, Penna. Indian Trader. June 7, 1745/6. March 14, 1749. J.235.
Friends: Edward Shippen, Rees Thomas' eldest daughter and William Kelly's second son. Servant: Jacob. Exec: Edward Shippen.
Witnesses: Isaac Bellanger, John Mackarall, Robt. Gibbs.

BEDDOME, ELIZABETH. Wife of Joseph Beddome. Merchant. City of Philadelphia. Sept. 24, 1749/50. March 16, 1749. J.236.
Children: Elizabeth Stone, James Stone and Sarah Sallows. Exec: Evan Morgan, Ebenezer Kinnersley, Samuel Hazzard.
Witnesses: Deborah Franklin, Emanuel Rouse, Lewis Evans.

PARRAT, JOHN. Bensalem, Co. of Bucks, Penna. Feb. 27, 1749/50. March 16, 1749. J.238.
Friends: John Williamson and wife, Septimus Robeson, Joseph Hough, Patrick Kelly, Cornelius Vanosten, widow of William Roberts and her children. Exec: Septimus Robeson.
Witnesses: Joseph Walton, John Howard, Thos. Robinson.

ROBERTS, WILLIAM. Whitpan, Co. of Philadelphia. Yeoman. 9 mo. 2, 1749/50. March 9, 1749. J.239.

Wife: Jane. Children: Joseph, Margret and Jacob. Brother: Edward. Overseers: Edward Roberts, Joseph Jones. Exec: Jacob Roberts. Witnesses: Job Pugh, Griffith Hugh (his mark), James Wood.

HUFTE, JOHN. Abington, Co. of Philadelphia. March 8, 1749/50. March 20, 1749. J.240.
Mother: ---. Nephew and Niece: John and Mary Hufte. Brother: Jacob. Sisters-in-Law: Sarah and Mary Hufte. Friends: Phole and Cathrine Vandyke. Exec: Jacob Hufte, Abraham Coffing.
Witnesses: John Webster, Abel Marple.

MORGAN, DAVID. Blockley, Co. of Philadelphia. Yeoman. Feb. 26, 1748/9. March 25, 749. J.241.
Wife: Anne. Friends: James, John, Isaac, and Jacob Jones; Ellin Roberts; Lewis Jones children - David, Anne and Joseph; James Jones children - Jesse, Richard, James, Isaac and Hannah; William Lewiss children - Gideon, Gwen, William and Susannah; William Roberts; John Martin; David Davis Skinner's four children; Martha Chapman; Mary Moore; Evan James' four children; Merion Meeting House and Graveyard. Exec: James Jones.
Witnesses: John Brooks, Mary Clark.

ORPEN, ABRAHAM. Late of Kingston, Jamaica, now of City of Philadelphia. Mariner. March 23, 1749/50. March 27, 1750. J.242.
Codicil:
Wife: Judith. Brother: Raymond. Sister: Isabella. Brother-in-Law: Thomas Wright. Nephews: Love Orpen, James Orpen. Friend: John Mifflin. Negro: Dick. Exec: John Mifflin.
Witnesses: Sarah Read, James Trotter, Silas Pryor.

KELCHNER, GEORGE. Oly, Co. of Philadelphia. Blacksmith. Nov. 15, 1747/8. March 28, 1750. J.243.
Wife: Margaretha. Exec: Margaretha Kelchner. Trustee: Samuel Gulden.
Witnesses: Henry Bruner, Daniel Worley, Johannes Wagener.

ERB, LAWRENCE. City of Philadelphia. July 25, 1747/8. March 29, 1750. J.244.
Wife: Anna Margaretha. Children: Lodowig and Casper. Exec: Anna Margaretha Erb.

Witnesses: Frederick Hillegass, Felix Bruner, Johannes Hood, Adam Hillegass.

ALBER, GEORGE. Germantown, Co. of Philadelphia. Yeoman. Jan. 4, 1749/50. April 5, 1750. J.245.
Wife: Katherine. Daughter: Katherine. Grandchildren: Children of Katherine Shelleberg. Son-in-Law: Abraham Shelleberg. Exec: Abraham Shelleberg, William Stadellman.
Witnesses: Battes Refer, Christ. Lehman.

STILFEALT, MAGDALENE. Germantown, Co. of Philadelphia. [Widow of Henry Stilfealt]. March 20, 1749/50. April 11, 1750. J.246.
Children: Henry, John, Sophiah and Mary. Exec: Henry and John Stilfealt.
Witnesses: Alexander Mack, Daniel Henricks, Anthony Tunis.

WILLIAMS, OLIVER. City of Philadelphia. Glover. March 13, 1749/50. April 24, 1750. J.248.
Wife: Jane. Son-in-Law: James Hawkins. Grandchildren: William, John and Jane Hawkins. Friends: Rev. Jenkin Jones, John Snowden, Junr., Rebecca Shoemaker, Catherine Fielding, Anne Hanks, Benjamin Price, Atty., Oliver Rees, Joseph Crane, David Owen. Exec: Jane Williams.
Witnesses: John Bleakley, Andrew Bankson, Jonathan Shoemaker.

KETTLER, ANDREW. White Marsh, Co. of Philadelphia. Dec. 22, 1749/50. April 28, 1750. J.248.
Father: ---. Brothers: David, John and Philip. Nephew: Andrew Sharp. Attys. and Exec: Edward Stroud, Nathan Potts.
Witnesses: Christopher Robins, Johannes Duffel, Pat. Menan.

MAY, ROBERT. Hanover, Co. of Philadelphia. Blacksmith. March 4, 1747/8. May 1, 1750. J.250.
Wife: Elizabeth. Children: Mary, Elizabeth, Sarah, Hannah, James and Thomas. Exec: Elizabeth Mary.
Witnesses: James Brooke, Jacob Frick, John Lunday.
Codicil: Aug. 1, 1749/50.
Witnesses: Jno. Campbell, Valentine Hann, James Brooke, Jacob Frick.

LAMB, JOHN. City of Philadelphia. April 3, 1750/1. May 5, 1750. J.253.
Sister: Frances Geary. Exec: Samuel Johnson, John Thornell.
Witnesses: John Head, D. Chambers.

SHINDLER, YOST. Francony, Co. of Philadelphia. March 29, 1749/50. May 12, 1750. J.254.
Sister's children in Germany. Cousins: Yost Pfannenkuenen, Hartman Tettermer and Margarett Tettermer. Exec: Hartman Fetterer.
Witnesses: Jacob Funck, John Frey.

THOMPSON, DAVID. Horsham, Co. of Philadelphia. Yeoman. March 9, 1749/50. May 19, 1750. J.255.
Wife: Sarah. Children: Ann, William, David and Elizabeth. Son-in-Law: Zacharias Faris. Servant: Hannah Herret. Exec: William Thompson.
Witnesses: John Crag, William Henry, Archibald McClean.

BURGESS, THOMAS. City of Philadelphia. Merchant. May 12, 1750/1. May 26, 1750. J.257.
Wife: Jane. Mother: Mary Hartford Engd. Brother-in-Law: Thomas Shaw. Sisters: Elizabeth, Margaret and Ann. Brothers: Francis, Genase, Samuel and Thos. Shaw, Junr. Nieces and Nephews: Sarah Bickham; children of John Deaker; children of Luke Budworth; Thomas, John, Ann, and Margaret Beckman; John and Thomas Burgess. Cousin: Samuel Shaw of Pennypack. Friends. Children of Rees Meredith. Negro: Caeser.
Witnesses: Rees Meredith, Samuel Neare, Thomas Davis.

JACKMAN, THOMAS. City of Philadelphia. March 14, 1749/50. June 5, 1750. J.259.
Wife: Elizabeth. Children: John, in Barbadoes and Thomas. Exec: Elizabeth Jackman. Ass't. Exec: John Kinsey.
Witnesses: Stephen Vidal, Mary Dallas.

KNIGHT, ISAAC. Abington, Co. of Philadelphia. 2 mo. 5, 1750/1. June 8, 1750. J.261.
Wife: Mary. Children: John, Isaac, Sarah, Ann, Mary, Rebecca and Elizabeth. Exec: Isaac and Nathan Bewly.
Witnesses: Nicholas Austin, Isaac Tyson, Griffith Davis.

MUMBAUR, WILLIAM. Frederick Township, Penna. May 19, 1750. June 11, 1750. J.262.
Wife: Margaretha Barbara. Children: ---. Exec: Margaretha Barbara Mumbaur, Johannes Yost.
Witnesses: Peter Hauch, Nicholas Kemmer.

FITZWATER, GEORGE. City of Philadelphia. Gentleman. Oct. 11, 1748/9. June 15, 1750. J.263.
Sons-in-Law: Joseph House, Isaac Griffiths, William Coleman, Francis Richardson and Joseph Morris. Children: Hannah, Mary, Martha, Sarah and Elizabeth. Grandchildren: George Clymer, Phebe and George Morris, Mary and Elizabeth Griffiths, Peregoine and Mary Hogg, Mary, Grace and Hannah Richardson. Exec: William and Hannah Coleman, Francis and Mary Richardson.
Witnesses: Thomas Hopkinson, Tench Francis, Junr., Thomas Biles.

TRAUT, JEREMIAS and TRAUT, JOHN BATHAZER. Germantown, Co. of Philadelphia. May 26, 1747/8. June 21, 1750. J.275.
Sons and Couzins: Jacob, Balthazer and Jeremias. Exec: Jacob Traut, John Frederick Ox, John Shinfeld.
Witnesses: Mathias Adams, John Roberts.

ROBERTS, ANNE. Gwynedd, Co. of Philadelphia. Widow. 10 mo. 30, 1749/50. July 2, 1750. J.277.
Children: William and Daniel. Grandchildren: Sarah Davis, Mary Williams, Anne Jones, Amos, Daniel, Hannah and Prasilla Davis, Hezekiah, Humphrey, Martha, Prasilla and Hannah Williams; James, Mary and Hannah Roberts. Sons-in-Law: Eldeed Roberts and John Davis. Exec: John Davis. Overseers: John Jones, Daniel Williams.
Witnesses: William Jones, Jesse Morgan, John Evans.

JONES, CATHRINE. Gwynedd, Co. of Philadelphia. Widow. June 15, 1750/1. July 3, 1750. J.278.
Children: John, Elizabeth Evans, Cathrine, Jane, Gainor and Humphrey. Son-in-Law: David Laurence. Exec: David Jones, Edward Foulke. Guardians: Thomas Evans, Junr., William Foulke.
Witnesses: John Evans (his mark), John Flatcher, Jno. Evans.

KNILL, ROBERT. City of Philadelphia. Nov. 27, 1747/8. July 10, 1750. J.280.
Mother: Ann. Sister: Mary. Exec: Charles Willing.

Witnesses: Ann Willing, Thos. Gilbert.

EDGELL, REBECCA. City of Philadelphia. Widow. July 10, 1750/1. July 13, 1750. J.281.
Children: Rebecca and William. Friends: Mary Glentworth, Sarah Jones, Margaret Holland, Patience Mifflin, Elizabeth Slive, Widow of John Wilkins, Susanna and Francis Ashton, Samuel Smith [of Donegall], Elizabeth Morris, Sarah, Samuel and Mary Edgell, Mary Dwadyhouse. Exec. and Guardian: Jonathan Mifflin.
Witnesses: Jno. Lynn, David Hall, Wm. Forsyth.

PHILIP, HENRY. Willistown, Co. of Chester, Penna. Yeoman. Sept. 6, 1749/50. July 19, 1750. J.282.
Wife: ---. Children: Morys, Mary, Martha, Thomas, Ann and Joseph. Exec: Wife ---. Trustees: Morys Griffith, Joseph Jones, Mark Morys.
Witnesses: John Evans, Wm. Evans.

GRIFFITH, KATHERINE. Merrion, Pro. of Penna. Widow. Proved July 19, 1750. J.283.
Children: Elizabeth, Sarah and Margaret Evans, and Thomas. Grandchildren: Children of Elizabeth and Margaret Evans, children of Katherine Jones decd., Owen and Peter Evans, Katherine Jones, Katherine Williams, children of Sarah Williams. Exec: Elizabeth Evans, Sarah Williams.
Witnesses: Thamer Thomas, Thos. Thomas, Rebecca George.

BETTLE, JOHN. City of Philadelphia. Cordwainer. 4 mo. 14, 1750/1. July 23, 1750. J.284.
Wife: Lydia. Children: Josiah, Elizabeth, Hannah, Abigal and Lydia. Exec: Lydia Bettle.
Witnesses: John Jones, Isaac Moss, Jno. Reily.

STUBER, BALTHASER. City of Philadelphia. April 16, 1750/1. July 26, 1750. J.286.
Wife: Barbara. Children: Philip and Barbara. Exec: Barbara Stuber, Valentine Steinmetz.
Witnesses: Johannes Hanny, Valentine Steinmetz, John Hanny.

LEWIS, HENRY. City of Philadelphia. Shopkeeper. 3 mo. 20, 1750/1. July 28, 1750. J.287.

Wife: Jane. Children: Henry, Barbara and Catherine. Brother: Jacob. Exec: Jane and Jacob Lewis.
Witnesses: William Warner, Isaac Warner, Jno. Reily.

BROWN, JEREMIAH. City of Philadelphia. Dec. 27, 1748/9. Aug. 4, 1750. J.288.
Wife: Bridgett. Exec: Bridgett Brown.
Witnesses: Dianna MacCulla, John McCulla.

MC QUIN, ---. Late of Scotland. Dated at sea, July 19, 1750/1. Mariner, on board ship "Earle." Aug. 11, 1750. J.289.
Brother: William McQuin. Friends: John Hamilton, Junr., Arthur Hurrey, Elizabeth Green, Archibald Hamilton. Exec: John Hamilton [Master of ship "Earle"].
Witnesses: William Young, Thos. Lorenore (his mark), Archibald Hamilton.

FINNEY, CHARLES. Oxford, Co. of Philadelphia. Yeoman. July 16, 1750. Aug. 13, 1750. J.290.
Children: Elizabeth Todd, Mary Bringhurst, Samuel, William and Richard. Grandchildren: Hannah Finney, Thomas and Hannah Tresse. Daughter-in-Law: Rebecca Jones. Exec: Samuel Richard, William Finney.
Witnesses: R. Greenway, Ann Tresse, Roby. Greenway.

WILKINSON, GABRIEL. City of Philadelphia. Shipwright. Oct. 11, 1749/50. Aug. 15, 1750. J.293.
Wife: Sarah. Children: Anne, Sarah, Daniel and Mary. Exec: Sarah [wife], Anne and Sarah Wilkinson.
Witnesses: William Vanderspiegel, John Ser. Clarkson, Roby. Greenway.

ASHMEAD, JOHN. Germantown, Co. of Philadelphia. Blacksmith. July 14, 1750/1. Aug. 18, 1750. J.294.
Wife: Ann. Children: William, John and Rachel. Exec: Ann Ashmead.
Witnesses: Daniel Potts, Thos. Rose, Saml. Potts.

RAKESTRAW, JOSEPH. City of Philadelphia. House carpenter. July 23, 1750/1. Aug. 23, 1750. J.295.
Wife: Elizabeth. Children: Joseph, John, Elizabeth and Hannah.

Witnesses: Joseph Marriott, John Lownes, Jos. Fox.

DURBOROW, JOSEPH. Wecaco, Co. of Philadelphia. Ship carpenter. Aug. 14, 1750/1. Aug. 28, 1750. J.296.
Wife: Mary. Children: Joseph and Mary. Sister: Sarah. Cousin: Daniel Durborow. Exec: Mary Durborow. Overseer: Daniel Durborow.
Witnesses: William Allen, Paul Isaac Voto, Jane Blany (her mark).

EATON, JACOB. Mountgomery, Co. of Philadelphia. Cordwainer. Aug. 3, 1750/1. Sept. 20, 1750. J.298.
Mother: Uriah. Brother: Isaac. Sister: Hannah. Friends: Charles [son of Thomas Humphrey], Deborah [daughter of Thomas Dungan]. Exec: Uriah [wife] and Isaac Eaton.
Witnesses: John Marks, Rachel Bartholomew, Si Butler.

THOMPSON, JAMES. Norriton, Co. of Philadelphia. Yeoman. Sept. 10, 1750/1. Oct. 1, 1750. J.300.
Brother: Archibald. Sister: Martha Ball. Brother-in-Law: William Bull. Cousins: Archibald, James, Mark, Martha, Agnes and Rebecca Thompson. Exec: Archibald Thompson. Trustee: William Bull.
Witnesses: John Chien, John Stevenson, Samuel Scott.

LIVEZEY, DAVID. Lower Dublin, Co. of Philadelphia. Blacksmith. Nov. 1, 1748/9. Oct. 1, 1750. J.301.
Brother: Jonathan. Children: Thomas, Rachel, Elizabeth and Hannah. Exec: Jonathan and Thomas Livezey.
Witnesses: Jacob Taylor, Joseph Thomas, Abraham Leech.

UPDEN GRAFF, JACOB, Pergwomie, Co. of Philadelphia. Weaver. Sept. 21, 1750/1. Oct. 1, 1750. J.302.
Children: Elizabeth, Catherine, Abraham, Edward, Margret and Eneken. Son-in-Law: Richard Gable. Exec: Abraham UpdenGraff, Richard Gable.
Witnesses: William How, Nichos. Bunn.

WILEY, JOSEPH. Maiden Creek, Co. of Philadelphia. Yeoman. June 16, 1750/1. Oct. 1, 1750. J.303.
Wife: Abigal. Children: Jane, Sarah and Ann Penrose, John. Grandchildren: Thomas Penrose. Exec: John Wiley.
Witnesses: Moses Starr, Jacob Lightfoot, Nathaniel Houllton.

RAMBO, ELIEAS. Upper Merrion, Co. of Philadelphia. Sept. 4, 1748/9. Oct. 1, 1750. J.305.
Children: Jeremiah, Jonas, Andrew, Gunner, Ann, Peter, George and Elias. Exec: Peter and George Rambo.
Witnesses: Matthias Rambo, William White, Jas. Curry.

DEAVS, ISAAC. Creesom, Co. of Philadelphia. Yeoman. 7 mo. 1, 1750/1. Oct. 1, 1750. J.306.
Wife: Martha. Children: Thomas, Samuel, Abraham, Sarah Gomery and Mary Streper. Grandchildren: Margaret, Mary, Isaac, and Agnes Deavs. Exec: Samuel and Abraham Deavs.
Witnesses: John Hammer, Jacob Shoemaker, Thos. Rose.

CRIMLY, SOLOMON. Upper Salforth, Co. of Philadelphia. Aug. 31, 1750/1. Oct. 1, 1750. J.307.
Wife: Anna Christina. Children: Feina, Durrety, Solomon and Barbara. Exec: Soloman Crimly, Christian Stoufer.
Witnesses: Peter Penebacker, Lodwick Pickle.

PHILPOT, MARY. City of Philadelphia. Widow. May 15, 1750/1. Oct. 1, 1750. J.309.
Children: Rachel Foster, William, Sarah Blacklidge and Phebe Atkins. Grandchildren: Mary and Rachel Foster and Mary Atkins. Exec: Philip Tillier, William Tillier.
Witnesses: Alexr. Parker, John Evans, Lewis Evans.

JOHNSON, MATHIAS. Hatfield, Co. of Philadelphia. Weaver. June 20, 1750/1. Oct. 8, 1750. J.310.
Wife: Ficken. Children: Johannes and Halanca. Exec: Ficken and Johannes Johnson.
Witnesses: Han Nicholas Tellp (his mark), William Nash.

MC KAY, ADAM. City of Philadelphia. Oct. 2, 1750/1. Oct. 8, 1750. J.311.
Friend: John Gay. Poor of Philadelphia. Exec: John Gay.
Witnesses: James Cusick, John Ross.

GRASSKOPF, JACOB [alias GREATHEAD]. Creesham, Co. of Philadelphia. Mason. Oct. 3, 1750. Oct. 11, 1750. J.312.
Wife: Anne Mary. Children: Margaretha, Christopher, Jacob and Paul. Exec: Anne Mary Grasskopf, Peter Heysler.

Witnesses: Mathias Millan (his mark), Michal Seamon (his mark), Christn. Lehman.

ZIMMERMAN, CHRISTIAN. Salford, Province of Penna. Oct. 27, 1749/50. Oct. 12, 1750. J.313.
One child. Brother-in-Law: Andrew Riess. Exec: Andrew Riess, Michael Shleer.
Witnesses: Christopher Keilback, Mathias Kelchner, Christian Merckel (his mark).

CUNRADT, HANS. Late of Wallishueed, Canton of Bern, now of City of Philadelphia. Yeoman. Nov. 11, 1749/50. Oct. 16, 1750. J.314.
Wife: Maria. Children: Ulrich, Johannes, Barbara, Elizabeth and Maria. Exec: Maria Cunradt.
Witnesses: Joseph Crell, Petrus Nygh, Andreas Boshart.

MORTON, ABIGAL. City of Philadelphia. Widow. Proved Oct. 26, 1750. J.315.
Children: Elizabeth Custard, John Hood and Rebecca Scattergood. Grandchildren: Ann Watson and Elizabeth Custard. Son-in-Law: Joseph Scattergood. Friends: Prudence and Sarah West [daughters of Charles and Sarah West]. Exec: John Hood, Joseph Scattergood.
Witnesses: James West, Charles West, Junr., Alexr. Seaton.

STAPLEFORD, ELIZABETH. City of Philadelphia. Maiden. Sept. 8, 1750/1. Nov. 1, 1750. J.316.
Brother-in-Law and Exec: Thomas Gordon.
Witnesses: Charles Vandick, Enoch Hobart, Rd. Allison.

THOMAS, JOHN. Whitpain, Co. of Philadelphia. Yeoman. Oct. 4, 1750/1. Nov. 5, 1750. J.317.
Wife: Margaret. Children: Owen, Evan, Jane, Sarah and Robert. Exec: Margaret Thomas. Guardians and Overseers: William Foulke, Rowd. Evans, Samuel Evans.
Witnesses: Jacob Levering, Abraham Evans, Owen Evans.

KNOWLES, ANN. Merion, Co. of Philadelphia. Widow. Oct. 9, 1750/1. Nov. 5, 1750. J.318.
Brother: James Paul. Children: Margaret Jones, Hannah Lewis and John. Son-in-Law: Robert Jones. Grandchildren: Ann and Jane Garret, Ann Jones, John and Elizabeth Lewis, Rachel and Martha

Levezely, Hannah and Sarah Buckingham, Ann Obourn. Exec: James Paul, Robert Jones.
Witnesses: Edwd. Price, Lewis Jones.

WEGER, PETER. City of Philadelphia. Oct. 21, 1750/1. Nov. 15, 1750. J.319.
Wife: Anna Margaretha. Children: Elizabeth, William, Johannes and Philip. Exec: Christian Snyder.
Witnesses: Jacob Winey, Jno. Bergen.

LINDERMAN, SAMUEL. Whipton, Co. of Philadelphia. Husbandman. Oct. 26, 1750/1. Nov. 24, 1750. J.320.
Wife: Susannah. Children: John, Christane, Mary and Rachel. Brother-in-Law: Thomas Been. Exec: Susannah Linderman, Thomas Been.
Witnesses: Stenrick Levering, Garret Levering.

COOPER, SAMUEL. Morland, Co. of Philadelphia. Yeoman. June 1, 1750/1. Nov. 24, 1750. J.322.
Brother: William. Sisters: Rebecca Kelly and Ester Hussey. Sister-in-Law: Mary Cooper. Nephews: Joseph, Samuel, Thomas and James Cooper. Couzin: James Cooper. Friend: Rachel Brittin. Exec: William Brittin, Senr., John Butcher, Samuel Swift.
Witnesses: John Atkins, Phebe Atkins, Tabitha Ashton.

NICOLLS, PATRICK. City of Philadelphia. April 11, 1746/7. Nov. 29, 1750. J.324.
Friend: David Montgomery [City of Glasgow, North Brittian]. Exec: William and David McIlvaine.
Witnesses: John Williams, Jno. Phillips.

DEAVES, MATTHAR. Germantown, Co. of Philadelphia. 9 mo. 16, 1750/1. Nov. 30, 1750. J.324.
Children: Thomas, Samuel, Abraham, Sarah Gomery and Mary Streeper. Grandchildren: Margaret, Mary, Isaac and Agness Deaves. Exec: Abraham Deaves.
Witnesses: John Hammer, Killean White, Isaac Hammer.

HILL, MARY. City of Philadelphia. Widow. Sept. 2, 1750/1. Nov. 30, 1750. J.326.
Mother: Esther Hoodt.

Brothers and Sisters: Daniel and Esther Hoodt, Elizabeth Trotter.
Exec: Esther Hoodt, Joseph Oldman.
Witnesses: Jeremiah Elfreth, Junr., Saml. Oldman, Rebecca Wells.

WELLS, THOMAS. City of Philadelphia. Shipwright. June 20, 1750/1. Dec. 4, 1750. J.327.
Wife: Rebecca. Children: Thomas, Junr., James, Rebecca and Elizabeth. Anne Collum and son. Exec: James and Thomas Wells, Junr.
Witnesses: Elizabeth Robeson, Ricloff Albertson, Roby. Greenway.

CLINE, MICHAEL. Whitpain, Co. of Philadelphia. Cordwainer. Feb. 22, 1749/50. Dec. 12, 1750. J.330.
Wife: Susannah Elizabeth. Children: Martha, Philip, Conrad, Margret, Elizabeth and Susannah. Son-in-Law: George Kastner.
Exec: Susannah Elizabeth Cline, George Kastner.
Witnesses: Jacob Levering, John Davis.

MULLIN, KATHERINE. City of Philadelphia. Widow. Proved Dec. 12, 1750. J.331.
Child: Ann Perdew. Grandchildren: Saran Mullen and Mary Parkhouse. Exec: Ann Perdew, Benjamin Franklin.
Witnesses: Wm. Nicholson, Thomas Say, Alexr. Seaton.

BROWN, JOHN MICHAEL. Late of West Indies, now of Co. of Philadelphia. Doctor of Physick. Dec. 5, 1750/1. Dec. 19, 1750. J.332. [Estate in Ireland and Philadelphia]. Mother: ---. Sisters: Mary [Clumbo, Ireland], Joan Brown [alias Maning], Bridget Brown [alias Kelley], Eleanor Murphy, Anatasia Dillon. Child: John. Son-in-Law: Thadee Murphy. Godson: Samuel Lynch of Barbadoes. Friends: Theodore Snyder, Dominick Blake, George and Robert Meade, Robert Kernan [of Bonnatollar], Edward Luther, Esq. Exec: Edward Luther, Esq. [of Montserrst], Rev. Theodore Snyder, Robert Meade.
Witnesses: Paul Miller, John Michael Somers.

JAMES, THOMAS. Tredyfrunn, Co. of Chester, Pa. Yeoman. Dec. 8, 1750/1. Dec. 24, 1750. J.334.
Wife: Anne. Child: Thomas, in Great Britain. Nieces: Mary and Anne Jenkins [in Cerrigee, South Wales]. Nephew: George James [in Virginia]. Kinsman: Lewis James, Junr. Friend: Anne Owen. Exec: Anne James.

Witnesses: Geo. Aston, Joseph Bartholomew, John Rowland, John Williams (his mark).

THOMAS, RICHARD. Moorland, Co. of Philadelphia. Fuller. Dec. 13, 1750/1. Dec. 26, 1750. J.336.
Wife: Mary. Child: Rachel. Exec: Mary Thomas, Robert McKee.
Witnesses: James Hawkins, Junr. (his mark), Thomas Lewis, Richard Treat.

MICELMO, JOHN. Moreland, Co. of Philadelphia. Weaver. Dec. 14, 1750/1. Jan. 2, 1750. J.337.
Wife: Mary. Uncle: Adam Willman. Cousin: John Willman. Exec: John Michener, Mary Micelmo.
Witnesses: Robert Cather, John Yerkes.

PARR, SAMUEL. City of Philadelphia. Merchant. -- day of -- 1750/1. Jan. 4, 1750. J.338.
Brother: Caleb of Nottingham, England. Kinsman: Nathaniel Parr. Friends: Lydia Warder, Joseph Trotter, Rachel Catherill, Rebecca Jervis, Hannah Evans, Sarah Sandwith, Anne Bantiff, Sarah Reynells, Margaret Cedgg, William Parr, William Pearson, Daniel Free, Junr. and sister of Daniel. Nephews and Niece: John, Caleb and Anne Parr. Poor of City of Philadelphia. Poor Quakers of Philadelphia. Exec: John Reynells, Joseph Trotter, William Parr.
Witnesses: Thos. Stretch, Joseph Stretch, Nathan Trotter.

SHEWELL, ROBERT. City of Philadelphia. Baker. Dec. 14, 1749/50. Jan. 22, 1750. J.340.
Wife: Elizabeth. Children: Stephen, Joseph, Mary, William, Elizabeth and Robert. Exec: Elizabeth, Stephen and Joseph Shewell. Guardian: Evan Morgan.
Witnesses: P. Sonmans, Jno. Reily.
Codicil: Dec. 18, 1750/1.
Trustee and Guardian: Joseph Fox.
Witnesses: Samuel Sansom, Jno. Reily.

LISTER, ADAM. City of Philadelphia. June 16, 1743/4. Jan. 23, 1750. J.343.
Wife: Ann. Exec: Ann Lister.
Witnesses: John Wright, Philip Hulbeart.

TENNIS, ANTHONY. Towamensing, Co. of Philadelphia. Nov. 24, 1749/50. Jan. 24, 1750. J.343.
Child: Christian. Stepmother: Christian Tennis. Sisters: Elizabeth Morris and Bathsheba Yeocum. Poor of this Township. Exec: Jacob Gatshalick, Isaac Crawl.
Witnesses: Daniel Morgan, Daniel Williams.

MC KEE, ROBERT. Moorland, Co. of Philadelphia. Jan. 7, 1750/1. Jan. 26, 1750. J.344.
Wife: Margaret. Children: John, Jennet and Robert. Exec: Margaret McKee, Robert Miller, Collin McSwiney.
Witnesses: John Campbell (his mark), Thomas Hutchinson (his mark), Peter Dubois.

FREE, GEORGE. Moorland, Co. of Philadelphia. Yeoman. Aug. 9, 1749/50. Jan. 26, 1750. J.346.
Wife: Susannah. Brother: Jacob. Exec: Susannah Free.
Witnesses: Thomas Marple, James Hawkins, Thos. Austin.

COX, PETER. Passyunk, Co. of Philadelphia. Yeoman. Oct. 2, 1748/9. (Oct. 22, 1748 in recorded copy) Jan. 28, 1750. J.347.
Children: Israel, Elianor (Dupee), Rebecca (Wise, Weiss), (John-Jacob) and Margaret (Many). Exec: Israel Cox.
Witnesses: Adam Andres, Jereh. Elfreth, Alexr. Seaton.

JAMES, JANE. Radnor, Chester Co. Penna. Jan. 19, 1750/1. Jan. 30, 1750. J.348.
Stepdaughter: Sarah Thomas. Nephews and Nieces: Mary, Susannah, Margaret, Joseph, Isaac, James and David Davis, Evan James.
Ministers: John Davis, Owen Thomas.
Witnesses: Rees Thomas, Evan David.

MORRIS, JAMES. City of Philadelphia. Merchant. Jan. 27, 1750/1. Jan. 30, 1750. J.349.
Children: Isaac, Anthony, Mary. Brothers: Samuel, Anthony and John. Sisters: [no names given]. Exec: Anthony and John Morris and his children, Isaac, Anthony and Mary. Guardians: His father and mother [no names].
Witnesses: Tho. Bond, C. Brockden, Sarah Morris.

THOMAS, GRIFFITH. Plymouth, Co. of Philadelphia. Oct. 6, 1750/1. Jan. 31, 1750. J.350.
Children: Philip, Elizabeth, Miccah, Ann, Mary and Griffith. Exec: David Cornock, Griffith Thomas. Trustee: Griffith Llewellen.
Witnesses: John Gruber, Anthony Levering, Pat. Menan.

WHITE, THOMAS. Bristol T., Co. of Philadelphia. Yeoman. Aug. 29, 1747/8. Jan. 26, 1750. J.352.
Children: Thomas, John, Joseph, Grace, Sarah, Mary and William. Children of son Robert dec'd. Exec: William and Mary White.
Witnesses: Isaac Shoemaker, Samuel Potts, Christn. Lehman.

DAVID, JOHN. Merion, Co. of Philadelphia. July 27, 1750/1. Feb. 2, 1750. J.354.
Wife: Elizabeth. Children: Mary, Enoch, John and Ann Nathan.
Exec: Elizabeth and Nathan David.
Witnesses: John Enoch, G. Lewellin.

JONES, GRIFFITH. Gwynedd, Co. of Philadelphia. Feb. 3, 1749/50. Feb. 14, 1750. J.355.
Wife: Katharine. Exec: Katharine Jones.
Witnesses: Sarah Davis (her mark), Owen Evans.

BRIGHT, JOHN. Upper Socunk, Co. of Bucks, Penna. May 12, 1750/1. Feb. 15, 1750. J.356.
Wife: Margaret. Children: John and Margaret. Exec. and Trustees: John Gezell, Lawrence Eartbugh.
Witnesses: Peter Cryling, John Beadler.

BRINGHURST, JOHN. City of Philadelphia. Cooper. 4 mo. 16, 1750/1. Feb. 16, 1750. J.358.
Wife: Mary. Children: Joseph, James, John, Mary Fulke and Elizabeth. Son-in-Law: Judah Fulke. Sister-in-Law: Elizabeth Claypoole. Trustees: Anthony Morris, Joshua Crosby. Exec: Mary and John Bringhurst.
Witnesses: John Nelsson, John Dunker, Thos. Hallowell.

ZIEGLER, JACOB. Germantown, Co. of Philadelphia. Jan. 23, 1750/1. Feb. 18, 1750. J.361.
Wife: Anne Catherine. Evangelic Church, Germantown. Exec: Johannes Mourer, Martin Houser.

Witnesses: Peter Brunholtz, George Seyder, Anne Catherine Seyder (her mark).

HENCKEL, ANTONY. Germantown, Co. of Philadelphia. Jan. 17, 1750/1. Feb. 22, 1750/1. J.362.
Wife: Anna Margreta. Children: John and Mary Barbara. Evangelical Church, Germantown. Trustees: John Grethausen, Anthony Gilbert. Exec: Anna Margreta and John Henckel.
Witnesses: Peter Brunholtz, Anthony Gilbert, Baltzer Hoffman.

RIGWAY, EDWARD. White Marsh, Co. of Philadelphia. Yeoman. Feb. 10, 1750/1. Feb. 25, 1750/1. J.363.
Wife: Margret. Children: Edward, John, Job, Elizabeth and Hannah. Brother: Job Ridgway. Exec: Job Ridgway, Edward Stroud.
Witnesses: [of unsigned will] Samuel Jones, John Harry, James Johnston.

FOSTER, THOMAS. Lower Dublin, Co. of Philadelphia. Yeoman. Nov. 1, 1750. March 1, 1750/1. J.365.
Wife: Mary. Child: John. Granddaughters: Sarah Tillyer, Mary and Rachel Foster. Exec: Mary Foster, Philip Tillyer [of Moreland].
Witnesses: Wm. Brittin, Daniel Kelly, Joseph Kelly.

HAAS, JOHAN HENRY. City of Philadelphia. Dec. 31, 1750. March 1, 1750. J.366.
Wife: Anna Elizabeth. Children: Johan Valentine, Johan Henry and others. Father: Hieronymus Haas. Vestry of Lutheran Church at Providence, Penna. Exec: Johannes Schrack, Jacob Miller, --- Livers [of Providence].
Witnesses: Peter Buhl, Jno. Peter Reinhard.

YERKES, HERMAN. Moreland, Co. of Philadelphia. Yeoman. May 2, 1750. March 4, 1750. J.368.
Wife: Elizabeth. Children: Anthony, John, Josiah, Herman, Sarah, Elizabeth, Silas, Stephen, Elias and Titus. Exec: Elizabeth and Silas Yerkes.
Witnesses: David Foulton, Elizabeth Brown, Andrew Patterson.

CLAYPOOLE, ABRAHAM. City of Philadelphia. Merchant. July 4, 1750. March 9, 1750. J.370

Mother: Deborah. Friends: John Swift, Dr. John Kearsley, Junr., Elizabeth Redman, Mary Parker, Robert Ellis, Junr., Samuel Mifflin, Thomas Cross, James Wright, Judah Foulke, Elizabeth Booth. Cousins: George and James Claypoole, Abraham Falconer. Library Company of Philadelphia. Exec: Deborah Claypoole, William Coleman, John Swift.
Witnesses: Isaac Griffitts, Hugh Forbes.

ROBERTS, AWBREY. Gwynedd, Co. of Philadelphia. Aug. 20, 1750. March 18, 1750/1. J.373.
Wife: Ellin. Children: Jacob, Elizabeth, Hannah and Cathrine. Brother-in-Law: Isaac Jones. Exec: Ellin Roberts, Isaac Jones. Trustees: George Lewis, Edward Hughes, John Jones, Jacob Jones.
Witnesses: George Boland (his mark), Rowd. Evans.

TREGO, JACOB. Whiteland, Co. of Chester, Pa. Yeoman. Nov. 24, 1749. March 20, 1750. J.374.
Mother: Elizabeth. Brother: William. Sisters: Elizabeth and Sarah Simcock. Nephew: James Simcock. Brother-in-Law: Samuel Simcock. Uncle: Richard Barry. Exec: Elizabeth Trego, Richard Barry.
Witnesses: Daniel Goldsmith, Saml. Gray.

GARRET, MORTON. Blockley, Co. of Philadelphia. Yeoman. 7 mo. (Sept.) 8, 1750. March 23, 1750. J.376.
Wife: Bridget. Children: John, Jacob, Magdalane and Christian. Exec: John and Jacob Garret.
Witnesses: Joseph Williams, Edward Williams.

SNOWDEN, JOHN. City of Philadelphia. Tanner. Feb. 5, 1750/1. March 28, 1751. J.377.
Wife: Ruth. Children: James, Jedediah, John, Isaac and Mary Keen. Sister: Mary Wright. Grandchild: James Snowden. Friend: Charles Edgar. Exec: John and Isaac Snowden. Trustees: Edward and Joseph Shippen.
Witnesses: Joseph Stretch, Charles Jervis, Paul Isaac Voto.

BLOOM, LUDWIK. Coventry, Co. of Chester, Pa. Innkeeper. March 20, 1750/1. March 28, 1751. J.381.
Wife: Catherine. Children: Elizabeth, Ephriam, John, Christiana, Mary and Catherine. Exec: James Ingels, George Grup.

Witnesses: Jacob Engers, Johannes Brower, Jeremiah Jordon.

VENABELES, THOMAS. Northern Liberties, City of Philadelphia. May 21, 1750. April 1, 1751. J.382.
Wife: Rebecca. Exec: Rebecca Venables.
Witnesses: Edward Jones, Lethea Howell.

HAMER, ADAM. New Providence, Co. of Philadelphia. Cordwainer. April 6, 1751/2. April 10, 1751. J.383.
Brothers: James, Samuel and Lewis. Sisters: Hannah and Elizabeth. Exec. and Friends: Henry Pawling, John Jacobs, Junr. Trustees: John Jacobs, Edward Richardson.
Witnesses: Mary Comings (her mark), John Diener, Peter Boyce (his mark).

MAY, JAMES. Hanover, Co. of Philadelphia. Blacksmith. Jan. 3, 1750/1. April 20, 1751. J.384.
Wife: Margret. Children: Robert and Rachel. Exec: Margret May, Samuel Brooke.
Witnesses: Jacob Fricke, James Brooke, James Brooke, Junr.

ROBERTSON, ALEXANDER. City of Philadelphia. Silversmith. April 4, 1751. April 26, 1751. J.386.
Children: John, Alexander, Margaret, Jane, Sarah, Mary and Catherine. Exec: Philip Syng, Joseph Richardson.
Witnesses: Alexr. Alexander, Paul Isaac Voto.

BROWN, MICHAEL. City of Philadelphia. Silk Dyer. April 17, 1751. April 30, 1751. J.387.
Wife: Sarah. Exec: Sarah Brown, John Hutton.
Witnesses: Edward Evans, Joseph Warner, Nathaniel Brown, Philip Adamson.

ROBERTS, RACHEL. Abington, Co. of Philadelphia. Spinster. May 8, 1750. March 30, 1751. J.388.
Brother: Charles. Brother-in-Law: Morris Gwyn. Niece: Izable Parks. Exec: Morris Gwyn, Samuel Boulton.
Witnesses: John Mason, Barbara Cassel (her mark), Jno. Doreland.

CONSER, GEORGE. McCalls Manor, Pro. of Penna. Jan. 13, 1749/50. April 9, 1751. J.389.

Wife: Anna Barbara. Children: Conrad, Christiana, Catarina, Elizabeth, Nicholas and Andrew. Exec: Anna Barbara and Conrad Conser.
Witnesses: Peter Specht, Yockern Nogell, Mathias Richard.

FINNEY, WILLIAM. Germantown, Co. of Philadelphia. Cordwainer. March 27, 1751/2. April 16, 1752. J.390.
Brothers: Samuel and Richard. Sisters: Rebecca Jones, Elizabeth Todd and Mary Bringhurst. Brother-in-Law: John Bringhurst. Nephews and Nieces: Thomas and Hannan Tresso, Hannah Finney. Exec: Elizabeth Todd, John Bringhurst.
Witnesses: Charles Bensel, Leonard Steinbruner, Danl. Potts, Roby. Greenway.

ASHTON, JOSEPH. Lower Dublin, Co. of Philadelphia. Yeoman. Oct. 31, 1750. April 24, 1751. J.392.
Children: Thomas, Isaac, Hannah Thomas, Mercy Williard and Rachel Roberts. Nephew: John Ashton. Exec: Thomas Ashton.
Witnesses: Samuel Mickle, Thomas Brooks, Nathaniel Walton.

CLYMER, WILLIAM. City of Philadelphia. Merchant. March 22, 1749/50. April 29, 1751. J.393.
Wife: Margaret. Nephews: William, George and Daniel Clymer. Minister and Wardens of Christ Church for poor widows. Exec: Margaret Clymer, Charles Willing.
Witnesses: Daniel Magee, Jos. Fox, William Fisher.

POEK, ARCHIBALD. Abington, Co. of Philadelphia. Taylor. Oct. 23, 1749. May 1, 1751. J.395.
Brothers and sisters: Moses, Elizabeth, Andrew, Jane Wilson, Mary Calwall, John and Mary Lockhard. Nephew: Moses Lockhard. Cousins: Archibald Wilson, James Galloway.
Witnesses: Henry Shellenberg, Thomas Clifford, Alexr. Seaton.
Codicil: April 18, 1751.
Witnesses: John Thaw, Margaret McKee (her mark), Richard Treat.

SANDERS, JOHN. Lower Milford Twp., Co. of Bucks, Pa. Sept. 26, 1747. May 1, 1751. J.397.
Wife: Anne. Children: Samuel and Jacob. Brother-in-Law: Jacob Musselman. Exec: Jacob Musselman, Jacob Sanders.
Witnesses: Johannes Funk, George Ackerman.

BRUNER, PAUL. City of Philadelphia. April 8, 1751. May 4, 1751. J.398.
Wife: Gertrude. Children: ---. Brother: Henry. Exec: Frederick Marshtattler, Henry Bruner.
Witnesses: John Keppinger, Christian Weber.

RICHARDSON, AWBREY. Providence, Co. of Philadelphia. Yeoman. April 30, 1751/2. May 7, 1751. J.399.
Wife: Margret. Children: Daniel, Amos, Abrey, Jonathan, Elizabeth, Hannah and Susanna. Brothers: Richard, Edward. Exec: Richard Richison. Trustee: Edward Richison.
Witnesses: Thomas Reese, Peter Boyle (his mark).

PHILIPS, OWEN. Tredyfrun, Co. of Chester, Penna. Feb. 18, 1751/2. May 11, 1751. J.401.
Brothers: Thomas, John, Joan and Jennet. Nephews and Nieces: John and Grace Griffith [in England]. Cousins: Esther William, Mary and Catherine William. Poor of Congregation [of Anabist]. Friends: John Thomas, Sarah David, Rachel James, George George, Thomas Waters. Exec: Thomas Waters. Trustee: George George.
Witnesses: Thomas Godfrey, William Melchoir, William Godfrey.

BENEZET, JOHN STEVEN. Germantown, Co. of Philadelphia. Merchant. Nov. 10, 1750. May 20, 1751. J.403.
Wife: Judith. Children: Anthony, James, Philip, Judith, Marianna and Susanna. Exec: Judity Benezet. Witnesses: Christopher Sower, Senr., John Adam Gruber, Christopher Sower, Junr.

JONES, GEORGE. City of Philadelphia. Yeoman. Sept. 22, 1743. May 28, 1751. J.404.
Sister: Elizabeth Clay [City of Worcester]. Nephews and Nieces: Children of James Jones decd. [Brogmore Green, Great Brittain]. Friends: Sarah Toms, Thomas Howard, Mary Howard, Andrew Robertson, Kattrine Hinton, Abraham Pratt. Exec: Jonathan Robertson, Esq., Laurence Anderson, Jacob Duchee.
Witnesses: William Cunningham, Warwick Coats, John Chapman.

MOYER, CHRISTIAN. Franconia, Co. of Philadelphia. Yeoman. Jan. 18, 1748/9. June 6, 1751. J.407.
Children: Christian, Jacob, Samuel, Elizabeth Oblinger and Barbara Reiff. Poor of Menonite Meeting of Salford and Fraconia. Grandchild:

Esther Funck. Son-in-Law: Henry Funck. Exec: Christian Moyer, Henry Funck.
Witnesses: Jacob Funck, John Frey, George Bachtall.

HASSELL, SAMUEL. City of Philadelphia. June 10, 1751. June 24, 1751. J.408.
Wife: Anne. Children: Samuel, Elizabeth Huston, Anne Benezet, Jane, Hannah, Sarah and Thomasine. Exec: Anne and Samuel Hassell, Elizabeth and Alexander Huston, Anne and James Benezet, Jane, Hannah, Sarah and Thomasine Hassell.
Witnesses: Townsend White, Benj. Price, Benj. Bagnell, Junr.

THOMAS, JOHN. City of Philadelphia. Baker. June 9, 1751. July 8, 1751. J.410.
Daughters: Mary and Catherine. Friend: William Whitehead. Exec: William Whitehead, Mary and Catherine Thomas.
Witnesses: Thos. Maule, John Head, Junr., Paul Isaac Voto.

CORDERY, HUGH. City of Philadelphia. Block maker. June 16, 1741. July 24, 1751. J.411.
Children: Esther Mifflin, Senoir, Mary and Deborah. Grandchildren: John, George and Sarah Mifflin. Exec: Deborah Cordery.
Witnesses: Wm. Heaslton, Barth Penrose, Job Goodson.

BENBRIDGE, JAMES. City of Philadelphia. Gentleman. Nov. 6, 1749/50. Aug. 6, 1751. J.413.
Wife: Mary. Child: Henry. Exec: Mary and Henry Benbridge.
Witnesses: Robert Tempest, James Stephens.

DAVID, THOMAS. Plymouth, Co. of Philadelphia. Farmer. July 18, 1751. Aug. 14, 1751. J.414.
Wife: Mary. Children: David (only son), Ann, Rachel, Elizabeth, Sarah, Jane, Mary Pugh and Kathrine Bartholomew. Brother: Richard. Friend: John David [Baptist minister at Tredyrun]. Exec: Mary and David David, Samuel Davis.
Witnesses: Hannah Yerkes, George Harkness, Benj. Davis.

BOURNE, ALICE. City of Philadelphia. Widow. June 14, 1751. Aug. 21, 1751. J.416.
Elders of the Presbyterian Church. Indian School in New Jersey. Friend: Ann Benet. Exec: John Clifton.

Witnesses: Peter Bard, Alexr. Crukshank, Alexr. Seaton.

STRICKLAND, MILES. City of Philadelphia. Shopkeeper. 3 mo. 1, 1751. Aug. 22, 1751. J.418.
Wife: Mary. Children: Thomas, John, Rachel Hillbourn and Amos. Nephews and Nieces [grandchildren?]: Children of Thomas Strickland, children of John Naylor and children of Joseph Strickland, decd. Son-in-Law: John Naylor. Exec: John Strickland.
Witnesses: Joseph Chattham, Alexr. Seaton, Rebekah Seaton.
Codicil: 3 mo. 8, 1751.
Witnesses: William Mornington, Alexr. Seaton.

RUSH, JOHN. City of Philadelphia. Gunsmith. July 18, 1751/2. Aug. 27, 1751. J.420.
Wife: Susannah. Brother: William. Children: Rachel, Rebecca, Benjamin, Jacob and John. Cousin: William Rush. Brother-in-Law: Jacob Hall. Exec: Susannah and William Rush. Trustees: Jacob Hall, William Rush.
Witnesses: Daniel Rees, John Elton, Alexr. Seaton.

NICHOLAS, ANTHONY. City of Philadelphia. Blacksmith. 6 mo. 24, 1751/2. Aug. 30, 1751. J.422.
Brother: John. Children: Samuel, Mary and Sarah. Brother-in-Law: Attwood Shute. Exec: John Nicholas, Attwood Shute.
Witnesses: Samuel Webster, Jno. Reily.

MORRY, WILLIAM. City of Philadelphia. Yeoman. March 25, 1750/1. Sept. 3, 1751. J.423.
Wife: Barbara. Children: Elizabeth, Maria, Anna, Hannah, Jacob and William. Exec: Jacob and William Morry.
Witnesses: John Stillwaggon, Hannes Kuncell (her mark).

CLASS, ALEXANDER. City of Philadelphia. Mariner. July 21, 1751/2. Sept. 12, 1751. J.425.
Friend and Exec: John Dickson, mariner.
Witnesses: John Leverly, John Smith, Gregory McCarty.

SMITH, MARGARET. Wife of Armstrong Smith. Shipwright. Wiccacoe, Co. of Philadelphia. Oct. 14, 1750/1. Sept. 19, 1751. J.426.
Husband: Armstrong Smith. Nephews: John and Andrew Reese, Joseph Horsey. Nieces: Rebecca Roberts, Elizabeth Feegan, Rebecca

Sutton, Elizabeth Horsey, Elizabeth Reese. Friend: Thomas Penrose. Exec: Thomas Penrose, John Palmer.
Witnesses: Plunket Fleeson, Catherine Fleeson, Mary Holland.

SLIGER, JOHN. McCalls Manor, Prov. of Penna. Nov. 7, 1750. May 18, 1751. J.430.
Wife: Catharine. Children: [names not given]. Exec: Catherine Sliger.
Witnesses: Conrad Reber, John Adam Kline, John Hart (his mark), Marlin Sell.

WILLIAMS, ELEANOR. Blockley, Co. of Philadelphia. Widow. 8 mo. 22, 1749/50. Oct. 1, 1751. J.431.
Children: Sarah, Jane and Daniel. Grandchild: Ellin Humphrey. Exec: Daniel Williams.
Witnesses: Hugh Evans, Robt. Roberts, Lewis Jones.

NEGLEE, JOHN. Northern Liberties, City of Philadelphia. Yeoman. Aug. 20, 1751. Oct. 7, 1751. J.432.
Wife: Catherine. Children: Mary, Henry, John, Jacob and Ann. Son-in-Law: Alexander Forbes. Exec: Catherine, John and Jacob Neglee.
Witnesses: Richard Collings, Jno. Reily.

BRIGHT, JANE. City of Philadelphia. Widow. Oct. 1, 1751. Oct. 15, 1751. J.433.
Son-in-Law: James Bright. Friends: Randall Yeaton, William Gisling. Exec: Philip Syng, William Lawrence.
Witnesses: Joseph Johnson, Benjn. Hooton, Randall Yeaton.

SMITH, SEBASTIAN. Kipback, Prov. of Penna. Blacksmith. Sept. 16, 1751. Oct. 19, 1751. J.435.
Wife: [name not given]. Children: John, Leonard, Anna Margaretha, Anna Maria and Catharine. Exec: Anna Barbara Smith.
Witnesses: Frederick Gotz (his mark), Christian Weber.

NAYLOR, MARY. Southampton, Co. of Bucks, Penna. Widow. 8 mo. 16, 1751. Oct. 26, 1751. J.437.
Children: John, Hannah, Samuel and Lane. Grandchildren: Edward and Rachel Edwards. Sons-in-Law: Thomas Edwards, John Carver. Friend: Jeremiah Wolston. Exec: John and Rachel Carver.
Witnesses: Robert White, Jacob Scott, John Carver.

CLEMMER, JACOB. City of Philadelphia. March 20, 1749/50. Nov. 11, 1751. J.438.
Wife: [name not given]. Children: Henry, Esther, Christian, Catherine, Valentine, Jacob, Mary, Barbara, Anne and Elizabeth. Brothers: Christian and John Jacob. Exec: Christian and Valentine Clemmer.
Witnesses: Jacob, Johannes and Barbara Funck (her mark).

RICHARDSON, EDWARD. New Providence, Co. of Philadelphia. Yeoman. 8 mo. 6, 1751. Nov. 15, 1751. J.440.
Wife: Ann. Children: William, Joseph, John, Sarah, Mary, Isaac and Jacob. Father: Joseph. Friend: David Lewis. Exec: Ann and Joseph Richardson. Trustees: Henry Powling, John Jacobs, Junr.
Witnesses: Jon. Jacobs, Junr., Joseph Jacobs, Benj. Jacobs.
Codicil: 8 mo. 28, 1751/2.
Witnesses: Jno. Jacobs, Junr. and Joseph Jacobs.

DAVIS, RICHARD. Vincent, Co. of Chester, Pa. Yeoman. Nov. 2, 1750. Dec. 20, 1750. J.443.
Brothers: John, Morris, Elijah and Elisha. Sisters: Mary Mathias and Elizabeth Griffith. Sister-in-Law: Margaret Davis. Friends: Mary Pugh [widow], Mary Pugh, Junr., Evan, Daniel, Margaret, Elizabeth, Hannah and Rachel Pugh, Owen Thomas. Exec: Morris, Elijah and Elisha Davis.
Witnesses: James Roberts, William James, Jno. Thomas.

NICHOLAS, THOMAS. West Nantmell, Co. of Chester, Pa. Farmer. July 10, 1750. Nov. 20, 1751. J.445.
Children: Elinor, Edward, Mary, Ann and Thomas. Exec: Thomas Nicholas.
Witnesses: William Mackey, Anne Thomas, Hedges Vaines.

MILLER, THOMAS. City of Philadelphia. Nov. 9, 1751. Nov. 26, 1751. J.446.
Wife: Mary. Child: Catherine. Son-in-Law: Charles Rowtt. Exec: Catherine Miller. Asst. Exec: Robert Rawlinson.
Witnesses: Jno. Jones, John Philip Bertholt, Will Hamilton.

SHEWBERT, MARY. City of Philadelphia. Widow. Nov. 27, 1751. Dec. 9, 1751. J.449.

Children: Richard Hockley, Robert, Philip and John. Daughters-in-Law: Mary Armitage and Ann Janvier. Sister: Ann Reaves [in Hartfordshire]. Exec: Richard Hockley, Isaac Zane, Sarah Brown. Witnesses: Geo. Heap, Davis Bassett, David Clerck.

ULRICH, CASPER. City of Philadelphia. Innholder. Nov. 22, 1751. Dec. 10, 1751. J.451.
Wife: Eve. Children: Susanna, Rutter and Philip. Exec: Eve Ulrick. Witnesses: James Bell, Johanes Gottringer, Robert Owens.

DRISCOLL, ALEXANDER. City of Philadelphia. Mariner. Nov. 30, 1751. Dec. 20, 1751. J.452.
Friend and Exec: Richard Palmer [Practitioner of Physick].
Witnesses: Elizabeth Kerr, Jas. Tapscott.

HOPKINSON, THOMAS. City of Philadelphia. Gentleman. Sept. 11, 1751. Nov. 25, 1751. J.450.
[Part of estate in Island of Antigua]. Wife: Mary. Children: Francis, Thomas, Elizabeth, Jane, Mary and Anne. Niece: Elizabeth Boore. Guardians and Exec: Mary Hopkinson, Thomas Cadwalader, Richard Peters, Charles Willing, Esq.

LEGAY, JACOB. City of Philadelphia. Merchant. June 8, 1751. Sept. 20, 1751. J.455.
[Part of estate in St. Michal's, Barbadoes]. Wife: Mary. Children: Jacob and Benjamin. Friends: James Butcher and wife Mary [of St. Michaels Town], Thomas Perkins and wife Ann, Mary Charnock [of St. Michaels Town]. Exec: James Butcher, Thomas Bond, Joseph Grover, Mary Legay.
Witnesses: Nahl. Mager, D. Chambers, Elizabeth Weyman.

PHERIS, JOHN. Passyunk, Co. of Philadelphia. Dec. 7, 1748. Dec. 23, 1751. J.457.
Wife: Margaret. Child: Thomas Zachariah. Exec: Margaret Pheris, David Chambers.
Witnesses: Wm. Shippen, Ross Hall.

HIBY, PETER, Senr. Maxethama, Co. of Philadelphia. Yeoman. July 5, 1751. Dec. 3, 1751. J.458.
Wife: Anna Barbara. Friends: Erhard Fusselman, Casper Winck, Catrina, Anna Barbara and Philip Peter Fusselman, Mary, Christiana

and Peter Seiber, George Adam Kremer, Anna Barbara and Peter Winck, Anna Barbara Ehrist [Christ?], George Ruch, Peter Wirtz, David Fraree. Exec: Anna Barbara Hiby, Jacob Levan, Erhard Fusselman.
Witnesses: Casper Wirick (his mark), Nicholas Jermany.

CREBS, MARGARETA BARBARA. Hanover, Co. of Philadelphia. Widow of Michael Crebs. March 18, 1751/2. Oct. 21, 1751. J.460.
Children: Simon, Henry. Exec: John Campbell, John Peter Bougher.
Witnesses: Peter Conrad, Thomas Yerger.

EVANS, DAVID. Tredyfrin, Co. of Chester, Penna. Yeoman. April 28, 1751. May 17, 1751. J.461.
Brothers: Joshua, Richard, Joel and William. Sisters: Mary, Sarah Wayn, Hannah and Magdalena Morgan. Exec: William Evans.
Witnesses: Joseph Mitchell, Ann Rees, Isaac Davis.

MILLER, PATRICK. Haverford, Co. of Chester, Penna. July 22, 1751. Nov. 13, 1751. J.462.
Wife: Anne. Children: Joseph, Ruth, Mary, Patience, Susannah and Anne. Exec: Anne Miller, Edward Humphreys.
Witnesses: Obadiah Weldy (his mark), Thos. Weldy (his mark), Chas. Humphreys.

POTTS, THOMAS. Colebrook Dale, Co. of Philadelphia. Iron master. Sept. 25, 1747. Jan. 10, 1752. J.464.
Wife: Magdelene. Children: Thomas, Junr., David, John, Mary Clever and Elizabeth Walker. Grandchildren: Sarah Potts, Stephen and Edward Yorke. Son-in-Law: Thomas Yorke. Exec: Magdalene, John and Thomas Potts, Thomas Yorke.
Witnesses: Edward West, Jacob Barnard, Isaac Bernard.
Codicil: Sept. 28, 1747.
Witnesses: Henry Switzer, Darby Sullivan (his mark), Edward West.
Codicil: Sept. 28, 1747.

RICHARDSON, JOSEPH. Providence, Co. of Philadelphia. Yeoman. Dec. 6, 1745. Jan. 14, 1752. J.468.
Children: Samuel and wife, Obrey, Edward and Richard Richardson, Ellinor Harmer, Barbara Davis and Elizabeth Pugh. Nephews and Nieces: Eldest son of Edward Richardson, Elizabeth, James and John

Richardson, eldest son of John Richardson [decd.], Samuel Richardson.
Exec: Obrey, Edward and Richard Richardson.
Witnesses: Thos. Yorke, John White, Jno. Bourne (his mark), David Thomas.
Codicil: Dec. 6, 1745/6.
Witnesses: Thos. Yorke, Jacob Levering, John Davis, David Thomas.
Codicil: 1 mo. 3, 1749/50.
Witnesses: David Thomas, John Jacobs, Francis Hobson.
Codicil: Nov. 9, 1751/2.
Exec: Henry Pawling.
Witnesses: Jon. Jacobs, Isrl Jacobs, Henry Vanderslice.
Codicil: Nov. 9, 1751/2.
Trustee: John Jacobs, Junr.
Witnesses: Jon. Jacobs, Junr., Henry Vanderslice, Isrl. Jacobs.

CLARE, GEORGE. City of Philadelphia. Cordwainer. Jan. 27, 1752/3. Feb. 18, 1752. J.473.
Wife and Exec: Kathrin. Children: [no names given].
Witnesses: Michl. Conner, Andrew Cowen, John Jones (his mark).

FORBES, ALEXANDER. City of Philadelphia. Merchant. Jan. 2, 1752/3. Jan. 31, 1752. J.474.
Wife: Ann. Children: Margaret and Catherine. Brother-in-Law: John Neglee. Exec: Ann Forbes, John Neglee.
Witnesses: Stephin Carmick, Daniel Fergusson.

ARMITT, STEPHEN. City of Philadelphia. Joyner. Dec. 1, 1751/2. Jan. 18, 1752. J.475.
Wife: Sarah. Children: John, Richard, Samuel, Sarah, Ann and Mary. Brother: John. Exec: Sarah and John Armitt.
Witnesses: Thos. Eastwicke, Joseph Trotter, Junr., Jno. Reily.

KAMM, CASPER. New Hanover, Co. of Philadelphia. Blacksmith. Nov. 3, 1741/2. Jan. 17, 1752. J.477.
Wife: Catharine. Children: Catharine Emertin, Vronica and Barbara Paltsgravin. Sons-in-Law: Philip Emert, George Paltsgrave. Grandchild: John Shelleberger. Exec: Philip Emert, George Paltsgrave.
Witnesses: Valentine Geiger, Bernard Dudderer.

VANDERSLICE, ANTHONY. New Providence, Co. of Philadelphia. Yeoman. Oct. 29, 1751/2. Jan. 21, 1752. J.478.
Wife: Martha. Children: Henry, Ann, Catharine, Evea and Anthony. Brother-in-Law: John Pennebacker. Exec: Martha and Henry Vanderslice. Overseer: John Pennebacker.
Witnesses: William How, Nicholas Bunn, John Herrick (his mark).

ATKINS, JOHN. Oxford, Co. of Philadelphia. Yeoman. Dec. 20, 1744/5. Jan. 15, 1752. J.480.
Wife: Ann. Child: John. Grandchildren: Jonathan, John, Joseph and Benjamin Atkins. Friends: Samuel Wells, Benjamin Taylor and Exec.
Witnesses: John Drinker, Henry Drinker.

BONSALL, BENJAMIN. Kingsess, Co. of Philadelphia. Yeoman. April 11, 1750/1. Jan. 20, 1752. J.482.
Wife: Elizabeth. Children: Nathan, Richard, John, Sarah, Hannah, Martha and Benjamin. Son-in-Law: William Horne. Grandchild: Edward Bonsall. Exec: James and Benjamin Bonsall. Overseers: William Horne, Isaac Pearson.
Witnesses: Joseph Fordham, John Pearson, Jacob Webber.
Codicil: Jan. 3, 1751/2.
Witnesses: Abram. Bonsall, Jno. Hunt.

WALDER, JACOB. Germantown, Co. of Philadelphia. Mason. Dec. 18, 1751/2. Jan. 27, 1752. J.486.
Wife: Gertrude. Children: [no names given]. Exec: Gertrude Walder, Christopher Meng.
Witnesses: William Wice, Richard Robb.

PASHASHEE, GEORGE. Co. of Philadelphia. Cordwainer. Feb. 11, 1752/3. March 12, 1752. J.487.
Wife: Margaret. Children: George, Michael and Catherine. Sister-in-Law: Susanna Hillegas. Exec: Michael Deal, Michael Ege.
Witnesses: Michael Hillegas, Paul Isaac Voto.

ENGLE, WILLIAM. Worcester, Co. of Philadelphia. Tanner. March 4, 1752/3. March 18, 1752. J.489.
Wife: Catherine. Child: Jacob. Exec: Catherine Engel, Jacob and Arnold Zimmerman.
Witnesses: Rudolph Bunner, Malcher Wagoner.

EDWARDS, MARTHA. City of Philadelphia. Tayloress. Feb. 11, 1752/3. March 11, 1752. J.490.
Sister: Tamer Edwards. Exec: Thomas Say.
Witnesses: George Wescott, Isaac Bartram.

LEWIS, DAVID. Tredyfrun, Co. of Chester, Penna. Jan. 23, 1752/3. Jan. 29, 1752. J.491.
Wife: Sarah. Brother: John. Nephews and Nieces: [John Lewis' children]. Friends: Abijah, Jesse and Benjamin Stephens, David Davis, Judith Jones, Stephen Evans. Exec: Stephen Evans.
Witnesses: Thomas Water, Thomas Otley, Adam Funk (his mark).

PAULL, WILLIAM. City of Philadelphia. Jan. 13, 1752/3. March 30, 1752. J.492.
Father: William Paul, Tanner, Glasgow, Scotland. Exec: John Nelson.
Witnesses: Daniel Goodman, Dougall Ferguson.

WISTER, CASPER. City of Philadelphia. Brass button maker. Feb. 13, 1752/3. March 28, 1752. J.493.
Wife: Catherine. Children: Richard, Casper, Margaret, Rebecca, Sarah and Catherine. Sisters: Dorothy, Alberthia and Maria Barbara Hitner. Brother: Lodowick, in Germany. Nephew: Martin Ulmer. Brother-in-Law: Richard Johnson. Guardians: Catherine Wister, Dance Deshler, Hugh Roberts. Children of Lodowick in Germany. Children of Dorothy Genshozn [Geushozn?] in Germany. Children of Alberthea Ulmer in Germany.
Witnesses: Jacob Shoemaker, John Wister, Thos. Shoemaker, Paul Isaac Voto.

BRINGHURST, GEORGE. Germantown, Co. of Philadelphia. Saddler. Jan. 21, 1752/3. March 21, 1752. J.503.
Wife: Anna. Children: John, George, Hester, Samuel, William and Sarah. Son-in-Law: George Palmer. Exec. and Guardian: Anna Bringhurst. Trustees: John Bringhurst, George Palmer.
Witnesses: John Jones, Danl. Mackenet, Thos. Rose.

SMITH, SIMON. White Marsh, Co. of Philadelphia. Taylor. Feb. 17, 1752/3. April 25, 1752. J.506.
Wife: Catherine. Children: Christopher, Anna Maria and others [names not given]. Trustee: John Morris. Exec: Catherine Smith.
Witnesses: Christian Lesser, Richard Jackson, Pat. Menan.

SIEGEL, JACOB. City of Philadelphia. Aug. 14, 1751/2. April 27, 1752. J.508.
Wife: Susannah. Children: Benjamin, Catherine and Mary Elizabeth. Godfather: Jacob Walder. Exec: John Nicholas Kressman, Susannah Siegel.
Witnesses: Christopher Shibele, John Nicholas Kressman.

GREEN, CHRISTOPHER. City of Philadelphia. Feb. 27, 1747/8. April 7, 1752. J.509.
Wife: Ann. Exec: Ann Green.
Witnesses: Jno. Reily, Robt. Forde.

LOGAN, JAMES. Stenton, Prov. of Penna. Gentleman. Nov. 25, 1749/50. May 1, 1752. J.510.
Wife: Sarah. Children: James, William and Hannah Smith. Grandchildren: Sarah and Mary Norris. Brother: Dr. William Logan. Brother-in-Law: Israel Pemberton. Sons-in-Law: Isaac Norris, John Smith. Niece: Mary Norris. Public Academy of the City of Philadelphia. Friends: John Kinsey, Richard Peters, Israel Pemberton, Junr., Edward Shippen. Poor Quakers in Philadelphia. Poor Quakers in Germantown. Cousin: Andrew Read. Exec: Sarah, William and James Logan, John Smith. Overseers: Isaac Pemberton, Israel Pemberton, John Kinsey.
Witnesses: Thomas Armstrong, Jared Irvine, Richd. Peters.

HANG, PAUL. Upper Dublin, Co. of Philadelphia. Jan. 16, 1751/2. Jan. 29, 1752. J.533.
Wife: Maria Veronica. Children: [no names given]. Exec: John Martin, Valentine Puff, Maria Veronica Hang.
Witnesses: Peter Wilhelm, Valentine Huschlin.

RICHARD, WILLIAM. Oley, Co. of Philadelphia. Dec. 6, 1751/2. Feb. 15, 1752. J.534.
Wife: Elizabeth. Children: William, Ruth, Sarah, Mary Ball, Owen, Margaret and James. Exec: Peter Weaver, Elizabeth Richard.
Witnesses: James Norrell (his mark), Benj. Langworthy, Jane Norrell.

STEPHENS, DAVID, JUNR. New Brittain, Co. of Bucks, Pa. Cordwainer. Jan. 18, 1752/3. Feb. 18, 1752. J.535.
Father: David. Brother: Samuel. Cousin and Exec: John Stephens.
Witnesses: William Davies, Junr., David Stephens, William Davies.

KLEINERD, JOHN. Maconce, Co. of Bucks, Penna. Yeoman. Dec. 2, 1751/2. April 10, 1752. J.535.
Wife: Jarly. Children: Philip and Anna. Exec: Philip Kleinard.
Witnesses: Geede Grim, Johannes Carchinburgh, Nicholas Jermany.

SHILBERT, ANNE. Germantown, Co. of Philadelphia. Widow of Peter Shilbert, yeoman. June 18, 1746/7. June 20, 1752. J.537.
Poor of Germantown. Grandchildren: Hannah Englehard, Henry, George and John Thomas. Exec: John Theobold End, John Frederick Ax.
Witnesses: Imanuel Kalkglasser, John Bertolet, Philip Benezet.

DEHAVEN, HERMAN, SENR. Providence, Co. of Philadelphia. Oct. 1, 1749/50. April 23, 1752. J.538.
Wife: Annica. Children: Isaac, Edward, Abram, John, Harmond, Katherine, Mary Seidly (Seiely), Elizabeth Paulin and Margaret Davis.
Son-in-Law: John Paulin. Exec: Annica Dehaven.
Witnesses: John Harpole, Ludwick Harpole (his mark), Rogr. North.

DICKINSON, JOSHUA. Whitpain, Co. of Philadelphia. Yeoman. April 20, 1752/3. May 6, 1752. J.539.
Wife: Elizabeth. Children: Mary Richards, Joseph, Benjamin, Joshua, Cadwalader, Jonathan and David. Father-in-Law: Richard Morris.
Exec: Elizabeth and Joseph Dickinson. Trustees and Guardians: Joseph Jones, Job Pugh, Rowland Evans.
Witnesses: Jno. Roberts, John Bell, Rowd. Evans.

KIRK, Thomas. Moorland, Co. of Philadelphia. Taylor. 1 mo. 6, 1752/3. April 22, 1752. J.540.
Wife: Mary. Children: Joseph, Ann, Mary, Susannah and Sarah.
Exec: Mary Kirk.
Witnesses: John Shaw, David Griffith (his mark), John Hart.

HUGH, ROWLAND. Gwynedd, Co. of Philadelphia. Yeoman. 3 mo. 27, 1752/3. April 14, 1752. J.541.
Wife: Ellin. Children: Ellis and Jane Lea. Grandchildren: Atkins Hugh, Jane Roberts. Cousin: Thomas Evans, Junr. Brother-in-Law: Owen Evans. Exec: Ellis Hugh. Overseers: Owen Evans, Thomas Evans, Junr.
Witnesses: Robert Roberts, David Humphrey, Jacob Jones, Jno. Evans.

FALKNER, THOMAS. Bethlehem, Co. of Bucks, Penna. Farmer. Feb. 20, 1752. May 8, 1752. J.542.
Wife: Joan. Children: Jesse, Mary, Susannah and Eve. Nieces: Eve Green, Mary Green. Nephew: James McCayston Pond. Exec: Thomas Downing, Jesse Falkner.
Witnesses: Jas. Ralston, James Perrey.

STORY, ELIZABETH. City of Philadelphia. Widow. March 1, 1752. May 7, 1752. J.544.
Children: Three daughters and one son. Exec. and Guardians: Edward Evans, Thomas Say, Anthony Benezet.
Witnesses: Joseph Marriott, Isaac Bartram, Hannah Roberts.

PANNEBAKER, JACOB. Perkyome, Co. of Philadelphia. Dec. 12, 1751/2. June 8, 1752. J.545.
Wife: Margaret. Children: Matthias, Cornelius, Henry, Elizabeth and Barbara. Brothers: Peter and John. Brother-in-Law: Cornelius Tyson. Exec: Peter and John Pannebaker. Trustees: Cornelius Tyson, Peter Kuster.
Witnesses: Jacob Umstat, Abraham Englin (his mark), Robert Jones.

MOYER, CASPER. Bristol, near Germantown, Co. of Philadelphia. June 12, 1752. June 16, 1752. J.548.
Wife: Barbara. Four children [no names given]. Exec: Henry Shelleberg, Rudolph Surber.
Witnesses: John Dewald End, Charles Hay, John Zacharias.

EDGELL, WILLIAM. City of Philadelphia. Merchant. Feb. 3, 1752. June 24, 1752. J.549.
Wife: Sarah. Brothers-in-Law: John Mather and Joseph Davis. Friend: Mary Devaryhouse. Exec: Amos Strettell, John Mifflin.
Witnesses: Henry Harrison, John Lynn, Paul Isaac Voto.

SMITH, JOHN. Northern Liberties, City of Philadelphia. Inn holder. June 12, 1752. July 30, 1752. J.550.
Wife: Margaret. Sister: Barbara Hyson. Son-in-Law: George Smith. Exec: Margaret Smith.
Witnesses: Wm. Cooper, Andrew Paterson, John Simons.

SEIGEL, SUSANNAH. City of Philadelphia. Widow. May 9, 1752. July 31, 1752. J.551.

Children: Benjamin and Catharine. Exec: Nicholas Kressman, Benjamin Seigel.
Witnesses: Christopher Shibler, John Simons.

WHEATLY, JOHN. Abington, Co. of Philadelphia. Cordwainer. March 11, 1752. Aug. 1, 1752. J.552.
Wife: Charity. Son-in-Law and Exec: James Hunter.
Witnesses: Isaac Evans, Henry Lewis.

LANDER, ANDREW. City of Philadelphia. School master. April 16, 1752. Aug. 13, 1752. J.557.
Exec: Jane Grivel.
Witnesses: Paul Isaac Voto, William Trotter, Francis Many.

DAVID, ELINOR. Tredyfrun, Co. of Chester, Penna. Spinster. March 14, 1752/3. Aug. 15, 1752. J.558.
Sister: Jane James. Nephews: James David, Isaac Abram and Thomas Waters. Nephews and Nieces: Elizabeth Hackett, Mary Owen, Jonathan, Nathan, Jesse, Ruth and Lydia Roberts, Gaziah Philips, Mirriam David, Abigal Buxon, Elizabeth Thomas, John, Mary, Hannah and David Parry, Rachel James. Friends: John Thomas and his three sons and one daughter [no names given]. Exec: Thomas Waters.
Witnesses: Edward Roberts, Samuel John, Stephen Evans.

SECKENBARGER, PETER. Germantown, Co. of Philadelphia. Aug. 12, 1752/3. Aug. 20, 1752. J.560.
Wife: Catharine. Cousins: Catherine, Hannah and Summer Laden.
Exec: Daniel Buddone.
Witnesses: George Begus, Christopher Brust, John Andrews.

REES, EVAN. Merion, Co. of Philadelphia. Yeoman. June 24, 1752. July 25, 1752. K.1.
Wife: Gwenn. Daughter: Mary. Exec: Wife Gwenn, Joshua Humphreys, Samuell Williams. Legatees and Trustees: Joshua Humphreys of Merion, Daniel Williams, Philadelphia, baker, Overseers of poor of Philadelphia, and Friends belonging to Merion Meeting (names not given).
Witnesses: John Smith, Allen Poke (his mark).

DUFFIELD, PETER. Moorland, Co. of Philadelphia. Aug. 12, 1752. Aug. 24, 1752. K.3.
Father: Thomas. Sisters-in-Law: Martha, wife of brother John, Mary Mills. Daughter: Elizabeth. Beneficiaries: Hester, wife of Peter Slots; Elizabeth, wife of Edward Collins; Baptist Meeting, Lower Dublin, Philadelphia Co. Exec: Crispin Collett of Byberry, Peter Peterson Van Horn.
Witnesses: Philip Tellyer, William Brittin, Edward Tellyer.

CRESSON, SARAH. City of Philadelphia. Widow. Jan. 20, 1748. Aug. 24, 1752. K.6.
Children: Caleb and Joshua. Brothers and Sisters: George, Samuel and Joshua Emlen, Rebecca Lobden, Ann Miller and Mary Armitt. Cousins: Mary, wife of Obadiah Eldridge; Mary Oldman, daughter of Mary Eldridge. Nieces: Hannah and Mary Miller. Beneficiaries: Susanna Medcalf, and sister Mary in trust for the poor Friends of the Monthly Meeting of Philadelphia. Guardians: Brother, Joshua, and brother-in-law John Armitt. Exec: Samuel and Joshua Emlen, John Armitt.
Witnesses: Joseph Stretch, Mary Moon, Charles Brockden.

HOLT, SAMUEL. City of Philadelphia. Sadler. Aug. 29, 1752. Sept. 14, 1752. K.8.
Brother: Rives Holt, Esquire. Wife and Exec: Elizabeth.
Witnesses: Charles How, Jr., John Stow, Sarah Browne.

FIELDING, WILLIAM. City of New York. Mariner. May 9, 1728. Aug. 4, 1752. K.10.
Wife and Exec: Leitje.
Witnesses: John Van Pelt, John Buckhoeen, T. V. Demeyer.

WILLIAMS, JOHN. City of Philadelphia. Cooper. Nov. 17, 1750. Oct. 7, 1752. K.11.
Wife: Anne, late Edwards. Beneficiaries: Friends, Stephen Vidal, Mathew Forster, a son of James and Hannah Forster, Joel and Mary, son and daughter of Jonathan Evans, cooper, and Hannah, his wife. Exec: Jonathan Evans, Joseph Trotter.
Witnesses: Zacharia Whitpaine, John Reily.

HURTT, REBECCA. City of Philadelphia, late of Newtown, Maryland. Singlewoman. July 26, 1751. Oct. 30, 1752. K.13.

Sister: Ann. Brother: John. Exec: Mary, wife of Richard Merian.
Witnesses: John Pickles, Richard Primmer.

POWELL, THOMAS. Lower Dublin, Co. of Philadelphia. Yeoman. Sept. 15, 1752. Oct. 20, 1752. K.14.
Wife: Elinor. Children: Mary, Samuel, Rebecca, Isaac, Joseph, William, Thomas and Benjamin. Exec: Wife Elinor, Joshua Jones, John Daniel.
Witnesses: Enoch Morgan, David Pinkerton, Jane Holme.

HANNA, JACOB. Gwynedd, Co. of Philadelphia. Yeoman. Feb. 26, 1747/8. Oct. 28, 1752. K.15.
Brothers: Isaac, William, Grace (Trump), Bees, Abraham, Mary, Sarah, Ann, Elizabeth. Exec: Brother William.
Witnesses: John Potts, John Lukens.

LLEWLIN, GRIFFITH. Lower Merion, Co. of Philadelphia. 8 mo. 6, 1750. Nov. 6, 1752. K.16.
Wife: Marianna. Children: John and ---. Exec: Wife Marianna and son John.
Witnesses: David Harry, Jr., James Truman, Mary Davis.
Codicil: 8 mo. 8, 1750.
Witnesses: William Thomas, David Harry, Jr.

YSERTO, OTTO. Upper Hanover, Co. of Philadelphia. Proved Nov. 7, 1752. K.18.
Wife and Exec: Maria, who renounced as such and Letter of Administration c.t.a. granted to son, Bernard.
Witnesses: Henry Beck, Peter Loup, Jacob Vanamaker, George Sholtze.

GRESS, JOHANNES. Germantown, Co. of Philadelphia. Aug. 20, 1752. Nov. 9. 1752. K.19.
Wife: Anna Magdalena. Children: Elizabeth and Anna Magdalena.
Exec. and Guardians: Wife and John Zachary, of Germantown, tanner.
Witnesses: George Herger, John Theobald Ent.

ACKER, HENRY. Oct. 12, 1752. Nov. 8, 1752. K.20.
Wife: Anna Catherine. Children: John and Mary Magdalena. Exec: Philip Gavy, Samuel Mummy.

Witnesses: Abraham Beck, schoolmaster, John Goodshires of Philadelphia, who testify that the said will was reduced to writing at the request of the Testator Oct. 12, 1752 and he was unable to sign.

MATLACK, TIMOTHY. City of Philadelphia. Brewer. Aug. 14, 1752. Nov. 10, 1752. K.22.
Wife: Name not given. Children: Seth, White and Josiah. Exec: Son-in-law, Ruben Heines.
Witnesses: John Sayre, Rachel Sayre, Josiah Jackson.
Codicil: Aug. 15, 1752.
Witnesses: Elizabeth Matlack, Josiah Jackson.

NORWOOD, JOHN. Nov. 29, 1748. Dec. 13, 1752. K.24.
Wife and Children: Names not given. Exec: Solomon Fussel, Jeremiah Warder and wife.
Witnesses: Benjamin Hooton, Elizabeth Rosedds (her mark), William Lawrence, Jr.

CRAMER, CASPAR. Co. of Bucks, Pa. Nov. 16, 1752. Dec. 15, 1752. K.25.
Wife and Exec: Elizabeth. Children: Names not given.
Witnesses: Baltus Carbough, Philip Fluck.

RICHEY, JOHN. Philadelphia. Weaver. Dec. 5, 1752. Dec. 19, 1752. K.26.
Children: Mary (Boid), Darcus (Sterling), Mathew and Edward. Exec: Son Edward.
Witnesses: William Aduddell, Benjamin Mason, John Lyons.

LEWIS, GEORGE. Montgomery, Co. of Philadelphia. Yeoman. 7 mo. 10, 1750. Dec. 23, 1752. K.27.
Daughter: Elizabeth, wife of Isaac Jones. Grandchildren: Daniel, Jane, Ruth and Isaac Jones. Exec: Isaac Jones, son-in-law, and Edward Hugh, cousin. Overseers: Rowlan Evans, John Williams.
Witnesses: Daniel Morgan, John Evans, John Evans, Jr.

BOONE, JANE. City of Philadelphia. Innholder. Dec. 15, 1750. Dec. 28,1752. K.29.
Children: William and Elizabeth (Turner). Sisters: Mary Pearce and Catherine Adams. Exec: Thomas Say.
Witnesses: Edward Drinker, Alexander Crukshank, Abraham Bickley.

JAMES, JAMES. City of Philadelphia. Late of Newtown, Maryland. Tanner and Currier. Nov. 17, 1752. Dec. 22, 1752. K.30.
Brother: Jervis James. Uncle and Exec: Thomas Jervis of Philadelphia. Witnesses: Mark Huhl, Charles Moore, Mary Dallas, John Reily.

SMITH, ULRICH. Salford, Co. of Philadelphia. Laborer. Dec. 24, 1752. Jan. 12, 1753. K.31.
Brother and Sister: Jacob and Elizabeth Rebin, wife of John Conrad Cramer of Switzerland.
Exec: Jacob Hoffman, William Schooler of Philadelphia, yeoman.

ROBERTS, EDWARD. New Providence, Co. of Philadelphia. Yeoman. Dec. 19, 1748. Jan. 16, 1758. K.32.
Children: Samuel, Jane, Ann, wife of Thomas Turner, Susannah, wife of William Edward, Edward and Febe. Grandson: Edward Roberts.
Exec: Samuel Roberts.
Witnesses: Lewes Morgan (his mark), Thomas Davis, James Curry.

RAMBO, PETER. New Providence, Co. of Philadelphia. Yeoman. Aug. 24,1744. Jan. 10, 1753. K.34.
Children: John, Peter, Guner, William, Ann, wife of Roger North, and Mary, wife of John Copling. Exec: Son John.
Witnesses: Edeth Adams (her mark), Richard Jacob, Thomas Bull.

SMITH, THOMAS. Co. of Philadelphia. Clothier. April 24, 1751. Feb. 5, 1753. K.36.
Son: John. Exec: Nathan Gibson and David Gibson, his son, who are made legatees contingent upon the death of said son, John.
Witnesses: Benjamin Lobb, Joseph Bonsall, Sarah Bonsall.

TOY, MARY. Lower Dublin, Co. of Philadelphia. Widow. Jan. 24, 1753. Feb. 5,1753. K.37.
Children: Elias, Nicholas, Elenor, Sarah, John, Jacob, James, Margaret and Josiah. Exec: Samuel Wells, John Vanhorn.
Witnesses: Abel Holme, Thomas Stammers.

YERGER, PETER. Co. of Philadelphia. Jan. 10, 1753. Jan. 12, 1753. K.38.
Wife: Barbara. Children: Tobeas, Peter and names of others not given. Exec: Brothers, Vert Yerger and John Yerger.

Witnesses: George Michael Frederick, Nicholas Kribiler.

ENGERS, JACOB. Co. of Chester, Pa. Husbandman. Jan. 20, 1753. Feb. 16, 1753. K.39.
Wife: Easter. Children: Easter and Fronica. Exec: Wife Easter, Christian Brower, Christian Beary.
Witnesses: Jacob Bosart, Andrew Height (his mark), Joseph Engers.

PRESTON, WILLIAM. City of Philadelphia. Mariner. April 14, 1746. Feb. 21, 1753. K.41.
Children: Mary Hannah, Mary, wife of Thomas Coatam, Margaret, Samuel and Belcher. Exec: Margaret and Hannah Preston, Joseph Wharton, Joseph Parker, David Ranken.

GRAFF, JOSEPH. City of Philadelphia. Nov. 15, 1752. Jan. 21, 1753. K.42.
Wife: Catherine. Children: John, John Jacob, Joseph, Samuel, Magdalena, Maria and Susanna. Beneficiaries: Overseers of the Poor of the People called Quakers, Philadelphia, elders of the Meeting of Meninites at Skippnack, in trust for the poor, Christopher Sout, John Eckstine, in trust for the poor of Germantown. Exec: Daniel Mackanet, shopkeeper, Philadelphia, and son, John Jacob.
Witnesses: John Oswaldt, Alexander Sexton.

SHRAGER, GERHART. Towamenson, Co. of Philadelphia. Weaver. Jan. 12, 1753. Feb. 21, 1753. K.44.
Wife: Janicken. Children: Goshen, Helena, Eve, Gertroude and Catherine. Exec: Jacob Gotschalk, Jr., son-in-law, and John Uly Stauffer.
Witnesses: Gabriel Shuster, John Hendricks, Andrew Ziegler.

PIGTIN, MARY BARBARA. Co. of Philadelphia. Widow. May 18, 1749. March 3, 1753. K.46.
Beneficiaries: St. Michael's Dutch Lutheran Church, Philadelphia, Anna Catherine, wife of George David Sigle, John Henry Piglin, Philadelphia Co. Exec: Lawrence Bast, farmer, John David Sigle, butcher, Philadelphia Co.

MONTGOMERY, ROBERT. New Providence, Co. of Philadelphia. Feb. 19, 1753. March 3, 1753. K.41.

Wife: Jane. Children: John, Mary, Robert (and an unknown child). Exec: John Edwards, David Told. Trustee: John Cammel. Witnesses: David Knox, William Connely, Israel Jacobs.

BETEW (BETUE), ANN. Co. of Bucks, Pa. Widow. June 20, 1748. March 7, 1753. K.49.
Daughter and Exec: Martha (Maclean).
Witnesses: William Brittin, Thomas Tillyer, Philip Tillyer.

MOORE, EASTER, City of Philadelphia. March 4, 1753. March 14, 1753. K.50.
Sisters: Elizabeth (Foord), Mary (Price). Beneficiaries and Exec: Jonathan Ogden, Mary Price.
Witnesses: John Roberts, John Cousens (his mark), George Wort (his mark).

STUART, THOMAS. City of Philadelphia. Shipwright. Sept. 18, 1753. March 14, 1753. K.51.
Wife and Exec: Hannah. Children: John, Thomas, Rachel, Joseph (and an unknown child).
Witnesses: Henry Rigby, John Reily.

PIERCE, THOMAS. City of Philadelphia. June 9, 1752. March 19, 1753. K.52.
Children: John, Thomas, Mary, wife of Joseph Inglis and Elizabeth, widow of Arnold Francis. Grandchildren: Thomas and Griffith Pierce; John Forrest; Thomas and David Francis; Jane Pierce; Sarah, Rachel, Hannah and Margaret Francis; Anthony, William and Ann Forrest; Israel, Mary and Thomas Inglis, children of Mathew Inglis. Niece: Rachel Hood. Legatee: Elizabeth, wife of Barnabas Pawling. Exec: Daughter Elizabeth Francis and her son, Thomas Francis.
Witnesses: Thomas Rodgers, Peter Hodgson, W. Jones.

SMITH, GEORGE. City of Philadelphia. Gentleman. Sept. 6, 1749. March 20, 1753. K.54.
Wife: Mary (former wife, Sarah). Children: Mary (Bassett), Archer and Josiah, minister. Exec: Revd. Jenkin Jones, Philadelphia, James Hinchman and wife Mary of estate in Penna. and the Jerseys. Exec. in South Carolina: Sons, Archer and Josiah, son-in-law, John Dart, Esq. Granddaughter: Dorothy Bassett.
Witnesses: Thomas Wills, Rebeak Wills, Elizabeth Robeson.

Codicil: Feb. 8, 1753.
Witnesses: Frances Jones, Edward Duffield, William Boddington.

MATTANE, MATHIAS. Cresson, Co. of Philadelphia. Yeoman. Oct. 13, 1748. Aug. 2, 1753. K.57.
Wife: Mary Barbarah. Children: John and Mathias Mallan, and Michael Steitz, step-son. Grandchildren: John, Emy, and other children (names not given) of John Mallane, Mathias and other children of Mathias Mallane (names not given). Beneficiary: Germantown Preparitive Meeting of Quakers. Exec: Jacob Levering, John Johnson.
Witnesses: Joshua Spycker, Mathias Barnstan (his mark).

VAN AKEN, HENRY. City of Philadelphia. Merchant. Dec. 3, 1751. April 4, 1753. K.60.
Wife: Rebecca. Brother-in-Law: Paul Kripner. Son: Paul. Exec: Wife Rebecca, Richard Johnson, Thomas Neudrow.
Witnesses: David Deshler, Moses Forster, Paul Isaac Voto.

SPENCER, JOHN. City of Philadelphia. Shipwright. April 4, 1753. April 7, 1753. K.62.
Wife and Exec: Diana. Children: Samuel, John, Daniel, James, William, Richard, Joseph, Ann and Mary. Father: Samuel.
Witnesses: John Sober, Joseph Grover, Margaret Pettiere.

GREEN, THOMAS. City of Philadelphia. House carpenter. Jan. 19, 1753. April 9, 1753. K.63.
Wife and Exec: Martha. Children: Thomas, Mary, Martha and Joseph. Trustees: Doctor Peter Sommans, Joseph Fox.
Witnesses: Joseph Arthur, Jr., Jean Arthur, Paul Isaac Voto.

TILEY, EDWARD. Deptford Township, Co. of Gloucester, West New Jersey. Yeoman. March 8, 1753. April 10, 1753. K.65.
Wife: Margaret. Daughter: Naome (and unknown child). Brother: John Tiley. Exec. wife and Brother-in-Law: Thomas Overend, cordwainer, and wife Margaret.
Witnesses: James McDonald, Jacob Spike, John Reily.

SHAURER, NICHOLAS. Co. of Bucks, Pa. March 30, 1753. April 10, 1753. K.67.
Wife: Anna Mary. Children: Jacob, Henry, Magdalena and John. Son-in-Law: Christian Henry and wife Anna Maria Shaurer.

Witnesses: Henry Mertz, Frederick Helwig.

GIRKEES, WILLIAM. Marlborough, Co. of Philadelphia. Tavern-keeper. March 12, 1753. April 10, 1753. K.68.
Wife: Anna Margaretha. Children: George, Jacob, Conrad, William, Abraham, Henry, Elizabeth, Anne, Mary and Salome. Exec: Wife and son George.
Witnesses: Charles Long, Joseph Keller.

GIGER, ANTHONY. Co. of Philadelphia. April 7, 1753. April 23, 1753. K.71.
Wife and Exec: Barbara. Brothers: Christopher and Valentine.
Witnesses: John Potts, John Ryan, Mathias Miller.

JACKSON, JOHN. City of Philadelphia. Cordwainer. Aug. 31, 1752. April 23, 1753. K.71.
Children: John, Elizabeth and Ann. Brother: Wilson. Exec: Alexander Moore, John Blackwood of Philadelphia.
Witnesses: Joseph Sears, William McCrea, John Johnson.

BEAT, GEORGE. Co. of Philadelphia. Yeoman. April 18, 1753. April 26, 1753. K.73.
Daughter-in-Law: Elizabeth Trego. Legatee: Elizabeth Morgan.
Exec: Elizabeth Morgan, Jacob Hall.
Witnesses: William Jones, John Sutton.

YOCOM, PETER. Upper Merion, Co. of Philadelphia. Yeoman. Oct. 30, 1750. April 28, 1753. K.75.
Children: Moses (and others, the names not given). Trustee: Andrew Holsten. Exec: Wife Elizabeth and son Moses.
Witnesses: Ezekiel Rambo, Michael Rambo, Mathias Holsten.
Codicil: Feb. 4, 1753.
Witnesses: Ezekiel Rambo, Mathias Holsten.

LAING, THOMAS. City of Philadelphia. Mariner. April 30, 1753. May 25, 1753. K.76.
Wife and Exec: Elizabeth.
Witnesses: John Meas, James Stevenson.

TUCKER, NICHOLAS. Manor of Moorland, Co. of Philadelphia. Yeoman. Feb. 6, 1753. May 28, 1753. K.77.

Wife: Mary. Legatees: Peter Peters on Van Horn, of Byberry, George Eaton, Sr., Lower Dublin, Stephen Gordon, Moorland, John Brooks, Southampton, Thomas Brooks, Byberry, Humphrey Brooks, Mary Brooks, widow of John Brooks, Southampton, Hannah Brooks, Rebecca Kelly, daughter of Calter Kelly, Moorland and Joshua Jones, Moorland. Exec: Wife Mary and Joshua Jones.
Witnesses: Nathaniel Brittin, Abel Walton, John Keen.
Codicil: Feb. 6, 1753.
Witnesses: Nathaniel Brittin, Abel Walton.

BYER, PHILIP. Amity, Co. of Bucks. Yeoman. April 21, 1753. May 28, 1753. K.79.
Wife: Elizabeth. Children: John, Michael, Benedict, Elizabeth, Catherine and Barbary. Grandchildren: Magdaline, John and Valentine Smith. Son-in-Law: Manonous Sansmans. Exec: Son John and John Gryner, Jr.
Codicil: April 25, 1753.
Witnesses: John Titerryner, John Sands, Elias Dagly.

FINNEY, SAMUEL. Co. of Philadelphia. Cordwainer. May 12, 1753. June 5, 1753. K.83.
Wife: Rebecca. Daughter: Hannah (names of other children not given). Exec: Brother Richard, brother-in-law Daniel Bristol and wife Rebecca.
Witnesses: Jacob Hall, Thomas Bristol, Hezekiah Bristol.

MONINGTON, WILLIAM. City of Philadelphia. Shop-keeper. 4 mo. 18, 1753. July 17, 1753. K.84.
Children: John and Rebecca. Grandson: Wm. Monington.
Beneficiaries: Negro Sam and negro woman, Parthenis and her daughter (name not given). Trustees and Exec: John Reynell, merchant, Thomas Stretch, hatter.
Witnesses: Thomas White, William Gough.
Codicil: April 20, 1753.
Witnesses: John Kidd, John Tseily.

FOGLY, GEORGE. Oly Hills, Co. of Berks, Pa. June 11, 1753. July 28, 1753. K.88.
Daughter: Catharina. Exec: Sons, George and Albrecht.
Witnesses: Frederick Helwig, Deobald Cart.

PELTS, SIMON. July 14, 1753. July 30, 1753. K.89.
Children: John Jacob, Christina and Mary Christine. Exec: Michael Kraws, John Koplin.
Witnesses: Henry Ovelman, Andrew Wise.

YOCOM, PETER. Co. of Philadelphia. Yeoman. Oct. 30, 1750. April 28, 1753. K.90.
Son: Moses (names of daughters not given). Exec: Wife Elizabeth and son Moses.
Witnesses: Ezekiel Rambo, Michael Rambo, Mathias Holsten.
Codicil: Feb. 4, 1753.
Trustee: Andrew Holsten.
Witnesses: Ezekiel Rambo, Mathias Holsten.

ROBERTS, ANN. Gwyned, Co. of Philadelphia. Widow. 4 mo. 15, 1752. Aug. 1, 1753. K.91.
Children: Robert, Edward, Jesse, Hugh and Margaret, wife of Robert Jones. (Former husband Hugh Evans). Trustees: Thomas Evans, Jr., David Humphrey. Grandchildren: Joshua and Margaret Foulke, Ann Davies. Exec: Son Robert.
Witnesses: Jacob Jones, Ellis Hughs, John Evans.

GODFREY, CESAR. City of Philadelphia. Gentleman. July 5, 1753. Aug. 9, 1753. K.92.
Beneficiaries: Catherine Barberrie of New Rochell, New York, widow; Alexander Allaire, Sr., of same place; Henrietta Marcellius, wife of Henry; Catherine Palmer, wife of Samuel; Heller Allaire; Peter Allaire, son of Peter, Sr.; Mary Stoler; Richard Hartley of Philadelphia; Mary Shirley, wife of Captain Shirley; wardens of Christ Church, Philadelphia, in trust for the poor; Alexander Allaire, Jr. Exec: Alexander Allaire, Jr.
Witnesses: John Clifton, Thomas Dermor, Benjamin Price.

JOLLEY, ANDREW. City of Philadelphia. Carpenter. Aug. 19, 1753. Aug. 27, 1753. K.93.
Exec. and wife: Esther. Brothers: John and Archibald. Sister: Margaret Scoby. Niece: Ann Scoby.
Witnesses: Anthony Beneset, Isaac Lobdell, John Wilson.

GREATON, JOSEPH. City of Philadelphia. Sept. 2, 1749. Aug. 30, 1753. K.93.

Exec., Legatee and Devisee: Robert Harding, Philadelphia, gentleman. Contingent upon his decease before Testator, estate to Thomas Digges, gentleman, Prince George's Co., Maryland.
Witnesses: Theodore Schneider, John Dixon, Patrick Carroll.

WATTKINS, ROBERT. Co. of Chester, Pa. Feb. 3, 1753. Nov. 7, 1753. K.94.
Signed at Augusta, Virginia. Exec. and wife: Jane. Children: Aaron, Moses, Reese, Philip, Enoch, Benjamin, Robert and Margaret.
Guardian: William Goarden.
Witnesses: Moses and Reese Wattkins, Robert Williams.

PIDGEON, RICHARD. City of Philadelphia. Mariner. Jan. 16, 1748/9. Sept. 11, 1753. K.95.
Exec. and sole Beneficiary: wife Sarah.
Witnesses: John Drinker, Alexander Seaton, Thomas Godfrey.

USHER, MATHEW. City of Philadelphia. Store-keeper. June 25, 1753. Sept. 7, 1753. K.99.
Father: James. Sisters: Jane, Rose and Margaret. Legatees: Abraham Usher; Elizabeth, daughter of Thomas Cummings; the Parish of St. Brides, Dublin, Ireland. Exec: Abraham Usher.
Witnesses: Persifor Frazer, James Harvey, Walter Shee.

HENRY, PATRICK. June 15, 1744. Sept. 12, 1753. K.100. Exec.: Wife Elizabeth.
Witnesses: Robert Mathers and James Alexander.

HENRY, PATRICK. City of Philadelphia. Mariner.
A marginal note states that there was an error in this [above] record. It is a Letter of Attorney to Elizabeth, wife of Patrick Henry, empowering her to collect data &c.

HENRICK, LOWRENTZ. Towamensin, Co. of Philadelphia. Tanner. Aug. 6, 1753. Sept. 22, 1753. K.101.
Wife: Yanicken. Children: Peter, Benjamin, John William, John, Mathias, Cornelius, Henry, Margareth, wife of Peter Tyson and Seydgen, wife of Walter Jansen. Exec: Wife and sons Cornelius and Henry.
Witnesses: Henry Ruth, Gossen Shrager, Andrew Ziegler.

ROBERDES, ELIZABETH. City of Philadelphia. Spinster. July 7, 1753. Sept. 25, 1753. K.103.
Brother: John. Mother: Elizabeth. Exec. and Sister: Blanch.
Witnesses: Samuel Smith, Andrew Reed, Thomas Smith.

COLLETT, CRISPIN, Bibury, Co. of Philadelphia. Feb. 23, 1743/4. Sept. 28, 1753. K.104.
Wife: Mary. Brothers and Sisters: Thomas, Richard, Elizabeth, Mary and Hester (Vinson). Nephews and Nieces: Elizabeth Huckman, daughter of Henry and Hester Huckman; Mary, William and John Vinson, children of Hester by her second marriage. Exec: Wife Mary, brother Thomas, brother-in-law Joseph Hart.
Witnesses: John Webster, William Marshall, Samuel Swift.

Dec 15, 1756. An obligation is recorded, Dec. 15, 1756, between Benjamin and Samuel Shoemaker who are bound unto Jacob Hoffman and William Shooler, to execute certain provisions of the will of Ulrick Smith of Philadelphia who named as his beneficiaries Elizabeth Reben alias Cramer and Jacob Smith of Germany and who empower the parties of the first part to receive and transmit monies due them from the executors of said will, viz., Jacob Hoffman and William Shooler.

DAVID, JOHN. Upper Merion, Co. of Philadelphia. Yeoman. Dec. 7, 1752. April 11, 1753. K.107.
Brother: Evan. Grandchildren: (names not given). Legatees: Joshua Edwards and to William Rees and James Davis, in trust for the support of the ministry. Trustees of Will: William Rees, James Davis. Exec: Wife Deborah and son Samuel.
Witnesses: Michael Thomas, John Francis, James Davis.

LEWIS, ELLIS. Upper Dublin, Co. of Philadelphia. 7 mo. 22, 1753. Oct. 1753. K.108.
Wife: Anne. Children: Ellis, Lewis, Jane and Elizabeth. Overseer: John Roberts. Exec: Son Ellis.
Witnesses: Ellis Hughs, Ellis Ellis, John Roberts.

SHOEMAKER, ABRAHAM. Bristol, Co. of Philadelphia. Yeoman. 9 mo. 21, 1753. Oct. 11, 1753. K.109.
Children: Abraham, William, Benjamin, George, Catherine and Sarah, wife of Daniel Pastorius. Brother: Arnold. Overseers: Brother-in-law

Anthony Williams, Thomas Rose. Cousin: Sarah Harris. Exec: Wife Amely and son William.
Witnesses: Benjamin Armitage, William White, Thomas Rose.

CLOSSON, ANN. City of Philadelphia. Widow. May 22, 1748. Oct. 12, 1753. K.113.
Granddaughter: Frances, daughter of George Heap, sadler.
Beneficiaries: (contingent upon the death of Frances Heap), William Branson Hockley, son of Richard Hockley; Elizabeth Sims, daughter of Joseph Sims; Mary Eyres, daughter of John Eyres, baker. Exec: Joseph Sims, Richard Hockley, Philadelphia, merchants.
Witnesses: Townsend White, Thomas Hockley, John Reily.

LEVERING, JACOB. Roxborrow, Co. of Philadelphia. Joiner. Dec. 22, 1752. Oct. 22, 1753. K.114.
Children: Magdalen, wife of Samuel Showter, Abraham, Wikkard, William, Jacob, Anthony, Benjamin and Septimus. Exec: Sons Abraham and Septimus.
Witnesses: Elizabeth Lickemont (her mark), John Houlgate, John Johnson.

GRUB, GEORGE. Coventry, Co. of Chester, Pa. Blacksmith. Sept. 2, 1752. Oct. 30, 1753. K.116.
Wife: Mary. Brother: Abraham. Sons: Abraham and David. Exec: Wife and brother Jacob, Martin Orner, John Switzher, Caspar Ingle.

EVANS, ELIZABETH. City of Philadelphia. Widow. 10 mo. 14, 1753. Nov. 1, 1753. K.117.
Grandson: David. Overseers: Edward Jones, Charles Jones, Owen Jones, Joseph Redman. Exec: Children Evan, Sidney and Sarah.
Witnesses: Samuel Movis, Jane Nicholas.

REESE, JOHN. Whitpain Township, Co. of Philadelphia. Yeoman. 8 mo. 25, 1753. Nov. 3, 1753. K.118.
Wife: Hannah. Children: John, Edward, Elin, Hannah, Rose (Malsby) and Jane. Son-in-Law: John Bell. Exec: Grandson John Bell.
Witnesses: William Morris, Isaac Ellis, Joseph Dickinson.

MARSTETTER, FREDERICK LUDWICK. Oct. 5, 1753. Nov. 10, 1753. K.120.

Wife: Barbara. Children: Henry, Daniel, Frederick, Philip and two others, names not given. Beneficiary: Church wardens for the benefit of Augustus Church, Providence. Exec: Sons Henry and Daniel. Witnesses: Stephen Boyner (his mark), Rudolph Banner.

SWARTZMAN, GEORGE. Co. of Philadelphia. Yeoman. Aug. 11, 1750. Nov. 10, 1753. K.122.
Children: Andrew, Marcus, Honegar, Katherine and Elizabeth. Exec: Wife Mary Angle.
Witnesses: Catherine Spanger, Andrew Englehard, John Green.

EDWARD, PHILIP. Charlestown, Pa. Oct. 3, 1753. Nov. 14, 1753. K.122.
Wife: Mary. Children: Edward, Sarah, Elisha and Philip. Guardians: Wife and Roger Martin. Overseers: Roger Martin and Philip Thomas. Exec: Wife and Thomas David.
Witnesses: David Maheas, Daniel Shea, Patrick Anderson.

PETERS, REES. City of Philadelphia. Shopkeeper. 11 mo. 30, 1752. Nov. 16, 1753. K.123.
Wife: Martha. Children: Rees, William, Elizabeth (Stytes) and Mary (Savery). Exec: Son William and son-in-law William Savery.
Witnesses: Alexander Seaton, Rebekah Seaton, Joseph Davies.

THOMAS, SAMUEL. Bristol, Co. of Philadelphia. Oct. 24, 1753. Nov. 24, 1753. K.124.
Daughter: Ann. Brothers: Joshua, Simon and Timothy. Cousins: Joseph, Malachi, Samuel and Elizabeth Treat. Exec: Wife (name not given) and brothers, Simon and Timothy.
Witnesses: Jane Armitage (her mark), John Restence, James Armitage.

DONALDSON, WILLIAM. Co. of Philadelphia. Mariner. Nov. 30, 1753. Dec. 10, 1753. K.126.
Son: Joseph. Exec: Wife Mary.
Witnesses: Martin Reardon, Jr., James McCreight, Paul Isaac Voto.

WALTON, BENJAMIN. Beberry, Co. of Philadelphia. Yeoman. 10 mo. 30, 1753. Dec. 15, 1753. K.126.
Children: Daniel, Benjamin, William, Hannah, Rebecca, Sarah, Esther, Elizabeth and Mary. Exec: Wife Rebecca and son Daniel.

Witnesses: James Thompson, Richard Walton, Joshua Walton (his mark).

EVANS, OWEN. Limerick Township, Co. of Philadelphia. Yeoman. Nov. 4, 1753. Dec. 18, 1753. K.128.
Children: David, Anne (wife of Edward Lane), Mary (wife of James Brooke), Jane, Gwenefried, Benjamin and Thomas. Exec: Wife Mary and son David.
Witnesses: George Brooke, William Davis, John Evans, George Evans.
Codicil: Nov. 8, 1753.
Witnesses: George Brooke, William Davis, George Evans.

KNIGHT, WILLIAM. City of Philadelphia. Carpenter. May 21, 1751. Dec. 19, 1753. K.131.
Niece: Sarah, daughter of brother-in-law Joseph Stretch. Nephew: John son of brother Henry Knight. Exec: Joseph Stretch.
Witnesses: Charles Jervis, John Leacock, Jr., Paul Isaac Voto.

LITTLE, JOHN. Co. of Philadelphia. Proved Dec. 19. 1753. K.132.
Exec: Wife Mary.
Witnesses: Mary Frayer (her mark), Mary Alexander.

PEEL, JOHN. City of Philadelphia. Mariner. Nov. 5, 1753. Dec. 19, 1753. K.132.
Brother: Benjamin. Brother-in-Law: James McKnight. Exec: Wife Margaret.
Witnesses: James Blair, Francis Jesson, John Reily.

RICHARD, JOHN. Co. of Bucks, Pa. Taylor. Sept. 5, 1751. Dec. 21, 1753. K.133.
Children: Jacob and Mary (Spigel). Exec: Wife Magdalen.
Witnesses: David Owen, James Thomas, Thomas Owen.

ARNET, JACOB. Salford Township, Co. of Philadelphia. Weaver. Jan. 15, 1751/2. Dec. 22, 1753. K.134.
Exec: Wife Elizabeth and John Haynes.
Witnesses: Christian Stauffer, William Nash.

TOEES, HANNAH. Whitpain, Co. of Philadelphia. 11 mo. 2, 1753. Jan. 4, 1754. K.134.

Children: Elin (Rhoads), Hannah (Bell), Rose (Maulsby), Edward and John. Grandchild: Hannah Rees. Exec: Son-in-Law John Bell.
Witnesses: Job Pugh, John Eastburn, Joseph Evans.

HASELL, WILLIAM. City of Philadelphia. Late of Barbadoes. Merchant. Sept. 14, 1753. Jan. 15, 1754. K.135.
Nephew: Samuel Hasell. Legatees: Margaret Settle, of Barbadoes, Samuel Stephen, Ann and Jane, children of James Benezet of Philadelphia, merchant. Exec., Guardians and Trustees: Alexander Hustin, Amos Settle.
Witnesses: Nathan Allen, Joseph Hewes, Philip Syng, Jr.

EVANS, ROBERT. Merion, Co. of Philadelphia. May 1, 1753. Jan. 22, 1754. K.137.
Children: Catherine, Anne (Tillbury), Jane (Roberts), Cadwalader and Thomas. Grandchildren: Robert Evans, Amos Roberts, Sarah and Catherine Evans, daughters of Thomas Evans. Exec: Son, Thomas.
Overseers: Brothers Hugh and Owen, and Robert Roberts.
Witnesses: John Evans, Jr., Margaret and John Evans.

EVANS, ANN. Abington, Co. of Philadelphia. Widow of Rev. David Evans, late of Co. of Salem, N.J. Jan. 5, 1754. Jan. 23, 1754. K.138.
Son: Samuel. Grandchildren: Israel, Hannah and Samuel. Daughter-in-Law: Susanna Evans. Kinswoman: Ann Thomas. Brother: Joshua Jones (Hannah, his wife). Exec: Kinsmen, Richard Treat, Joshua Thomas.
Witnesses: Eleaner Thomas (her mark), Sarah Hewitt, Henry Sommer.

PLUMLY, GEORGE. City of Philadelphia. Cutler. Sept. 5, 1734. Jan. 24, 1754. K.140.
Brothers: James, John. Nephews: John and Charles Plumly. Exec: Wife Sarah.
Witnesses: William Shippen, Amy and Josiah Lawrence.
Codicil: Aug. 20, 1753.
Wherein Mary, daughter of Thomas Lord, and William, son of Edward and Elizabeth Freeman are made legatees.
Witnesses: Joseph Davis, Thomas Janvier, Thomas Gregory.

MORREY, RICHARD. City of Philadelphia. Gentleman. Aug. 30, 1753. Jan. 30, 1754. K.141.

Overseers: Jenkin Jones, Dr. William Chancellor of Philadelphia.
Exec: Wife Sarah and brother-in-law Jacob Beazly.
Witnesses: James Graisbury, Paul Isaac Voto, Abraham Gardiner, Stpehen Howell.

DAVIS, GEORGE. City of Philadelphia. Mariner. Feb. 26, 1747/8. Feb. 20, 1754. K.142.
Children: Elizabeth, James, Mary, George and William. Overseers: William Plumstead, William Allen, merchants. Exec: Mary Grafton, Mary Plumstead of Philadelphia.
Witnesses: John Searll, Samuel McCall, Peter Hodgson.

PEMBERTON, ISRAEL. City of Philadelphia. Merchant. 10 mo. 17, 1751. Feb. 22, 1754. K.143.
Wife: Rachel. Father: Phineas. Grandchildren: Mary, Rachel, Sarah, Israel, Joseph and Charles. Sons: Israel (wife Mary), James and John. Brother-in-Law: Stephen Jenkins. Sister: Priscilla Waterman. Cousins: William, Phineas, Stephen, Charles and Abigail, children of Israel and Priscilla Waterman. Beneficiaries: Friends, Daniel Stanton, John Armitt, in trust for the Monthly Meeting of Friends of Philadelphia, overseers of Friends Public School, Anna Cross, widow, and negro, Betty.
Witnesses: Owen Jones, Thomas Hallowell, Joseph Wharton, Jr., Samuel Emlin, Jr.

GETCHELL, ELISHA, SR. Co. of Chester, Pa. 12 mo. 6, 1753. Feb. 26, 1754. K.153.
Wife: Rachel. Children: Elisha, Elizabeth (Mitchell), Easter (Brown), Hannah (Brown), Ann (Urik or Kirk), and Abigail (Price).
Witnesses: John White, Rowland Rogers, Archibald Job.

BARNARD, JACOB. Co. of Berks, Penna. Yeoman. Feb. 23, 1754. March 7, 1754. K.155.
Exec. and legatees: Brothers: Thomas and Isaac. Sister: Mary, wife of John Hughes. Witnesses: Edward West, Thomas Potts.

UDRE, MARY. City of Philadelphia. Widow. Dec. 15, 1753. March 4, 1754. K.156.
Children: Catherine, Jacob, Fanny (Wincey) and Mary (Lawerwaylor).
Exec: Leonard Melchor, of Philadelphia, innholder.
Witnesses: Adam Clampffer, Joseph Chatham, Paul Isaac Voto.

JONES, JOHN. City of Philadelphia. Blacksmith. Feb. 1, 1754. March 4, 1754. K.157.
Wife: Sarah. Exec: Son, Daniel.
Witnesses: John Wilkinson, Samuel Huhl, John Reily.

HARRIS, ANDREW. Moyamensing, Co. of Philadelphia. Gentleman. Nov. 24, 1753. March 7, 1753. K.158.
Wife: Sarah. Children: Margaret, Andrew, John, Dorothy (Adamson), Rachel and Sarah. Brothers: John and William. Grandchildren: Margaret and Sarah Peile. Exec: Joseph Trotter, Sr., Joseph Stretch, Isaac Lane of Philadelphia.
Witnesses: Edward Weyman, Amos Jones, Paul Isaac Voto.

ARNOLD, GEORGE. City of Philadelphia. Victualler. March 15, 1754. March 20, 1754. K.164.
Wife: Catherine. Children: Catherine, Margaret and Maria Barbara and Samuel Eater. Exec: ---.
Witnesses: John Baron, Christian Snyder, Robert Rawlison.

HECK, CHRISTOPHER. Co. of Chester, Penna. Laborer. Jan. 12, 1754. April 9, 1754. K.165.
Sister: Elizabeth Heck. Legatees: Susana Brower, Elizabeth Ecker, Markus Oberholt, children of Jacob Bach (names not given), all Friends. Exec: Jacob Bach.
Witnesses: Andrew Hight (his mark), John Brower.

PUGH, JOHN. Co. of Chester, Penna. Yeoman. 10 mo. 7, 1753. April 9, 1754. K.165.
Wife: Abigaiel. Brother: Jonathan. Exec: Children: John, Amelia and Mary. Trustees and Guardians: Trustees and Guardians: Brother-in-law, Mordieca Morgan and kinsman Evan Evans of Radnor.
Witnesses: Samson Davis, Nathaniel Miles, James Miles.

HOLT, ELIZABETH. City of Philadelphia. Widow. Jan. 8, 1754. April 10, 1754. K.166.
Brother: Jedediah Snowden. Mother: Ruth Snowden. Exec: Sister Sarah Browne.
Witnesses: Abigall Acetuer[?], Abel James.

PHILIPPRES, MARY. Co. of Chester, Penna. Widow. 1 mo. 23, 1753. April 10, 1754. K.167.

Brother-in-Law: Evan Jenkin. Sister: Ann. Nieces and Nephew: Elizabeth and Jacob Jenkin, Mary Roberts and Ann James. Exec: Mary Roberts.
Witnesses: Thomas Thomas, Levi Lewis.

LAWRENCE, THOMAS. City of Philadelphia. Merchant. Sept. 18, 1753. April 29, 1754. K.168.
Wife: Rachel. Exec: Children: Thomas, John and Mary.
Witnesses: Henry Elwes, Richard Swan, Stephen Carmick.

ZACHARY, JOHN. Germantown, Co. of Philadelphia. Tanner. March 29, 1754. May 4, 1754. K.170.
Wife: Catherine Roop. Children: Catherine, Elizabeth and unknown child. Exec: Wife, brother-in-law, Jacob Rupp and Baltes Reser.
Witnesses: John Dedier, Augustus Neiser, Philip Worner.

MILLER, PETER. Germantown, Co. of Philadelphia. Cordwainer. Nov. 6, 1753. May 4, 1754. K.171.
Wife: Mary. Children: John, Peter, George and Margaret. Grandchildren: Anthony and Annie Lander. Exec: Wife Mary and son Peter.
Witnesses: Augustin Neisser, Michael Bullinger.

GRAFTON, MARY. City of Philadelphia. Widow. Oct. 13, 1753. May 9, 1754. K.173.
Daughter-in-Law: Mary Dulany (husband Walter). Aunt: Mary Plumstead. Sister: Jane Davis. Grandchildren: Daniel, Rebecca, Mary and Margaret Dulany. Niece: Elizabeth Davis. Nephews: William, James and George Davis. Brother-in-Law: John Davis. Brothers: Robert and James Currie. Beneficiaries: Ann and Margaret, daughters of friend William Allen, and Christian Glean.
Witnesses: William Allen, Joseph Turner, Esquire, of Philadelphia.

OLLINGER, CHARLES. Jan. 18, 1754. May 10, 1754. K.175.
Wife: Anne Catherine. Children: Names not given. Exec: Johannes Frick, Johannes Staiffer.
Witnesses: Lawrence Erbach, John Redrook.

LLOYD, THOMAS. City of Philadelphia. Merchant. Jan. 5, 1748/9. May 13, 1754. K.176.

Sisters: Mary and Ann (Mathews). Sister-in-Law: Hannah or Joanna Kearney. Children: Sarah and Susannah. Nieces: Hannah and Sarah, daughters of Mordieca and Susannah Lloyd. Nephew: Thomas Lloyd. Beneficiaries: Samuel Greenman, apprentice, Dening Oliver, housekeeper. Exec: John Henry, Charles Willing, William Coleman. Witnesses: Robert Moore, Amos Strettell, Wright Massey.

TERRY, JAMES. May 16, 1754. May 20, 1754. K.178.
Sister: Julian Terry. Exec: Wife Susannah.
Witnesses: Maur Nikell, James White, John Coneely.

BACHMAN, GEORGE. Co. of Northampton, Penna. Yeoman. Oct. 15, 1753. May 29, 1754. K.179.
Children: Henry, John, Samuel, Abraham and Susanna. Overseers: Son Henry, Abram Clemens, John Joeder, Jr. Beneficiaries: "The poor of our congregation." Exec: Wife Anna Maria.
Witnesses: Jacob Mussleman, George Ackerman, John Hooker.

THOMAS, MARGARET. Garlhbulch, Parish of Lansanfrayd, Co. of Montgomery, Dioces of St. Asaph. Widow.
Legatees: Nephew Thomas Morris of Langhange; Elizabeth Howe wife of Morris David; cousin Catherine Morris; cousin Margaret Griffith; cousin Elizabeth Griffith; Mary Morris; Elizabeth wife of Ellis David; Morgan Howell; Marie Howell; Tacy wife of Jacob Endon of Cloddrecochion; and Elizabeth daughter of John Li---. Exec: Thomas Morris. NOTE: The above will was recorded from a copy sent with a requisition under the seal of the Prerogative Court of the Principality of Wales, engrossed in Latin and signed. In the original will, the name John Li is thus written, as above.

EVANS, STEPHEN. Co. of Chester, Penna. Yeoman. Feb. 21, 1754. June 12, 1754. K.181.
Exec: Wife: Mary. Sons: Jesse and Abijah. Children: David, Ruth (Hayle), Benjamin, Abijah and Jesse. Granddaughter: Prudence Hayle. Trustees: David (brother) and Thomas Waters.
Witnesses: David Stephens, Thomas Walter, William Godfrey.

FUHRMAN, JACOB. April 4, 1748. June 22, 1754. K.182.
Children: Mary, Catherine and John. Exec: Son John.
Witnesses: John Peter Lutz, Yost Volmers (his mark).

ATTWOOD, WILLIAM. City of Philadelphia. Merchant. Feb. 6, 1750. June 27, 1754. K.185.
Cousins: Mary Penly, Mary Penly Jr., Atwood Cowman, Barnaby Shute, brewer of Philadelphia, Samuel, Sarah and Mary children of Anthony and Mary Nichols, and Edward Penly. Exec: Attwood Shute.
Witnesses: Reese Meredith, Samuel Noave, William Fishbourne and Joseph Saunders.

HOPKINS, JOHN. City of Philadelphia. Merchant. July 11, 1754. July 16, 1754. K.185.
Sisters: Four in number, names not given. Nephew: James Hopkins son of brother William. Niece: Sister of James, name not given.
Beneficiaries: Patrick Drawson, mariner; Benjamin Price, Attorney-at-law; negro Emanuel. Exec: Attwood Shute, merchant, Patrick Drawson, James Hopkinson.
Witnesses: Aaron Jenkins, John Pole, Benjamin Condy.

LOGAN, SARAH. City of Philadelphia. 4 mo. 8, 1754. July 27, 1754. K.186.
Children: William, James and Hannah wife of John Smith. Brother-in-Law: Dr. William Logan of Bristol, England. Granddaughters: Sarah and Mary Norris. Sisters: Rachel Pemberton and Sarah Read.
Beneficiaries: Sarah Morris in trust for the use of the Women's Meeting in Philadelphia and Ann Cross. Exec: Son-in-law John Smith, and sons William and James.
Witnesses: Jonah Thompson, Sarah Morris, Joyce Benezet.

JENKINS, SISSILY. Co. of Chester, Penna. Widow. July 22,1754. Aug. 6, 1754. K.187.
Children: James, Mary, Ann, David, John and Isaac. Grandchildren: John, James and Isaac (parents, Mary and David Thomas); Mary and James (parents, Ann and John Lucas); John (son of John Jenkins); Sissily (daughter of testator's brother, Thomas). Beneficiaries: Friends John Bowen and David Jenkin in trust for the support of the Baptist meeting "kept near the Yellow Springs." Exec: Son-in Law David Thomas and John Lewis.
Witnesses: Thomas Mergan, Amos and Owen Thomas.

MEADE, ROBERT. City of Philadelphia. Merchant. July 16, 1754. Aug. 26, 1754. K.189.

Signed at St. Croix. Children: Garret, George and Catherine. Brother-in-Law: George Stretch of Barbadoes. Beneficiaries: Under Codicil - The Danish Church, and the English Church of St. Croix. Exec: Island of St. Croix, Dr. Mathias Farrell and Theobald Bourke, in Barbadoes; George Stretch; and in Penna., John Reardon and John Reily, Attorneys-at-Law.
Witnesses: Robert Jesson, Jonathan Brood.
Codicil: July 18, 1754, at St. Croix.
Witnesses: The same.
Codicil: Aug. 13, 1754, City of Philadelphia.
Robert Harding, Alice Hutchison.

SPAFFORD, GEORGE. City of Philadelphia. Merchant. Aug. 19, 1754. Aug. 28, 1754. K.191.
Wife: Sarah. Brother: William. Daughter: Sarah. Nephews: William and George Drury. Beneficiary: Samuel Hazard in trust for the new Presbyterian Church in Arch Street, Philadelphia, Rev. Mr. Gilbert Tennent, Pastor. Overseers: Brother William and Thomas Browne. Exec: Wife and David Chambers, stone cutter.
Witnesses: Samuel Purviance, Thomas Charlton, John Redman.

GRIFFITH, GRIFFITH. Bristol, Co. Philadelphia. Mason. Sept. 3, 1754. Sept. 12, 1754. K.192.
Brother: Joseph. Brother-in-Law: George Eaton. Nephews: Robert and Griffith. Nieces: Mary Davis and Mary Rush, daughter of Joseph Rush. Sisters: Margaret, Mary (Easton) and Ann (Claypoole). Beneficiaries: Jacob Hall and Isaac Ashton in trust for Trinity Church, Oxford Township, Philadelphia Co., Eneas Ross, rector; John Askins, Daniel and Benjamin Street; Thomas and Mary Harper and their children, Mary and Thomas; overseers of the Poor of Bristol Township; Mathias Han Mason and Sarah his wife; Ann Wells and her brother Josiah Harper, cordwainer; Sarah, daughter of Joseph Harper Jr.; William Vanderspegle, Govn. and Walter Goodman, Sheriff at Schoolkill Falls;, Fort St. George; John Skidmore; Thomas Jones, servant; and Elizabeth Welch, nurse. Exec: George Eaton, Thomas Carroll, Isaac Ashton.
Witnesses: William Morgan, John Skidmore (his mark), Jacob Hall.

BARTHOLOMEW, ANDREW. City of Philadelphia. Cordwainer. Sept. 14, 1754. Sept. 20, 1754. K.196.

Wife: Elizabeth. Children: John, Joseph and Mary. Exec: Brother Thomas and brother-in-law Jonathan Biers.
Witnesses: Caleb Cash, Edward Bartholomew, Paul Isaac Voto.

ANNAND, ALEXANDER. City of Philadelphia. School master. May 1, 1752. Sept. 23, 1754. K.197.
Beneficiaries: Elizabeth Annand, Inverness, Scotland; Ann and Barbara, daughters of sister Ann; nieces Jane and Betty Graeme, daughters of Dr. Graeme; Isabel McCall, daughter of Samuel McCall; James, son of John Leech; Rev. Mr. George Craig; Rev. Colin Campbell; Mrs. Graeme Tillotson; Alexander, son of Rev. Mr. Curry of Radnor; Samuel McCall Sr., merchant of Philadelphia and Mrs. McCall; Alexander Annand. Sisters: Ann and Barbara. Exec: Samuel McCall and Charles Stedman, merchants of Philadelphia.
Codicil: Aug. 3, 1753.
Additional Beneficiaries: Mrs. Graeme, Mrs. Ann Stedman, Rev. Dr. Robert Jenney and William Harper (Edinburgh). The will and codicil were admitted to probate on Sept. 23, 1754 upon the affidavits of Rev. Dr. Jenney, Dr. Thomas Graeme and Daniel Roberdean, who testified that they believed the signatures thereto were in the handwriting of the testator.

VANLOUVENING, MARY. City of Philadelphia. Aug. 14, 1754. Sept. 30, 1754. K.199.
Exec. and Legatee: Daughter, Mary.
Witnesses: William Dawson, Nicholas Leir.

MOORE, GAWIN. Co. of Chester, Penna. June 5, 1754. June 22, 1754. K.200.
Wife: Elender. Children: John, James, William, Gawin, Jane, Ester, Sarah, Charity and Mary. Grandchild: Sarah, daughter of Robert McCoy. Exec: William Wright, John Wall.
Witnesses: John White, William Gregory, David McKrorye (his mark).

POTTS, NATHAN. Whitemarsh, Co. of Philadelphia. Blacksmith. May 31, 1754. Oct. 1, 1754. K.201.
Children: Stephen, Nathan, Zebulon, Alse and Isaiah. Exec: Wife, Hester and brother John Potts.
Witnesses: Barnabas Coulston, James Stroud.

SHOEMAKER, CHRISTIANIA. Cheltenham, Co. of Philadelphia. Widow. Sept. 11, 1747. Oct. 1, 1754. K.202.
Children: Mary (Livezey), Samuel, Catherine (Thompson), Sarah (Williams), Barbara (Roberts), Arnold and Susannah (Phipps). Exec: Son Arnold.
Witnesses: John Thomas, Jonathan Livesey, Stephen Jenkins.

RUSSELL, JAMES. Commander of Ship Edinborough. Aug. 14, 1741. Oct. 9, 1754. K.203.
Daughter: Mary. Beneficiaries: Niece Sarah Brown, nephew James Anderson Brown and friends Benjamin and Samuel Shoemaker of Philadelphia. Exec., Trustees and Guardians: Benjamin and Samuel Shoemaker. When daughter Mary attains her majority, she to be sole Exec.
Witnesses: John Spurrier, Hugh Rose, David Wise.

PENNOCK, SAMUEL. City of Philadelphia. House carpenter. 9 mo. 26, 1754. Oct. 16, 1754. K.205.
Children: Joseph and Samuel. Exec: Wife Elizabeth.
Witnesses: John Pemberton, John Redman, Sarah Peters.

WARNER, ANN. Co. of Philadelphia. Widow. 11 mo. 23, 1746/7. Oct. 17, 1754. K.206.
Children: William, John, Isaac, Ann (Wynne), Mary, Esther, Hannah and Anne. Exec: Son-in-law, Richard George of Philadelphia.
Witnesses: Hugh Evans, Edward William.

PHIPPS, THOMAS. Abington, Co. of Philadelphia. Yeoman. 9 mo. 20, 1754. Oct. 17, 1754. K.207.
Wife: Mary. Grandfather: John Phipps. Children: Son John and daughter Margaret. Brother: Joseph. Exec: Sons Isaac and Peter.
Witnesses: Benjamin Mason, Isaac Shoemaker, John Pemberton.

HEAD, JOHN. City of Philadelphia. Joiner. 5 mo. 11, 1754. Oct. 18, 1754. K.208.
Wife: Rebecca. Children: Sarah (Brian), Martha (Lawrence), Samuel, John, Hannah (Heolen, Heoten?), Mary (Warder), Rebecca (Jones), Esther (Baker) and Susannah. Exec: Sons John and Samuel, son-in-law William Lawrence.
Witnesses: W. Montgomery, Joseph Johnson, Hezekiah Williams.
Codicil: 9 mo. 19, 1754.

Witnesses: Samuel Bell, Joseph Johnson, Hezekiah Williams.

WALMSLEY, THOMAS. Byberry, Co. of Philadelphia. Yeoman. 12 mo. 20, 1749/50. Oct. 21, 1754. K.212.
Wife: Mary. Children: William (Executor), Elizabeth (Walton), Agnes (Walton), Phebe (Carver), Martha and Ester, Mary (Worthington) and Abigail Comley. Sons-in-Law: John Worthington, Job Walter and Isaac Carver.
Witnesses: Thomas Rose, James Thornton, John Harker.

EMLEN, GEORGE. City of Philadelphia. Brewer. Feb. 7, 1749. Oct. 29, 1754. K.213.
Wife: Mary. Children: Hannah (Logan), Joseph and George.
Trustees: William Logan, John Armitt, John Mifflin. Beneficiaries: Said trustees for the benefit of the Poor of the Monthly Meeting of Quakers in Philadelphia. Exec: Son-in-law, William Logan, son George, brother-in-law John Armitt.
Witnesses: Thomas Jarvis, Charles Brockden, Paul Isaac Voto.
Codicil: April 20, 1750.
Witnesses: Paul Isaac Voto, Peter Miller Jr.
Codicil: April 1, 1751.
Witnesses: David Edwards, Paul Isaac Voto.
Codicil: March 2, 1754.
Witness: Paul Isaac Voto.

TILLYER, PHILIP. City of Philadelphia. Oct. 13, 1754. Nov. 5, 1754. K.217.
Wife: Ann. Children: Edward, William, Tamar, Thomas and Mary.
Legatees: Sylvania and Thomas Ledyard. Exec: Sons Edward and William. Exec: Sons Edward and William.
Witnesses: Benjamin Clift, Harman Vandergrift, John Watts.

BAST, HERMAN. City of Philadelphia. Yeoman. Nov. 22, 1754. Nov. 27, 1754. K.218.
Children: Maria Margaretta, Henry, John Henry, Anne and Lawrence.
Exec: Wife Judith and brother Lawrence Bast.
Witnesses: Peter Miller, Jacob Grief.

WARNER, EDWARD. City of Philadelphia. House carpenter. 11 mo. 4, 1754. Nov. 28, 1754. K.219.

Wife: Anna. Children: William, Rebecca, Catherine, Anna and Elizabeth. Grandchild: Anna Howell. Overseers, Trustees and Guardians: William Fisher, Joseph Fox. Exec: Wife Anna, son-in-law Joshua Howell and Catherine, his wife, and Rebecca Warner.
Witnesses: William Parr, George Robotham, John Reily.

BARTHOLOMEW, JOSEPH. Co. of Chester, Penna. Yeoman. Nov. 3, 1754. Nov. 30, 1754. K.222.
Wife: Sarah. Children: John, Benjamin, Hanah and Rachel. Brother: Benjamin and wife Sarah.
Witnesses: Isaac Davis, Thomas Water, Henry Ackerton.

GOZELL, JOHN. Co. of Bucks, Pa. Husbandman. Dec. 26, 1753. Dec. 5, 1754. K.225.
Wife: Catherine. Chiildren: Names not given. Exec. and Trustees: John Redtrock and George Okerman.
Witnesses: Nicholas Harwick, Christian Topar.

HARKER, ADAM. City of Philadelphia. 10 mo. 2, 1753. Dec. 5, 1754. K.226.
Children: Mary (Lloyd), Jane (Collison), Grace (Fisher), Rachel (Parry) and Samuel. Sons-in-Law: John Fisher, Thomas Lloyd, John Mitchenor. Grandchildren: James and Jehu Harker (sons of Samuel), John, Thomas, Samuel and James Lloydd, Mary Kirk, Sarah Tyson, Grance Longstreth, Jane and Elizabeth Mitchenor. Nephew: Adam, son of David Harker. Brothers: David and James. Sister: Sarah Scott. Beneficiaries: Friends Thomas Hackery, Israel Pemberton, Jr., John Smith (merchant), Joseph Hamton, John Linton in trust for brother James and Amy, his wife, and for a Free School in Wrightstown, Bucks Co., Pa.; also schools in Buckingham and Middletown, Pa. Trustees: Thomas Lloyd, John Mitchenor, James Thackery. Exec: John Harker, John Lloyd.
Witnesses: James Stephens, William Dunwick, Paul Isaac Voto.
Codicils: 10 mo. 7, 1753, 5 mo. 17, 1754, 11 mo. 15, 1754.
Witnesses: Same.

LIGHTFOOT, MICHAEL. City of Philadelphia. Proved Dec. 9, 1754. K.229.
Children: Mary, wife of Samuel Clarke, Katherine, Sarah (Hutton), Elinor (Parvin), Thomas and William. Exec: Wife Mary.
Witnesses: Anthony Benezet, Joyce Benezet, John Wilson.

WILLING, CHARLES. City of Philadelphia. Merchant. July 28, 1750. Dec. 10, 1754. K.231.
Father: Thomas, of Bristol, merchant. Children: Thomas, Charles, Richard, Ann, Dorothy, Mary, Elizabeth and Abigal. Brother: Thomas, of Londen, merchant. Sisters: Ann and Dorothy H---. Exec: Wife --- and son Thomas.
Witnesses: D. Martin, Thomas Hopkenson, John Price.

PASTORIUS, DANIEL. Germantown, Co. of Philadelphia. Sadler. 10 mo. 27, 1754. Dec. 13, 1754. K.234.
Children: Hannah, Abraham, Samuel and Daniel. Exec: Wife Sarah and brother-in-law George Shoemaker.
Witnesses: Richard Johnsen, Daniel Shiner, Thomas Rose.

PARKER, JOHN. City of Philadelphia. Dec. 1748. Dec. 16, 1754. K.235.
Brothers: William, Richard and Joseph. Sister, Mary. Exec: Brothers William and Richard.
Witnesses: Jonathan Paschall, Ralph and William Lewis.

EVANS, RICHARD. Co. of Chester, Penna. Yeoman. March 15, 1754. Dec. 18, 1754. K.236.
Brother: William. Nephews and Nieces: Joshua, Joel, William, Mary, Sarah (Wayn) and Hannah (children of William Evans).
Granddaughter: Elenir (John). Exec: Grandsons William and Richard.
Witnesses: David William (his mark), Elizabeth Jones (her mark), Isaac Davis.

JONES, MALACHI. Co. of Chester, Penna. Yeoman. Aug. 12, 1754. Dec. 18, 1754. K.237.
Children: Horasho, Chester, Martha, Malachia, Ruth, Stephen, William, Lynard and Abednego. Exec: Wife Mary and son Horasho.
Witnesses: Llewelyn David, William Roberts, John Griffith.

ELLIS, ELLIS. Upper Dublin, Co. of Philadelphia. Wheelwright. 11 mo. 26, 1754. Dec. 19, 1754. K.238.
Brothers and Sisters: Morris, Mordica, Rowland, Thomas, Enos and Elinor. Beneficiary: Members of Horsham Meeting. Exec: Brothers Morris and Mordica.
Witnesses: Ellis Lewis Jr., John Lukens.

MOORE, ELIZABETH. City of Philadelphia. Widow of Robert. Aug. 19, 1754. Aug. 29, 1754. K.239.
Mother: Middleton. Son: William. Sister-in-Law: Catherine Clarke. Brothers: Thomas and William Gibs. Brother-in-Law: John Moore. Nephew: Charles. Niece: Margaret. Sisters: Hannah, Mary and Anne. Beneficiaries: Israel Pemberton in trust for the execution of certain provisions of the will: negro woman Grace and her son; Ann Topp (now Sharswood); Thomas Topp; Esther Hulbert; Mary Nelson; Margaret Davis; Philip Hulbert; Thomas Necher. Exec: Son William. Witnesses: Charles Meredith, Mark Huhl, Jr. and Israel Pemberton.

ATKINSON, WILLIAM. Upper Dublin, Co. of Philadelphia. 8 mo. 15, 1754. Jan. 1, 1755. K.240.
Children: Susannah (wife of Samuel Davis), Phebe (wife of William Walton) and Hannah (wife of Ellis Hughs). Son-in-Law: Ellis Ellis. Exec: Samuel Davis and Ellis Hughes.
Witnesses: David Humphrey, Jacob Jones, Cephas Child.

CALVERT, MARY. City of Philadelphia. Widow. July 4, 1753. Jan. 1, 1755. K.242.
Child: Mary (wife of Hugh Roberts). Grandchild: Isaac Greenleaf. Beneficiary: The Monthly Meeting of Friends of Philadelphia. Exec: John Smith, Edward Catharell, merchants of Philadelphia, Mary Roberts.
Witnesses: Sarah Kirk, Enoch Fleuer, Robert Greenway.

HAGEMAN, JOHN ULRICK. Germantown, Co. of Philadelphia. Yeoman. July 24, 1754. Jan. 2, 1755. K.242.
Wife: Veronica. Beneficiaries: Kinsmen, Ulrick and John Freyhofer, to whom the estate is bequeathed after the decease of testator's wife, and the poor of the city irrespective of their religious belief. Exec: John Johnson, Ulrick Freyhofer.
Witnesses: Charles Witherholt, John Bowman, Elizabeth Bowman.

GOODMAN, MARTHA. Wife of Walter Goodman City of Philadelphia, merchant. Sept. 25, 1747. Jan. 9, 1755. K.244.
Sole Legatee, Devisee and Exec: Husband.
Witnesses: George Thompson, John Parrock, Robert Greenway.

POLE, JOHN. City of Philadelphia. Merchant. 1 mo. 3, 1755. Jan. 16, 1755. K.245.

Wife: Rachel. Exec. and Trustees: For benefit of children (names not given), William Callender, Edward Cathirel, John Smith.
Witnesses: Jonah Thompson, Thomas Clifford, Joshua Howell.

KRESSMAN, JOHN NICHOLAS. City of Philadelphia. Jan. 1, 1755. Jan. 21, 1755. K.246.
Wife: Mary. Brothers: George and John. Sister: Marrilies. Nephews: Frethrick, Nicholas and John (sons of George); Anthony and John (sons of John). Nieces and Nephews: Anna, Margreth, Marrilies, Nicholas and Katherine (children of Marrilies). Exec: John (son of George), Keil Jan Gangler and testator's wife.

PARROCK, JAMES. City of Philadelphia. Shipwright. May 4, 1754. Jan. 24, 1755. K.247.
Wife: Hannah. Grandchildren: John and Sarah. Beneficiaries: Lidia Cathcart, children of John and Sarah Smallwood (names not given); Monthly Meeting of Quakers at Philadelphia; Joseph and Richard Fordham; James Ashton (son of Isaac Ashton) and Sarah his wife; Susannah, Hannah, Mary, Sarah, Rebecca and William (children of William and Sarah Paschall); John, Manly, Richard, Joseph, Moses, James, Mary and Sarah (children of John Smallwood); children of Benjamin Richards (names not given); Lidia Cathcart's children (names not given); children of Mary Lee (no names given); John Spencer's children (names not given). Exec: Jeremiah Elfreth, blacksmith, and William Collander, merchant.
Witnesses: Benjamin Leigh, Joseph Warner, Nathaniel Brown, Peter Miller.

BOYCE, JOSEPH. Kingsess, Co. of Philadelphia. Yeoman. April 2, 1750. Jan. 31, 1755. K.252.
Wife: Mary. Grandchildren: Joseph, Mary and Margaret. Son-in-Law: Aaron Hibberd.
Witnesses: Isaac Pearson, John Rudulph, William Wood.

LASSELL, JOHN. Co. of Philadelphia. Glazier. May 29, 1754. Jan. 29, 1755. K.254.
Brother: Thomas. Sister: Mary. Nieces: Rachel Vernon and Mary Shaw. Grandchildren: Sarah and Mary (children of daughter Mary Morgan) and William Darvill. Kinsmen: Evan Morgan and Enoch Flower. Exec: Enoch Flower.
Witnesses: Joseph Gray, Jacob Shoemaker, Thomas Tillbury.

GALLOWAY, ANN. Oxford Township, Co. of Philadelphia. Widow. Jan. 17, 1755. Feb. 1, 1755. K.255.
Nephew: Samuel Johnson. Grandnephew and Nieces: Richard, Mary and Samuel Johnson, Ann Hill of Maryland. Brother: Francis Hill. Beneficiary: Rev. Aeneas Ross. Exec: Samuel Johnson.
Witnesses: William Ballard, Aeneas Ross.

PLUMSTED, MARY. City of Philadelphia. Widow. Aug. 12, 1754. Feb. 6, 1755. K.256.
Nieces and Nephews: Elizabeth, Mary and Jane Davis, Robert and James Curry. Grandnieces and Nephews: George, William, Elizabeth, and Mary (children of Jane Davis), Elizabeth, Thomas and Rebecca (children of son-in-law, William Plumsted). Beneficiaries: The Pennsylvania Hospital; Presbyterian Synod of Philadelphia; Christian Glenn, widow; Trustees of the Academy, Philadelphia.
Witnesses: Thomas Lawrence, Jonathan Evans, Alexander Stewart.

JONES, JOSHUA. Abington, Co. of Philadelphia. Jan. 9, 1755. Feb. 8, 1755. K.258.
Children: Mary and Abenezer. Exec: Wife Hannah.
Witnesses: Richard Treat, William Watkins (his mark), Joshua Thomas.

IDEN, JOHN. Abington, Co. of Philadelphia. Cordwainer. Nov. 4, 1752. Feb. 13, 1755. K.259.
Children: Elizabeth, Samuel, Jacob and John. Exec: Joshua Morris of Abington, yeoman, and son Samuel.
Witnesses: John Webster, Phineas Jenkins, Daniel Thomas.

BASTAIN, CHRISTIAN. Germantown, Co. of Philadelphia. Yeoman. Feb. 12, 1755. Feb. 26, 1755. K.260.
Children: Anne and Sybilla (wife of Jacob Rex). Step-son: Jacob Reep and Son-in-Law: Jacob Rex. Exec: Step-son Jacob Reep.
Witnesses: John Cunrades, Jr., Cornelius Conrades.

RAMBO, ANDREW. Lower Dublin, Co. of Philadelphia. Farmer. Nov. 2, 1753. Feb. 22, 1755. K.262.
Wife: Catherine. Brothers: John and Jacob. Cousins: Deborah, Cornelius and Hannah, (children of Daniel and Ann Jones), Elias and Peter (sons of brother Peter). Exec: Wife and Elias Rambo.
Witnesses: Andrew Boor, Thomas Stammers.

GRIFFITH, ALICE. Bristol, Co. of Philadelphia. Widow. Feb. 4, 1755. Feb. 24, 1755. K.263.
Children: Joseph, Mary (Caton), Ann (Claypool) and Margaret (Davis). Grandchildren: Griffith Griffith, Benjamin, Thomas and Daniel Street, Mary Davis and Mary Rush. Exec: Sons-in-Law: David Davis, George Caton [Eaton?].
Witnesses: Thomas Roberts, Jr., William Aduddell.

LOWRY, LAZARUS. City of Philadelphia. Indian trader. Feb. 6, 1755. Feb. 25, 1755. K.264.
Wife: Anne (former husband, Thomas Edwards). Children: Lazarus, Thomas, Benjamin, William and Martha Lowry, and John Edwards. Exec: Wife and Thomas Campbell, merchant, of Philadelphia.
Witnesses: Ebenezar Kinnersly, Benjamin Street, Thomas Say.

WITMER, JACOB. Co. of Philadelphia. Yeoman. Oct. 7, 1751. March 7, 1755. K.266.
Wife: Margretta. Children: Jacob, Margretha Elizabeth, Susana, Anna and Anna Barbara. Exec: Thomas Meyer of Philadelphia, potter.
Witnesses: Michael Egee, George Pasache.

COLLINGS, EDWARD. City of Philadelphia. Keeper of the Goal. Feb. 18, 1755. March 10, 1755. K.267.
Wife: Elizabeth. Beneficiaries: Brothers and sisters (names not given). Exec: Wife and James and John Paul.
Witnesses: Isachar Davids, William Nicholson, Peter Hodgson.

VIDAL, STEPHEN. City of Philadelphia. School master. Jan. 27, 1755. March 14,1755. K.268.
Sole legatee and Devisee: Exec: Abraham Robinson, son of testator's friends Thomas Robinson, Esq. of New Castle, Delaware.
Witnesses: William Murdock, Newburgh Chease, Samuel Morris, Jr., John Reily.

FINNEY, REBECCA. Co. of Philadelphia. Widow. Jan. 22, 1754. March 15, 1755. K.268.
Exec. and Trustee: Brother-in-Law: Daniel Bristol. Children: Names not given.
Witnesses: Jacob Hall, James Roberts, George Bartholomew.

LACY, THOMAS. City of Philadelphia. Baker. March 9, 1755. March 20, 1755. K.269.
Wife: Mary. Brothers: James and John. Sisters: Elizabeth and Mary. Father-in-Law: Benjamin Brittain. Exec: Father-in-law Benjamin Brittain, and testator's wife.
Witnesses: William Anderson, Caleb Evins, Paul Isaac Voto.

HAWKINS, JAMES. Moorland, Co. of Philadelphia. Yeoman. 2 mo. 18, 1755. March 22, 1755. K.270.
Children: James, William, John, Joseph, Isaac, Mary and Hannah (Hilton). Exec: Wife Mary and son James.
Witnesses: Jacob Randall, John George Gast, John Woolman.

TILLYER, EDWARD. Moorland, Co. of Philadelphia. Husbandman. Dec. 7, 1754. March 29, 1754. K.272.
Wife: Hannah. Children: Silas, Joseph, Sarah, Rachel and Ann. Exec: John and Silas Bedel.
Witnesses: William Tillyer, Harman Vandergrift, John Watts.

NASH, ANN. Co. of Philadelphia. Widow. April 13, 1753. March 31, 1755. K.273.
Daughters: Rachel Peichard, Mary Coddy, Rebecca Linsey and Ann Reynolds. Exec: Sons: William and Joseph. Grandchild: Hannah.
Witnesses: Thomas Austin, Grace Tyson.

ROBESON, JAMES. Franconia Township, Co. of Philadelphia. Yeoman. 4 mo. 7, 1754. March 31, 1755. K.274.
Children: James, John, Elizabeth, Mary and Rachel. Trustees: Daniel Williams, Robert Ellis, Daniel Morgan, John Fry. Exec: Son James and son-in-law Edward Edwards.
Witnesses: Thomas Evans (his mark), Richard Evans, Owen Evans.

STRUDWICK, NATHANIEL EDMUND. City of Philadelphia. (Army). March 24, 1755. April 1, 1755. K.276.
Legatees: Mary Fowler and her son John. Exec: Mary Fowler.
Witnesses: William Henderson, Jonathan Durell, John Reily.

COON, GEORGE. Co. of Bucks. Carpenter. Jan. 3, 1755. April 3, 1755. K.277.
Children: Five, names not given. Exec: Wife Catherine.
Witnesses: Henry Miller, John Zekroth.

DENTON, JOHN. City of Philadelphia. Carpenter. Dec. 24, 1754. April 4, 1755. K.277.
Wife: Mercy. Children: Thomas, John, Rebecca and Mary. Exec: Wife and Walter Goodman, gentleman, of Philadelphia.
Witnesses: Charles West, Michael Hulings, Brian Wilkinson, John Reily.

STEHLETON, JOHN. Co. of Berks, Penna. Yeoman. Dec. 2, 1754. April 5, 1755. K.279.
Children: John and Mary Elizabeth. Exec: Wife Mary Margareth and Casper Gressimer.
Witnesses: John Lesher, John Yoder, Jacob Geiger, John Gshwind.

SNELLBERG, HENRY. Roxborough, Co. of Philadelphia. Miller. March 22, 1755. April 7, 1755. K.281.
Children: John, Daniel, Elizabeth, Catherine and Henry. Exec: Wife Dorothea and Daniel Williams.
Witnesses: Nicholas Rapain, George Hast, Christian Lehman.

DAVID, THOMAS. Gwynead, Co. of Philadelphia. Yeoman. Nov. 1, 1754. April 8, 1755. K.282.
Wife: Elizabeth. Children: John, Robert, David and Gainer.
Grandsons: Thomas and Israel David.
Witnesses: Edward Foulke, William Foulke, Rowland Evans.

MILLER, JACOB. Germantown, Co. of Philadelphia. Wheelwright. Feb. 8, 1755. April 9, 1755. K.283.
Wife: Mary Magdalena. Children: John and Jacob. Exec: Wife, brother-in-law Jacob Sassmanhausen and John Dewald End.
Witnesses: Philip Martin Wernar, Jacob Herman, Christian Lehman.

URNER, MARTIN. Co. of Chester, Penna. March 24, 1755. April 10, 1755. K.284.
Wife: Barbara. Child: Mary. Grandchildren: David and Jacob Urner, John, Andrew and Martin Wolf. Daughter-in-Law: Barbra Urner. Son-in-Law: Andrew Wolf. Exec: Martin Urner, Jr. and Jacob Freek.
Witnesses: John Sliner, Stephen Bower, George Croft.

SCARTH, TIMOTHY. City of Philadelphia. Tanner. Feb. 17, 1749. April 12, 1755. K.286.
Exec. and sole Legatee: Wife Mary.

Witnesses: Thomas Green, Robert Rolison (his mark), Paul Isaac Voto.

MC VAUGH, JAMES. City of Philadelphia. Innholder. March 30, 1755. April 12, 1755. K.287.
Children: Benjamin, Rebecca, John, James, Sarah, and Mary (Mason).
Exec: Wife and Jacob Hall.
Witnesses: John Strickland, Edmund Skinner, Joseph Thornhill.

FISHER, JOHN. April 7, 1754. April 26, 1755. K.288.
Wife: Cunnichunto. Children: John Philip, Killian and Barbara.
Exec: Wife and Killian Goukle.
Witnesses: Jacob Noors, Vallentain Bringhoof.

BURNS, ANDREW. April 4, 1755. April 28, 1755. K.289.
Exec: Michael McIntyre (sole Legatee) and Mary McIntyre.
Witnesses: Richard Winter, John Reily.

SINGER, JOHN. Co. of Philadelphia. Carpenter. Nov. 22, 1754. April 30, 1755. K.290.
Children: Cathrain, Christian, Margaret, Philip, Barber, George, John, Samuel and Mary. Exec: Wife Catherine.
Witnesses: Philip Bame, Jacob Fisher, Jacob Levering.

ANDERSON, LAWRENCE. City of Philadelphia. Mariner. May 27, 1746. May 1, 1755. K.291.
Exec: Children: Lawrence and Hannah. Trustees: Capt'n William Clymer (mariner) and Jacob Duchee (shopkeeper) of Philadelphia.
Witnesses: Enoch Story, Stephen Potts.

HARKER, JOHN. Moorland, Co. of Philadelphia. Taylor. March 7, 1755. May 5, 1755. K.292.
Grandfather: Adam. Brother: James. Uncle: James Sidwell.
Legatees: James, Thomas, Samuel, Benjamin, and Susanna Loyd of Moorland, cousins; James Sidwell, cousin; friends, Martha and Hester Walmsley of Bybury; William, Isaac and Benjamin, sons, and Mary, Hannah and Martha, daughters of Johr Worthington; friends, Thomas Stapler and Joseph Atkinson of Bristol, Bucks County, in trust for the Quaker Meeting Houses at Bristol and Bybary; Jonathan Davis, apprentice; Joseph Hill, son of John Hill of Buckingham, and John Loyd. Exec: Joseph Hill, John Loyd.

Witnesses: John Worthington (his mark), William Homer, Thomas Worthington.

JONES, JOHN, SR. Co. of Philadelphia. Cordwainer. May 27, 1754. May 6, 1755. K.295.
Exec. and sole Legatee: Son John.
Witnesses: David Rees, Samuel Garrigues, Paul Isaac Voto.

EDWARDS, JOHN. Co. of Bucks. Yeoman. May 5, 1753. May 7, 1755. K.296.
Children: William, John, and Alice (Jemison). Son-in-Law: Thomas Christy. Exec: Wife Mary and son William.
Witnesses: Samuel Clark, Samuel Foulke, Joseph Phillips.

QUEE, ALEXANDER. Co. of Philadelphia. Yeoman. Nov. 8, 1753. May 7, 1755. K.297.
Wife: Sarah. Children: Alexander, Jonathan, Seth, Sophia (Beventon), Margaret (Ridgway), Mary (Cunnrads), Kattrin (Jenins), Sarah (Morton), Rachel, Esther and Abigal. Exec: Archibald McClean and son Seth.
Witnesses: John Barnes, William French, Mary McClean (her mark).

BONSALL, JAMES. Kingsess, Co. of Philadelphia. Yeoman. Proved May 15, 1755. K.298.
Sisters: Hannah Price, Sarah Elliot. Cousins: Edward Bonsall, Martha (daughter of Philip and Hannah Price). Brothers: Benjamin and Nathan. Overseers: Jonathan Paschall (uncle), cousin John Hunt. Exec: Brother Benjamin.
Witnesses: Jonathan Paschall, John Hunt, David Gipson, John Sellers and Jesse Bonsall, who testify they they believe the unsigned will to be in the handwriting of testator.

MILLS, MARY. City of Philadelphia. Widow. Sept. 1, 1753. May 24, 1755. K.300.
Grandchildren: Albertus and Mary Shockela, Anne Bromwick, Mary and Anne Mills. Niece: Rebecca Whitman. Exec: Evan Morgan, merchant.
Witnesses: John Kearsley, Jr., John Vicary, Margaret Yeo (her mark).

REARDON, JOHN. City of Philadelphia. Cordwainer. May 15, 1755. May 26, 1755. K.301.

Children: John, Elizabeth and Ann. Beneficiaries: Martin Welsh and Peter Boyles, servants. Exec: Wife Ann, James White and John Reily. Witnesses: John Cottringer, James Rock (his mark).

HENDRICKS, JOHN. Co. of Philadelphia. Yeoman. April 11, 1755. May 28, 1755. K.303.
Son: John, names of other children not given. Exec: Wife Magdalena and John Schrack.
Witnesses: John Pennebacker, Nicholas Schneder, Nicholas Bunn.

HESSELIUS, GUSTAVUS. City of Philadelphia. Face-painter. June 15, 1750. May 29, 1755. K.304.
Children: John, Elizabeth (Price), Mary, Lydia and Sarah (Porter).
Exec: Son John.
Witnesses: Thomas Walker, James Kinsey, Lewis Evans.

OLDMAN, JOSEPH. City of Philadelphia. Blacksmith. May 2, 1755. July 25, 1755. K.305.
Appraisers: Edward Cathrall, Daniel Williams, Abel James. Exec: Wife Sarah and son Samuel.
Witnesses: Thomas Hopkins, Daniel Williams, William Parr.

NUTT, CHARITY. Late of Parish of St. Paul, Shadwell, in the County of Middlesex, England. Widow. June 20, 1751. Oct. 10, 1760. K.306. Signed in England, proved in London. Brother: Thomas Maleigh (wife, Abigail). Sisters: Susan Russell and Anne Bacon (wife of John Bacon). Cousins: Thomas Maleigh (son of brother Thomas). Kinsmen and Legatees: John Mountford of Wapping, Middlesex County, Apothecary; Gilbert Seabrook (son of cousin John Seabrook); the Poor of Ratclife Meeting House; friends Elizabeth Clarke, widow and Mary Streett, the elder.
Witnesses: In England, James Cooper, Mary Watts, Edward Marlar. The copy of record under seal of the Commissary Court of the Bishop of London, England, was delivered by Israel Pemberton to the Register General's office at Philadelphia to be recorded on June 16, 1761.

MAYLEIGH, THOMAS. Late of the Parish of St. Benedict, London. Citizen and apothecary. Recorded June 16, 1761. K.309.
Children: Thomas, Samuel, Abigail (Fernley), Hannah and Sarah. Son-in-Law: Edward Fernley. Trustees and Beneficiaries: Humphrey Hill and Samuel Willson, merchants of London. Exec: Wife Hannah,

and at her death, the three daughters. (The above was recorded from a copy, under seal, of the Prerogative court of the Archbishop of Canterbury, which was delivered to Israel Pemberton who brought it to be recorded at the Register General's office, Philadelphia, June 16, 1761.)

SCHREDLIE, DANIEL. June 29, 1754. July 2, 1754. K.323.
Wife and Children: Names not given. Kinsman: Daniel Schredle, schoolmaster, Houkheimb, Germany. Exec. and Guardians: John Hoplin, Bastian Huhly.
Witnesses: Andreas Paul, Andreas Hock.

CLIFTON, JOHN. City of Philadelphia. Merchant. April 2, 1755. June 2, 1755. K.325.
Children: William, Elizabeth, Francis, Ann, and Eleanor. Exec: Wife Elnor and children.
Witnesses: Thomas Greene, John Kearsley, Jr., William Vanderspiegel.

JOHNSON, SAMUEL. City of Philadelphia. Painter. May 20, 1755. June 2, 1755. K.326.
Wife: Mary. Legatees: Niece: Name not given (wife of James Trumble). Nephews: John Johnson and Samuel Johnson. Exec: Wife Mary, Benjamin Franklin, Esquire, Thomas Bourne of Philadelphia.
Witnesses: William Sturgeon, Samuel Johnson, Paul Isaac Voto.

ROBINSON, WILLIAM. New Providence, Co. of Philadelphia. May 18, 1755. June 7, 1755. K.327.
Children: William, Thomas, Nicholas, Mary, Elizabeth, and Rebecca (Valentine). Exec: Wife Rachel and Francis Hobson.
Witnesses: Owen Evans, Thomas Valentine.

MOYES, JAMES. City of Philadelphia. Ropemaker. June 26, 1750. June 9, 1755. K.328.
Son: John. Grandson: James Carrear (son of Abraham Carrear, barber). Legatees: (contingent upon the death of James Carrear) William Garwood and Abraham Carrear. Exec: William Garwood, John Jenkins.
Witnesses: Edward Campbell, Robert Miller.

OTTWAY, THOMAS. City of Philadelphia. Attorney. June 8, 1755. June 10, 1755. K.330.

Legatees: John Beanbrige of Northamptonshire, England, and Lynford Lardner. Exec: Lynford Lardner of Philadelphia, gentleman.
Witnesses: James Trotter, Mary Henderson.

BARGE, JOHN. German Township, Co. of Philadelphia. Miller. May 31, 1755. June 14, 1755. K.330.
Wife: Elizabeth. Mother: Mary Farmer, wife of Samuel Farmer. Children: Joseph, Andrew, Mary and Elizabeth. Exec: Wife and brother William Barge.
Witnesses: Oliver Shortall, George Wasker, Christian Lehman.

ERWIN, SAMUEL. City of Philadelphia. Yeoman. June 14, 1755. June 23, 1755. K.333.
Children: John, Sarah, Jane and Susanna (wife of James Dickey). Exec. and Trustees: Jacob Dubre, yeoman, and son John.
Witnesses: George Bullock, David Bevan, Paul Isaac Voto.

CROSBY, JOSHUA. City of Philadelphia. Gentleman. Nov. 28, 1752. July 2, 1755. K.335.
Beneficiaries and Relatives: Elizabeth Crosby (widow of nephew John, late of Ratcliffe, England) and her son John Bromley and daughter Mary Crosby; Francis Hatt and Elizabeth, his wife, and Elizabeth and Joshua Hatt, their son and daughter; Rachel Broderick, niece; Rebecca Webster, niece; Mary Page, niece; Sarah Collier, grand-niece; grand-nephews, John and Stephen Collier; Thomas Allen, nephew; niece Mary Rowe (wife of James); Job Crosby, nephew; Hugh Crosby, cousin (wife Jane); Joshua Crosby, cousin (son of Hugh); Thomas Crosby, nephew (all of England). Other Beneficiaries: Friends Thomas Hyam and Thomas Whitehead in trust for Friends' Workinghouse, near London; Mary Drummond of Edinborough; to Executors, in trust for the Poor of Philadelphia, also for Friends' Meeting in Philadelphia; Pennsylvania Hospital; Friends Grammar School, Philadelphia; Mary Magdalen Kerns, housekeeper; Anthony Benezet, schoolmaster; Rebecca Berchall, schoolmistress; John Willson, usher of the grammar school; Elizabeth Gardner of Pennsylvania Hospital; Samuel Garrigue, barber. Exec: John Reynall, John Smith, and nephew Thomas Crosby, merchants.
Witnesses: Bartholomew Penrose, John Baynton, John Reily.

WORRALL, SARAH. Co. of Chester, Penna. 9 mo. 28, 1750. July 2, 1755. K.335.

Children: Elizabeth (Salkield), John, Sarah (Taylor), Peter and Thomas. Grandchildren: Mary Taylor and Egnes Salkield. Sisters: Mary James and Ann Goodwin. Cousin: Sarah Vor. Exec: Son Peter. Witnesses: James Black (his mark), Samuel Oliver.

WATKINS, WILLIAM. Abington, Co. of Philadelphia. April 2, 1750. July 26, 1755. K.340.
Children: Names not given. Exec: Wife Hesther and Symon Thomas. Witnesses: Joseph Jones, Joshua Thomas, Malachi Jones.

FRANKS, JONATHAN. Co. of Philadelphia. Carpenter. Oct. 20, 1750. Aug. 6, 1755. K.341.
Mother: Elizabeth Hauksworth (late Franks). Sisters: Mary and Hester Franks. Exec: Mother, Father-in-Law William Hauksworth and Abraham Daws, yeoman.
Witnesses: Archibald Chrystie, John Campbell, William Tea.

NEIDERMARK, MATHIAS. Co. of Philadelphia. Victualler. July 25, 1755. Aug. 12, 1755. K.342.
Wife: Jane. Daughter: Sarah. Exec: Wife and Henry Sparks, yeoman.
Witnesses: William Murdock, John Reily.

DAWSON, MATTHEW. Oct. 2, 1749. Aug. 15, 1755. K.348.
Exec. and sole Legatee: Brother, James Dawson.
Witnesses: John Reily, Robert Forde.

JONES, JOHN. Co. of Chester, Penna. Yeoman. Aug. 1, 1755. Aug. 16, 1755. K.343.
Exec: Wife, Lyddia, and brothers, Samuel and Thomas Jones.
Witnesses: John Johnston, John Harvard, Jr. and John Calaghan (his mark).

BRADFORD, CORNELIA. City of Philadelphia. Widow. Jan. 11, 1755. Aug. 25, 1755. K.345.
Nephews: James Hamm and George Smith (wife Cornelia). Nieces: Elizabeth Flew, and Catherine Degrowgh (daughter of sister Mary). Beneficiaries: Negroes, Henry and Sylvia. Exec: George and Cornelia Smith.
Witnesses: John Swift, George Claypool, Thomas Gordon.

ANTES, HENRY. Co. of Philadelphia. Wheelwright. July 20, 1754. Aug. 8, 1755. K.346.
Wife: Christina. Children: Frederick, William, Cathrina, Margaretta, Elizabeth, Henry, John, Mary and Beningna. Guardians: Adolph Mayer, David Bishoph. Beneficiaries: Abraham Bemper and Timothy Horsefield in trust for religious purposes. Exec: Wife and sons Frederick and William.
Witnesses: Conrad Duddarer, George Hipner, Jost Bitting.
Codicil: July 8, 1755.
Beneficiaries: The people called Unitas featrum (a religious denomination).
Witnesses: Same witnesses.

JONES, ELLIN. Gwynedd, Co. of Philadelphia. Spinster. 7 mo. 7, 1755. Sept. 1, 1755. K.349.
Cousins: Jane Darkins, Ruth Loyd, Sarah Loyd and Margaret Evans (daughter of John Evans.) Nieces: Margaret, Ellin and Hannah Jones. Sister-in-Law: Gainor Jones. Brother: John Jones. Beneficiaries: Friends, Ellin Williams and negro Harry. Exec. and Trustees: Cousins Rowland Evans and Abram Evans.
Witnesses: John Jones, Mathias Luken, John Evans.

PHILLIPS, THOMAS. City of Philadelphia. (Late of the Island of Antigua). Mariner. Aug. 23, 1755. Sept. 6, 1755. K.350.
Wife: Elizabeth. Children: Thomas and John. Exec: William Plumsted, Esq., and Captain John Phillips of Philadelphia, and Samuel Martin (merchant) and Robert Gray of the Island of Antigua.
Witnesses: Michael Lovell, George Houston, Benjamin Price.

HOLLAND, THOMAS. City of Philadelphia. Merchant. July 6, 1754. Sept. 12, 1755. K.351.
Children: Nathaniel, Thomas, Elizabeth, Mary, Sarah, Joanna, Samuel and Joseph. Exec: Son Nathaniel and son-in-law John Bankson.
Witnesses: Thomas Tilbury, William Standley, William Gray.

FOSTER, JOHN. City of Philadelphia. Victualler. Sept. 12, 1755. Sept. 15, 1755. K.353.
Wife: Mary. Daughter: Mary. Exec: Samuel Bettle (tanner) and Thomas Tilbury of Philadelphia.
Witnesses: Doughty Jones and Paul Isaac Voto.

HUNTER, JOHN GEORGE. Oley, Co. of Philadelphia. Tayler. Jan. 6, 1754. Sept. 16, 1755. K.354.
Children: Anthony and Nicholas. Exec: Nicholas.
Witnesses: Jacob Shoemaker, Henry Keppele, George Pasnshawa.

HITT, RICHARD, JR. City of Philadelphia. Gentleman. Aug. 20, 1752. Sept. 15, 1755. K.355.
Father: Richard. Aunts: Mary and Rachel Moore. Brother-in-Law: Dr. Samuel Preston Moore (wife Hannah). Brother: Henry. Sisters: Hannah, Mary, Deborah, Harriett, Rachel, Margaret, Sarah and Miltha.
Exec: Richard and Dr. Samuel Preston Moore and wife.
Witnesses: Reese Meredith, Redmond Conyngham, Edward Shippen.

HOLTZ, GEORGE. City of Philadelphia. Shopkeeper. Sept. 2, 1755. Sept. 17, 1755. K.356.
Children: John, George, Elizabeth, Andrew, Catherine (Age), Anne (Gerard), Margaret and Mary (Mathias). Exec: Son George and son-in-law Henry Mathias.
Witnesses: Peter Miller and Henry Potts.

MCCOMBS, JOHN. Co. of Philadelphia. Yeoman. Sept. 17, 1755. Sept. 20, 1755. K.357.
Legatee: R: D: Mr. Richard Treat. Exec: Son, John McCombs and Andrew Dunbar.
Witnesses: William Adams and Archibald McClean.

HALL, THOMAS. Blockley, Co. of Philadelphia. 7 mo. 6, 1755. Sept. 27, 1755. K.358.
Wife: Hannah. Children: James, Aaron, Hannah, Margaret, Martha, Rachel, and Lyddia (Hinds). Exec: Son James.
Witnesses: Joseph Lees, Daniel Hibbere, Thomas Marshall.

RAMBO, ANDREW. Upper Merion, Co. of Philadelphia. July 2, 1755. Oct. 1, 1755. K.359.
Legatees: Peter and George Rambo; Elias, Gunner, Jonas and Jeremiah Rambo (relationship not stated); and Ann Carsine ("brother's daughter").
Witnesses: William White, Sarah Priest, Andrew Holsten.

GRAY, JOSEPH. City of Philadelphia. Yeoman. Jan. 17, 1755. Oct. 10, 1755. K.360.

Wife: Mary. Children: Mary (wife of Charles Jenkins), Samuel and George. Grandchildren: William and Joseph (sons of son William, deceased). Legatee: Son-in-law Charles Jenkins. Exec: Daughter Mary (wife of Charles Jenkins).
Witnesses: John Galloway, John Ingham, Paul Isaac Voto.

EASTBURN, ROBERT. City of Philadelphia. Clothier. Nov. 21, 1752. Oct. 13, 1755. K.361.
Children: John, Esther (Livesey), Samuel, Robert, Sarah (Thomas) and Elizabeth (Clark). Nephew and Niece: John Eastburn and Elizabeth Walton. Grandsons: Joseph Eastburn and Jonathan Livesey. Sons-in-Law: Jonathan Livesey and David Clark. Exec: Samuel and Joseph Eastburn and Jonathan and Joseph Livesey.
Witnesses: Richard Peters and John Levers.

HALL, ANN. City of Philadelphia. Widow. Sept. 29, 1755. Oct. 17, 1755. K.363.
Sons: David and Charles. Exec: William Ball Goldsmith. David to be co-executor on attaining his majority.
Witnesses: John Benson, Daniel Jones, Alice Loadman.

KERR, JAMES. City of Philadelphia. House carpenter. Aug. 18, 1753. Oct. 22, 1755. K.364.
Legatee: Hester Allar, spinster, of Philadelphia. Exec: Mother Elizabeth and James Stevens (baker).
Witnesses: John Campbell, William Dunwick, William Harrison.

KEMPHER, JOHANNES. March 19, 1755. Oct. 24, 1755. K.365.
Exec: Sons John and Jacob and Jacob Reife.
Witnesses: Jacob Marckly and Philip Marckly.

GREEN, JOHN. City of Philadelphia. Mariner. May 6, 1747. Oct. 28, 1755. K.366.
Son: William. Sisters: Katharin and Hannah. Cousin: Sarah (daughter of Samuel Green). Guardians: Reese Meredith and Charles Norris. Exec: Wife Sarah.
Witnesses: Theophilus Grew, Henry Schleydorn, Elizabeth Shewell.

EYRE, JOHN. City of Philadelphia. Innholder. Sept. 26, 1755. Oct. 31, 1755. K.367.

Daughter: Mary (wife of James Price). Exec: Wife Mary and William Young.
Witnesses: Jonathan Shoemaker, Thomas Rogers, Peter Thomson.

MILLER, JACOB. New Providence, Co. of Philadelphia. Farmer. June 4, 1754. Dec. 13, 1755. K.369.
Exec: Wife Christiana.
Witnesses: Edward DeHaven, Frederick Hearing, Charles Cornelius Reboteace.

DE NYCE, WILLIAM. City of Philadelphia. Smith. Nov. 15, 1755. Nov. 25, 1755. K.370.
Legatees: Mary and Susanna DeNyce (nieces); John DeNyce (brother); friends, Thomas Jackman, Samuel Owen, and Jacob Cooper (baker).
Exec: Jacob Cooper.
Witnesses: Sarah Owen, Samuel Mergan, Paul Isaac Voto.

MARTIN, THOMAS. Co. of Chester, Penna. Laborer. April 22, 1754. Jan. 7, 1756. K.371.
Children: Lettice, Mary and Martha. Grandchildren: Rebecca and Hannah (issue of daughter Hannah, deceased) and Martha (issue of Lettice Jones). Exec: Wife Martha and Isaac Davis.
Witnesses: Richard Evans, John Gronon, William Evans.

ARNT, ELIZABETH. Co. of Philadelphia. Widow. Dec. 1, 1755. Jan. 23, 1756. K.372.
Beneficiaries: Yost Pannekugh and Philip Reed, Jacob Shouler, Elizabeth Shouler, Jacob Zelnar, Jacob Bower, Hannah Pannekugh, John Pannekugh, Jacob Stump, Presbyterian Church of Franconia, Pa., Lutheran Church (same place). Trustee: George Stump. Exec: Yost Pannekugh and Philip Reed.
Witnesses: Christian Moyer, Jacob Dettwiller, Robert Jones.

DIXON, JOHN. City of Philadelphia. Barber and Surgeon. Jan. 6, 1756. Jan. 28, 1756. K.374.
Beneficiaries: Children of Testator's late brother Martin (names not given); friends, Theodore Schneider; Mary and Margareth (daughters of Patrick Farrell); Christopher Bryan; Francis Farrell; Robert Harding, Philadelphia. Exec: Robert Harding and Patrick Farrell.
Witnesses: Andrew Farrell, Sarah Green, Robert Fleming.

KEYSER, DIRICK. City of Philadelphia. Cordwainer. Jan. 2, 1756. Feb. 4, 1756. K.375.
Brother: Andrew. Children: Alice, Hannah (Keyser), Elizabeth (wife of Andrew Wood), John, Peter, Dirick and Michael. Exec: Wife Alice and sons John and Peter.
Witnesses: Ludwick Englehard, John Ax, Christian Loehman.
Codicil: Jan. 4, 1756.
Witnesses: Same.

NICHOLAS, JOHN. City of Philadelphia. House carpenter. May 7, 1755. Feb. 4, 1756. K.378.
Wife: Jane. Sisters: Martha Roberts and Mary Evans. Niece: Sarah Loyd. Grand niece: ---. Samuel, Robert and Martha Loyd, Margaret Evans and Jane (daughter of Aubry Roberts). Cousins: Samuel, Mary and Sarah (children of Testator's deceased brother, Anthony Nicholas). Exec: Wife, cousin Hugh Roberts and Joseph Fox.
Witnesses: Rebecca Owen, Mary Griffiths, Joseph Galloway.

REED, MARGARET. City of Philadelphia. Widow. Oct. 12, 1751. Feb. 9, 1756. K.380.
Grandson: John Forrest Hammond. Exec: Daughter Ann (Hammond).
Witnesses: John Greenleaves, Josiah Jackson.

ZEIGLER, MARTHA BARBARA. Co. of Lancaster, Penna. Widow. April 16, 1753. Feb. 12, 1756. K.381.
Sisters and Legatees: Anna Marigretha Saltzgeber (wife of Ditereck), Anna Maria Kunigunda (wife of Jacob Frank). Exec: Jacob Frank.
Witnesses: Jacob Wise, Peter Miller.

RAWLINSON, ROBERT. City of Philadelphia. Victualler. Jan. 7, 1756. Feb. 14, 1756. K.382.
Wife: Hannah. Brother: Jeffery (of Liverpool). Legatees and Kinsfolk: Langston Carlisle and children of brother Jeffery (names not given). Exec: Wife and son-in-law, William Jones of Philadelphia, grazier).
Witnesses: Richard Davis, John Gill, John Reily.

INESON, ROBERT. City of Philadelphia. Shopkeeper. Sept. 18, 1753. Feb. 26, 1756. K.384.

Wife: Margaret. Children: William and Martha. Brothers: Richard and Hugh. Sister: Ann.
Witnesses: William Norton, Anthony Benezet.

JONES, THOMAS. Co. of Philadelphia. Yeoman. Feb. 20, 1756. Feb. 28, 1756. K.385.
Wife: Catherin. Children: Samuel, Martha, Rebeccah, Daniel, Thomas and Joshua. Grandchild: Mary. Exec: Sons Daniel and Thomas.
Witnesses: Robert Davies, Benjamin Griffith.

HEINZLEMAN, MATHIAS. City of Philadelphia. Minister. Feb. 7, 1756. March 11, 1756. K.386.
Wife: Margrette. Child: (unknown). Exec: Rev. Henrie Muhlenberg.
Witnesses: George Hilner, Henry Keppele.

EDWARDS, JOHN. Co. of Philadelphia. Yeoman. Jan. 28, 1756. March 17, 1756. K.387.
Wife: Margaret, nee Kirk. Father: Thomas. Children: John, Jesse and Sarah. Exec: Wife and brothers-in-law Reynear Kirk, yeoman, and William Loofbourrow, tayler.
Witnesses: Thomas and John Roberts and Christian Lehman.

BOUCH, JACOB. Co. of Chester, Penna. March 11, 1756. March 23, 1756. K.390.
Children: John, Jacob and Elizabeth (names of three other children and grandchildren not given). Exec: Wife Barbra and Henry Bener.
Witnesses: John Switzer and Andrew Hade (his mark).

THOMAS, LEWIS. Co. of Chester, Penna. Laborer. March 9, 1752. March 26, 1756. K.391.
Children: Lewis and Anne (Reese). Trustees: John William and Richard Evans. Exec: Wife Joan.
Witnesses: Joseph Mitchell, Ann Reese, William Evans.

KLAMPFFER, ADAM. City of Philadelphia. Shopkeeper. July 29, 1755. April 3, 1756. K.392.
Wife: Anna Maria. Children: William and Eva Margaretha (wife of John Conrad Schwickhaus). Grandchildren: Catherine, Louisa, and John Schwickhaus. Exec: Son William.
Witnesses: John Baynton, Michel Halling, Peter Miller.

NEFF, SEBASTIAN. Co. of Philadelphia. Cordwainer. March 29, 1756. April 12, 1756. K.396.
Wife: Anna Barbara. Son: Jacob. Exec: Wife and John Jones.
Witnesses: Jacob Frites, John Henry Juncken, Christopher Lehman.

BOULTON, HENRY. Co. of Philadelphia. Woolcomber. April 3, 1756. May 3, 1756. K.397.
Wife: Sarah. Children: Isaac, David, Sarah, Ann, Elizabeth, Mary, Hanna, William and Thomas. Exec: Son Thomas.
Witnesses: John Jordan, Samuel Brooke, Peter Rimbey.

RICHARD, MARY. Co. of Philadelphia. Widow. Jan. 28, 1755. May 3, 1756. K.398.
Children: Hannah (Sheyner), Casper and Mathias. Grandchildren: Rebecca Sheyner (other names not given). Exec: Sons Casper and Mathias.
Witnesses: Andrew Keppler, Michael Walther.

REES, MICHAEL. Co. of Chester, Pa. Taylor. April 5, 1756. May 5, 1756. K.399.
Wife: Sarah (former wife, Elizabeth Heans). Children: Tamar, Hannah, Rebecca and Abigel. Step-daughters and sons: Sarah, Mary, Joseph and Isaac Thomas. Beneficiary: St. Peters Church, Coventry, Chester Co. Exec: Wife Sarah.
Witnesses: Benjamin Thomas, John Llewellin.

GMELIN, MATHIAS. Co. of Philadelphia. Glazier. Jan. 1, 1755. May 14, 1756. K.400.
Children: Christian, Rosina, Sophia and Christiana. Grandchildren: Mathias and Sophia (issue of Christiana). Exec: Wife Maria Barbara and Jacob Wentz; and after their death, Balthas Reser.

BOND, SARAH. Horsham Township, Co. of Philadelphia. Widow. Jan. 11, 1756. May 19, 1756. K.402.
Children: Benjamin, Abraham, John, Edward, Isaac and Hannah.
Exec: Brother Jacob Cadwallader and brother-in-law Robert Comly.
Witnesses: William Lukens, Joseph Lukens, William Dunkan.

DAUB, JOHN WILLIAM. Sept. 19, 1755. May 22, 1756. K.404.
Children: Valentine, John, Henry, John Peter and Jacob, Mary, Catherina and Gertruyd. Exec: Wife Anna Barbara and Jacob Nuss.

Witnesses: Conrad Sneider, Valentine Nungesser.

MATHISON, HENRY. City of Philadelphia. Yeoman. Oct. 16, 1755. May 26, 1759. K.404.
Exec: Wife Mary.
Witnesses: Thomas Tilbury, Alexander Sadler, Christian Loehman.

REES, WILLIAM. Upper Merion, Co. of Philadelphia. Yeoman. Dec. 29, 1755. June 12, 1756. K.405.
Children: William and Margaret. Beneficiaries: George George and James Davis, in trust for the Friends Meeting and support of the ministry, contingent bequests to Sarah (daughter of Jonathan Davis) and Joan (daughter of Thomas and sister Margaret Lloyd). Exec: Wife Jenett and son William.
Witnesses: Thomas Rees, James Davis.

FUNCK, JACOB. Co. of Philadelphia. Yeoman. May 15, 1756. June 14, 1756. K.407.
Wife: Barbara. Children: Jacob, Samuel, Barbara and Maria. Exec: Wife and cousin Christian Funck.
Witnesses: Christian Meyer, Samuel Meyer, Henry Funck.

WALN, RICHARD. Noriton, Co. of Philadelphia. Yeoman. Dec. 1, 1753. June 16, 1756. K.409.
Children: Richard, Robert, Nicholas, Joseph, Ann, Susanna (Williams), and Mary. Grandchildren: Names not given. Exec: Son Joseph.
Witnesses: Josiah Wood, Rowland Evans.

BROCKDEN, RICHARD. City of Philadelphia. Gentleman. Jan. 22, 1754. June 18, 1756. K.410.
Children: Latitia, Ann and Mary. Grandchildren: Richard, Charles, Ann and Elizabeth Brockden; Latitia, Ann, Charles, Thomas Norton and Elizabeth Pryor. Son-in-Law: Nerton Pryor. Exec: Latitia Brockden.
Witnesses: Silas Pryor, Joseph Saunders, Daniel Rees, William Boddington.

BLACKWELL, HUGH. May 8, 1756. June 19, 1756. K.413.
Brother: John. Daughter-in-Law: Sary Babb. Son-in-Law: Steven Foulk. Beneficiaries: Joseph and his son Hugh and daughter Sary Carter; John and his son and daughter, Isaac and Sary Bogan;

Cadwallader and his children John and Anne Griffiths; John Burnett's sons John and Henry; John Hoopton's children (names not given); Easther Hopton; Robert Pyles' daughter Mary; Elizabeth Booth (wife of Robert); Joseph and Margarett (children of William Cloud). Exec: Wife Elizabe.
Witnesses: Joseph Cloud, Robert Pyle, Ann Carter and Robert Green, who testified that they were present on May 8, 1756 and heard said will read to testator and that he acknowledged it to be in accordance with his wishes.

WALN, MARY. Northern Liberties, City of Philadelphia. Widow. 11 mo. 19, 1745. June 23, 1756. K.415.
Children: Ann, Rebecca, Richard (and unknown child). Parents: George and Rebecca Shoemaker. Brother: Jacob Shoemaker.
Witnesses: Rebecah Minshall, Hannah Shoemaker.

HAYS, WILLIAM. Kensington, City of Philadelphia. Innholder. Sept. 5, 1753. June 24, 1756. K.417.
Children: William, John, Elizabeth and Mary. Grandchild: Catherine Brooks. Exec: Joseph Stennard (butcher) and Isaac Dutton (shipwright).
Witnesses: George Fox, William Pearson, Joseph Grover.

SHUEMAKER, GEORGE. Upper Melfort, Co. of Northampton, Pa. Yeoman. June 4, 1756. June 29, 1756. K.419.
Children: John, Frederick, Adam, Elizabeth, Barbara and Jacob. Exec: Wife Barbara and son Jacob.
Witnesses: Valentine Stinmeats, Frederick Karen, John Hooker.

EVANS, LEWIS. City of Philadelphia, late of Carnarvanshire, South Britain. Gentleman. May 26, 1756. Jan. 19, 1756. K.420.
Signed and proved in New York before Sir Charles Hardy, Knight, Captain General and Governor in Chief of the Province of New York and the Territories depending thereon in America, and Vice Admiral of the same. Daughter: Amelia Evans. Beneficiary: Martha Carwithy (servant). Exec: Brother John Evans and William Cox, merchant.
Witnesses: Patrick Carryl, Garret Noel, John Dies of New York.

POWELL, SAMUEL. City of Philadelphia. Carpenter. Signed Nov. 21, 1752. K.422

Wife: Abigail. Children: Sarah (Morris), Samuel and Deborah (Emlen). Grandchildren: Samuel, Deborah, Anthony, Israel, Sarah and Thomas Morris; Sarah and Samuel Powell; Abigail (Griffith) daughter of son Samuel, and Samuel Emlen. Beneficiaries: Samuel, Mary and Hannah (children of kinsman, Samuel Rhoads); Isaac Jenkins (apprentice); John Reynell and James Pemberton (merchants) in trust for the Poor of the Monthly Meeting of Friends; William Logan, John Smith (merchant), Samuel Rhoads and Samuel Wetherill (carpenters) in trust for said monthly meeting. Sons-in-Law: Joshua Emlen, Anthony Morris and William Griffiths. Daughter-in-Law: Mary Powell. Father-in-Law: Barnabas Wilcox. Overseers: Israel (and sons) Israel and James Pemberton. Exec: Grandson Samuel Emlen.
Witnesses: Asher Mott, Samuel Wetherell, Daniel Offley.
Codicil: June 14, 1755.
Witnesses: Same.
Codicil: 6 mo. 21, 1756.
The public school of Philadelphia through its overseer is made a beneficiary and Joshua Emlen is nominated Executor.
Witnesses: Same.

KROESEN, FRANCIS. Co. of Bucks, Pa. Farmer. May 1, 1756. July 3, 1756. K.435.
Wife: Elizabeth. Children: Elizabeth (Slaght), Leonard and Derrick. Grandchildren: John, Christian and Catherine Slaght. Exec: Wife and sons.
Witnesses: Derrick and John Kroesen, John Vanaredalen.

HUGHES, HUGH. City of Philadelphia. Gentleman. May 1, 1756. July 20, 1756. K.436.
Wife: Mary. Children: Hugh (of New York), John, Sarah (Dehaven) and William. Grandson: Hugh Dehaven. Son-in-Law: Peter Dehaven. Exec: John Hughes and Peter Dehaven.
Witnesses: Joseph Galloway, Benjamin Rumsey, Richard Smith.

BELLINGER, MICHAEL. Blockley, Co. of Philadelphia. June 5, 1756. July 3, 1756. K.438.
Wife: Margareth. Exec: Wife and brother-in-law Peter Miller.
Witnesses: Thomas Wynne, David Evans.

WILLHELM, JOHN. Co. of Philadelphia. Weaver. May 25, 1756. July 10, 1756. K.439.

Wife: Mary. Children: John, William, Catharin, Barbara, Mary and Elizabeth. Exec: Son John.
Witnesses: Ludwig Hinckle, John Tennis.

OX, ADAM. Co. of Philadelphia. Yeoman. June 1, 1756. July 29, 1756. K.441.
Wife: Elizabeth. Children: Mathias, Leonard, Peter, Elizabeth (wife of Peter Bieber), Catherine (wife of George Hunts [Kunts?]) and Anne (late wife of Abraham Weis). Exec: Son Mathias and George Yerger.
Witnesses: Elias Shryber, Peter Smith, Christian Lehman.

MC CALL, GEORGE. July 19, 1754. Aug. 3, 1756. K.443.
Wife: Lydia. Daughters: Catherine, Mary and Lydia. Exec: Wife, brother Samuel and nephew, Samuel McCall Jr., William Plumsted, and (by second Codicil) Redmond Conyinham of Philadelphia.
Witnesses: John Jourdain, Andrew Carsan, Robert Clerk.
Codicil: May 13, 1756.
Witnesses: John Cross, John Jenkins.
Codicil: July 2, 1756.
Witnesses: Phineas Bond, Robert Clerk.

FEND, FREDERICK. Germantown, Co. of Philadelphia. July 17, 1756. Aug. 4, 1756. K.445.
Children: Ferdinand, Anne, Magdalena (Weiss), Susannah (Graff) and Elizabeth (Lehman). Exec: Ferdinand (son), Christian Lehman (son-in-law) and daughter, Anne.
Witnesses: John Ekstein, Henry Ernst, John Adam Gruber.

REES, THOMAS. Co. of Bucks, Penna. Yeoman. June 19, 1756. Aug. 14, 1756. K.446.
Children: Hannah, John, Ann, John, and David. Niece: Mary (daughter of Daniel Rees). Exec: Wife, Elizabeth and son David.
Witnesses: George Shomaker, James Dunlap, William Davis.

MURATROYD, JAMES. City of Philadelphia. Merchant. Jan. 12, 1756. Aug. 16, 1756. K.447.
Children: John, Thomas and Mary. Exec: Wife Mary.
Witnesses: William Sturgeon, John Ord.

MILES, SARAH. Radnor, Co. of Chester, Penna. Widow of Richard Miles, yeoman. Oct. 6, 1756. Aug. 25, 1756. K.448.

Children: James, Evan, John, Jane, Abagail, Sarah and Hannah. Grandchild: Abigail Davis. Sons-in-Law: Joseph Powell, John Davis, Jonathan Pugh, Benjamin Griffiths.
Witnesses: David Davis, Isaac Wood, Joseph Stern.

ROBERTS, THOMAS. Germantown, Co. of Philadelphia. Yeoman. 5 mo. 5, 1753. Aug. 24, 1756. K.450.
Wife: Elinor. Children: Thomas, John, Mary (wife of Peter Tyson) and Sarah (Jones). Grandsons: Thomas Jones, Thomas Roberts Jr.
Exec: Thomas and John Roberts.
Witnesses: Thomas Rose, Margaret and John Michel Kriser.

NEWHOUSE, JOHN. Co. of Philadelphia. Yeoman. April 15, 1754. Aug. 31, 1756. K.453.
Children: By first wife, Antony; by second wife, John and Magdalene; by the third, Euphronica and Eva. Step-son: By third wife, Valentine.
Exec: Hannah (third and last beloved wife).
Witnesses: Jacob Umstat, John Hall.

FEAST, BASIL. City of Philadelphia, late of Santa Croix. Physician. May 5, 1756. Sept. 6, 1756. K.453.
Beneficiaries: Dr. Thomas Bond; Capt'n Thomas Riche; Gervase Burgess, merchant; Richard Taylor, London; George Appleby, London; Thomas Knight, cheesemonger, London; Elizabeth Painter; Dr. Phineas Bond; Dr. Castly, Sr.; Dr. Evans; George Beale; Mrs. Riche; Mrs. Graham; Mrs. McKnight; Miss Martha McKnight. Exec: Thomas Riche of Philadelphia, and Thomas McKnight, London.
Witnesses: George Beale, Walter Davis, Thomas Riche.

PENTER, JACOB. Co. of Philadelphia. Cordwainer. July 24, 1756. Sept. 18, 1756. K.457.
Children: Elias, Jacob, George, Mary Elizabeth (wife of Philip Fidler), Catherine, (wife of Bernhard Gilbert), Anne and Mary. Exec: Wife, Eve and son-in-law Bernhard Gilbert.
Witnesses: Johannes Frey, Jacob Landes, Andrew Ziegler.

GODFREY, THOMAS. Co. of Chester, Penna. Dec. 15, 1755. Sept. 18, 1756. K.458.
Children: William, Elizabeth (Thomas), Eleanor (Jones), Sarah, Rebecca (Hulen), Lucy (Jones), Hannah and John. Exec: Wife, Jane and son, William.

Witnesses: Thomas Water, Joseph Walker, William Currie.

DUFFIELD, JOHN. Co. of Philadelphia. Blacksmith. Aug. 19. 1756. Sept. 27, 1756. K.460.
Grandfather: Benjamin. Children: Phebe, John and Mary. Exec: Wife, Martha and John Paul. Brother: Peter.
Witnesses: William Foster, William Tillyer, Evan Thomas.

GARDNER, JOHN FREDERICK. Co. of Philadelphia. Weaver. Aug. 23, 1756. Sept. 29. 1756. K.461.
Wife: Anne Eve. Children: John, Hannah, Margaret (Heuss), John Henry, Susannah, John Jacob, George Jacob, John Frederick and five others (names not given). Exec: Wife, John George Gerster and son John.
Witnesses: John George Hellenbach, John Adam Gruber.

HILLES, HUGH. Co. of Bucks, Pa. Weaver. Aug. 6, 1756. Oct. 6, 1756. K.463.
Wife: Ann. Children: William, Ann, Mary and David. Exec: Brothers-in-law, George Brooks and George Evans.
Witnesses: Thomas, Theopholus and William Foulke.

JOHN, DAVID. Co. of Chester, Pa. April 27, 1756. Oct. 3, 1756. K.464.
Children: Mary, Elizabeth, David, Samuel, Hannah, Rachel, Lea and Benjamin. Exec: Wife, Katherine. Co-Exec: Isaac, David and Richard Evans.
Witnesses: John Chrystie, Thomas John, Thomas David.

KEYSER, PETER. Co. of Philadelphia. Tanner. Aug. 9, 1756. Sept. 30, 1756. K.466.
Wife: Susanna. Children: Peter, Andrew, Derick, Margareth and Hannah. Overseers: Brother-in-Law John Pennebacker and Peter Custer. Exec: Sons Peter and Andrew.
Witnesses: Gilbert Boors, Nicholas Bunn.

HOFFMAN, WILLIAM. Co. of Philadelphia. Aug. 16, 1756. Oct. 2, 1756. K.467.
Children: Five, whose names are not given. Exec: Wife Anna Mary and son-in-law John George Koch.
Witnesses: Augustine Neiser, John Conrad Steiner, Baltes Reser.

GRANT, WILLIAM. City of Philadelphia. Merchant. Nov. 14, 1753. Oct. 6, 1756. K.468.
Children: William, Mary and Margaret. Exec: Wife Mary, Samuel Smith, Thomas Bourne and John Wallace, merchants.
Witnesses: Joseph Trotter, John Howard, Paul Isaac Voto.

ROSEMAN, JACOB. Co. of Berks, Pa. Sept. 9, 1756. Oct. 12, 1756. K.470.
Son: Jacob (names of other children not given). Exec: Wife Annapolia and brother-in-law Henry Mertz.
Witnesses: Michael Moll, Henry Gabel.

MITCHELL, JOHN. City of Philadelphia. Mariner. Sept. 23, 1753. Oct. 15, 1756. K.470.
Children: John, Elizabeth and Sarah. Exec: Wife Jane.
Witnesses: Randall Mitchell, John Cowan.

DAVID, THOMAS. New Providence, Co. of Philadelphia. Yeoman. July 25, 1756. Oct. 16, 1756. K.472.
Children: John, Mary, Elizabeth, Elijah, Elisha and Morris.
Beneficiaries: Elizabeth and Anne (daughters of Paul Cartleberry); the Township of New Providence given a piece of land for public burial purposes. Exec: Son Morris.
Witnesses: David Castleberry (his mark), Nathan Davis, Benjamin Davis.
Codicil: July 27, 1756.
Gives to said Township an additional piece of land on which to erect a Baptist Meeting House.

LEHMAN, GODFREY. Germantown, Co. of Philadelphia. Potter. May 29, 1756. Nov. 2, 1756. K.473.
Children: Christian and John (by first wife, Anne Sophia), Hannah Loretta, Augustin, Daniel, Magdalen, Rosina, Lydia and Joseph. Exec: Wife Catherine and son Christian.
Witnesses: Hartman Adam, Eberhard Ludwig Gruber, Nicholas Christian Otto.

SCHRACK, EVA ROSINA. Widow of John Jacob. Aug. 22, 1754. Nov. 4, 1756. K.475.

Children: John, Elizabeth, Catherine, Eva, Mary, John Nicholas, Philip and Christian. Beneficiary: The Augustus Church of Providence Township, Pa. Exec: Son John.
Witnesses: Samuel Lane, Mathias Heinzelman, Michael Bunn.

MAYER, MICHAEL. Co. of Northampton, Penna. Farmer. Oct. 7, 1756. Nov. 8, 1756. K.478.
Wife: Mary Catherine. Children: Michael, Elizabeth, Magdalena, Conrad, Salome and Catherine. Exec: Wife, Abraham Bechtel, John Mayer.
Witnesses: Jacob Stahl, George Weiss.

LANDY, DAVID. New Providence, Co. of Philadelphia. Oct. 26, 1756. Nov. 9, 1756. K.479.
Daughter: Jane (wife of John Dunn). Trustee: John Edwards. Exec: Wife Mary.
Witnesses: Benjamin Chesnut, Thomas Major, William Beasley.

LEWIS, ANNE. Upper Dublin, Co. of Philadelphia. Widow. 6 mo. 29, 1754. Nov. 19, 1756. K.480.
Children: Elizabeth (Spencer), Lewis, Ellis and Jane. Exec: Ellis.
Witnesses: Mathew Tyson, John Hubbs, John Evans.

BARTHOLOMEW, JOHN. Co. of Philadelphia. Yeoman. Oct. 23, 1756. Nov. 20, 1756. K.480.
Children: Ann (Waters), Joseph, Thomas, Elizabeth, Rachel (Davis), John, Andrew, Benjamin, Mary, Augustine and Edward.
Grandchildren: Hannah (daughter of Isaac Davis), John, Mary and Joseph (children of Andrew Bartholomew). Trustees: Isaac James, Humphrew Bate, John Jones (carpenter), David Evans.
Witnesses: Joseph Ambler, Edward Ambler, Abel Griffith.

TULL, JOHN. Oct. 12, 1749. Dec. 4, 1756. K.483.
Exec. and sole Legatees: Brother James and sister Susannah Knowles.
Witnesses: William Moulder, John Hopkins, Josiah Warner.

ZACHARY, LOYD [Is the last name Lloyd?]. City of Philadelphia. Physician. Dec. 11, 1755. Dec. 6, 1756. K.483.
Beneficiaries: Cousins Dr. Thomas Loyd (and Peter, his son), Mary Loyd (and her sister, Ann Mathews, formerly Loyd); William, Sarah and Hannah (Pemberton), children of Mordecai and Hannah Loyd); Dr.

Richard Hill of Maderia; Abraham and Rebecca Brabius, London; Sarah and Susannah (daughters of Capt'n Thomas Loyd). Other legatees: Mary, John and Andrew (children of John and Margaret Simm); Andrew McNare; Doctors Greame, Thomas Bond, Phineas Bond and Thomas Cadwallader; the Pennsylvania Hospital; servants Jacob Smith, Peter and Margaret Steirwald; negroes, Rose, Molly and Dinah. Exec. and Trustees and Legatees: Isaac Norris, Hugh Roberts and Samuel Neave.
Witnesses: William Humphreys, Josiah Fisher, James Claypoole.

JENKINS, EVAN. Co. of Chester, Penna. Jan. 10, 1753. Dec. 8, 1756. K.486.
Weaver. Children: Jacob, Mary, Ann and Elizabeth. Exec: David Owen.
Witnesses: David Stephens, Jonathan Pugh.

MURSEN, BARNABAS. City of Philadelphia. Sadler. Dec. 1, 1756. Dec. 12, 1756. K.487.
Sole Legatees, Devisees and Exec: James Adams and wife (name not given).
Witnesses: Joseph Lownes, Benjamin Oxson (his mark).

LEE, JOHN. Dec. 5, 1756. Dec. 30, 1756. K.488.
Brothers: Thomas (of Glocester, England) and Francis. Nieces: Hannah Lee and Elizabeth Skinner (children of Francis). The estate bequeathed to all of above. Exec: Mathew Johns, Samuel Kirk.
Witnesses: Francis Sewer, Robert Kerr, William Horskins.
Codicil: Dec. 7, 1756.
Witnesses: Francis Seaver, Joseph Dobbins, Aulay McAulay.

THOMAS, DAVID. Co. of Philadelphia. Smith. Jan. 7, 1755. Jan. 12, 1757. K.489.
(Late wife, Anna). Children: Caleb, Sarah, Anna, Mary, Joshua and David. Father-in-Law: Abel Noble. Exec: David and Anna Thomas.
Witnesses: Patrick Gordon (his mark), Israel Jacobs, James Hamer.

MORRIS, DANIEL. Upper Dublin, Co. of Philadelphia. Miller. 12 mo. 13, 1756. Jan. 14, 1757. K.491.
Wife: Tacy. Children: Robert, Samuel, Owen and Ann. Exec: Wife and brothers Samuel and Joshua Morris.
Witnesses: William Foulke, Jonathan Rokson, John Roberts, Jr.

ROBERTS, JOHN. Montgomery, Co. of Philadelphia. 1 mo. 14, 1756. Feb. 8, 1757. K.493.
Children: John, Owen, Margaret, Katherine, Mary and Jane.
Guardians and Trustees: Brother Evan Roberts, brother-in-law Thomas Kenderdine and cousins, John Jones and John Evans. Exec: Wife Mary and son John.
Witnesses: Daniel Morgan, John Bartholomew, Evan Jones.

WEITMORE, BENJAMIN. Co. of Lancaster, Pa. Yeoman. Feb. 7, 1744. Proved in Lancaster, Dec. 18, 1756 and in Philadelphia, Feb. 10, 1757. K.495.
Children: John, Benjamin, Barbara, Abraham, Anna and Magdalena.
Exec: Son John.
Witnesses: Henry Bossler, Michael Fortunce, Thomas Cookson.

O'KILL, GEORGE. City ofPhiladelphia. Merchant. Feb. 5, 1757. Feb. 11, 1757. K.497.
Children: John, George, Jane and Ann. Exec: Wife Ann and Henry Harrison, merchant.
Witnesses: Thomas Bond, James Murray, John Reily.

FREDERICK, HENRY. July 29, 1755. Feb. 23, 1757. K.499.
Wife: Anne Barbara. Cousins and Legatees: Godfryd Henck, Joackim Henck of Philadelphia and William Hoffman, Germantown.
Beneficiaries: Poor house keepers in and about Germantown.
Witnesses: Nicholas Rousch, Jacob Enders.

HUFTY, BENJAMIN. Co. of Philadelphia. Jan. 18, 1757. Feb. 24, 1757. K.501.
Children: Jacob, John, Benjamin, Simon, Charles, William, Jonathan, Elenor and Catherine. Grandchild: Jane Hufty. Trustee: Isaac Ashton. Exec: Sons Jacob and John.
Witnesses: Silas Watts, Michael Grover, John Roberts.
Codicil: No date.
Witnesses: Same.

BYLES, DANIEL. Co. of Philadelphia. Jan. 7, 1757. Feb. 26, 1757. K.503.
Wife: Margaret. Son: Thomas. Exec: Wife, Moor Furman of Trenton, N.J., merchant, and William Ball, of Philadelphia, goldsmith.

Witnesses: Robert Roberts, Susannah Driver (her mark), John Roberts.

GEORGE, EVAN. Blockley, Co. of Philadelphia. May 29, 1756. March 2, 1757. K.584.
Children: George and Catherine (Evanson). Cousins: Jesse, Richard Jr. and Ann George. Brothers and sister: David, Richard and Jane Owen. All of the above are legatees together with grandchildren and five children of brother George George (names not given). Exec: Brothers Richard and George, and cousin Jesse George.
Witnesses: Jacob Zell, James Jones, Jr.

GIBSON, MATHEW. Co. of Philadelphia. Dec. 1, 1753. March 3, 1757. K.506.
Children: David, Joshua and Ann (wife of John Sellers).
Grandchildren: James and Hannah Gibson (children of Joshua).
Guardians and Legatees: Son-in-law Thomas Pearson and cousin Joseph Bonsall. Exec: Son David, son-in-law Thomas Pearson, Joseph Bonsall.
Witnesses: James Bartram, Robert Hanbest, Peter Yocum.

RANSTED, CALEB. Co. of Philadelphia. Turner. July 27, 1747. March 12, 1757. K.508.
Wife: Rachel. Children: William, Mary (wife of John White). Exec: In Great Britain, Elias Bland of London, merchant, and in Philadelphia, said son and daughter.
Witnesses: Charles Jones, Jeremiah Warder, Charles Brockden.

HASSERT, ARENT. City of Philadelphia. Merchant. Jan. 15, 1756. March 14, 1757. K.511.
Children: Elizabeth (Wiltsheet) and Arent. Grandchildren: Jannake Wiltsheet, Adriante and Jacob Hassert. Exec: In Great Britain and Holland, Abraham Heemioh of Holland, merchant, and in America, Samuel Shoemaker and Paul Keripner of Philadelphia.
Witnesses: Glover Hunt, Francis Richardson, Charles Brockden.
Codicil: Sept. 14, 1756.
Witnesses: Charles Brockden, Josiah Jackson.

HASELL, JANE. City of Philadelphia. Single woman. Jan. 7, 1757. April 2, 1757. K.514.

Brother: Samuel. Sisters: Elizabeth Huston, Ann Bennezet, Hannah Strettell and Sarah and Thomasin Hasell. Brother-in-Law: Amos Strettell, to whom a legacy was entrusted for charitable uses, and in event of his dying intestate the said sum so remaining to be given to Pennsylvania Hospital. Exec: Samuel Hasell, Amos Strettell.
Witnesses: Nathaniel and Hannah Allen, James Carmalt.

HOTTON, ELIZABETH. City of Philadelphia. Widow. 4 mo. 3, 1756. April 20, 1757. K.516.
Great grandchildren: Mary, John and Holton Jones; Elizabeth, Sarah and Arthur Howell; Elizabeth and Hannah Head. Grandsons-in-law: John Jones and Joseph Howell. All of the above are Beneficiaries, together with negroes, Nanney and Ishmael. Trustees and Overseers: Brother-in-law, Anthony Morris (brewer), sons-in-law Joshua Emlen (tanner) and Thomas Say (merchant), all of Philadelphia, who are to be Exec. upon the death of the Exec. nominated by testatrix. Exec. and granddaughters: Elizabeth (wife of John Jones, tanner), Hannah (wife of Joseph Howell, tanner) and Mary (wife of John Head, felt maker).
Witnesses: Joseph Chatham, James Gillingham, Alexander Seaton.

KOLB, DIETMAN. Salford, Co. of Philadelphia. Weaver. July 8, 1748. April 13, 1757. K.522.
Child: Elizabeth (wife of Andrew Ziegler). Grandchildren: Catherine and Dielman. Stepson: Mathias Sneavley. Beneficiaries: The Poor of the Dutch Mennonite Congregation of Salford, also of Perkyomie and Skipack. Trustees: Henry Funk, Ubriegh Bergher (yomen). Exec: Wife Elizabeth and Andrew Ziegler.
Witnesses: Robert Jones, Martin Kolb, Isaac Kolb.

PARKER, WILLIAM. New Providence, Co. of Philadelphia. April 18, 1757. April 30, 1757. K.525.
Children: Elizabeth, Alexander and Robert. Brothers: Archibald and James. Trustees: David Todd and Robert White. Exec: Wife Elizabeth and brother James Parker.
Witnesses: Robert Todd, John White, Benjamin Chestnut.

EVANS, OWEN. Gwynned, Co. of Philadelphia. Yeoman. 2 mo. 18, 1754. May 2, 1757. K.527.
Children: Samuel, Amos and Margaret. Grandchild: Owen Evans (and other children of Amos, names not given). Overseers: Cousins Thomas Evans, Jr., Roland and Evan Evans.

Witnesses: Abraham Evans, Jesse Jones, Amos Roberts.

WARDER, JOHN. City of Philadelphia. Feltmaker. May 5, 1746. May 9, 1757. K.529.
Legatees: Nephew, John Parsons, and his sons John and William Parsons. Exec: Wife Lydia. Assistant Exec: Kinsman Joseph Stretch.
Witnesses: John Riely, Robert Forde, Edward Williams.

LEWIS, THOMAS. Son of Thomas Lewis of New Britain, Co. of Bucks, Pa. Yeoman. June 11, 1751. May 18, 1757. K.530.
Children: Names not given. Exec: Wife Jane and brother Lewis Lewis.
Witnesses: Isaac William, Benjamin Griffith.

KENTNER, JOHN GEORGE. City of Philadelphia. April 21, 1757. May 23, 1757. K.531.
Legatees: Daughter of brother-in-law George Maister, Barbara Fleckin, Jacob Wasp, Philip Helsel, Owen Jones and Anthony Benezet, in trust for the Poor of the Monthly Meeting of Friends, Philadelphia.
Exec: John Wister and Thomas Say.
Witnesses: Anthony Benezet, David Leshler.

THOMAS, ROBERT. Mountgomery, Co. of Philadelphia. Yeoman. July 30, 1756. June 1, 1757. K.533.
Children: Samuel, John, Martha, Sarah, Mary and Barbara. Exec: Wife Grace and son Samuel.
Witnesses: Evan Roberts, Joseph Ambler, Joseph Walton (his mark).

HOOD, THOMAS. City of Philadelphia. Yeoman. Oct. 1, 1748. June 8, 1757. K.534.
Children: Thomas, Deborah (wife of John Johnson), Sarah (Morgan), John and Mary (Claypool). Guardians: Sarah and Elizabeth Johnson, Mary Claypool. Exec: John and Thomas.
Witnesses: John Hallowell, Jacob Dubre, William Peters.

HANES, JOHN. Co. of Philadelphia. Husbandman. Aug. 25, 1756. June 11, 1757. K.538.
Wife: Barbere. Children: John, Christrina (wife of Lennard Snider), Adam, Andrew, Jacob, Catherine (wife of Peter Loriekn) and Mary.
Exec: Peter Lovekx and Peter Carekeart.
Witnesses: William Mayer, William Nash.

HUGH, MARY. Co. of Chester. Widow. April 21, 1756. June 14, 1757. K.540.
Children: Elizabeth (wife of Joseph Watkin) and Mary (wife of Daniel Watkin). Exec: Daughter Elizabeth.
Witnesses: Gosport Seink, William John, James Davis.

ASSHERTON, WILLIAM. City of Philadelphia. Gentleman. June 7, 1757. June 22, 1757. K.542.
Sisters: Margaret and Frances. Cousin: Ann Powell. Brother: Ralph. All of above are legatees. Exec: Mother Susannah.
Witnesses: Ann Morrow, John Reily.

EVANS, JOHN. Gwneadd, Co. of Philadelphia. Yeoman. 9 mo. 16, 1756. June 22, 1757. K.543.
Wife: Ellin. Children: Jane (Hubbs), Margaret, Ellin, Elizabeth, Cadwallader, Rowland and John. Exec: The three sons.
Witnesses: Daniel Williams, Amos Roberts, George Maris.

JUSTICE, ANDREW. Kingsess, Co. of Philadelphia. July 7, 1748. June 24, 1757. K.545.
Legatees: Andrew Justice; sisters Ellinor Peterson and Mary; Mountie Justice; nephew, Samuel Flower. Exec: Wife Sarah.
Witnesses: James Bickham, Catherine Justice, Ann Beacon (her mark).

BROWN, THOMAS. City of Philadelphia. Baker. 6 mo. 15, 1757. June 27, 1757. K.547.
Children: Moses, Anne, Thomas, John, Martha (Harvey), Elizabeth (Ellecott), Mary, Priscilla and Samuel. Exec: Wife Magdalena and brother-in-law John Jones.
Witnesses: Samuel Caruthers, Paul Cripner.

RALSTONE, JOHN, SR. Co. of Chester, Pa. Yeoman. March 5, 1748. July 4, 1757. K.549.
Wife: Ann. Children: John, Margaret (Fitzseemons) and Robert. Grandchildren: Frances and Ann Hill. Brother-in-Law: William Thomson. Exec: Son Robert and Hugh Williams.
Witnesses: William Bell, Nathan Green.

BOWYER, SARAH. City of Philadelphia. Widow. May 4, 1757. July 5, 1757. K.550.

Children: Martha (Williams), Elizabeth (Austin), Hester (Boyt), Ruth (Bonham), Sarah (Brook) and Rebecca (Warner). Grandchildren: Sarah Williams, Boyer Brook, Elizabeth and Sarah Brook and Sarah Warner. Son-in-Law: Joseph Warner. Exec: Dr. Thomas Say, Hester Boyt.
Witnesses: Jeremiah Elfreth, John Parrock.

BISSETT, WILLIAM. City of Philadelphia. Blacksmith. July 15, 1750. July 19, 1757. K.552.
Mother-in-Law: Hannah Bissell. Brothers: Samuel and John. Sister: Hannah Dubre. Nephew: William Dubre. All are legatees. Exec: Brother Samuel and Oswald Peel.
Witnesses: Jacob Dubre, George Dorland, Jacob Howey.

HOODT, DANIEL. City of Philadelphia. 7 mo. 1, 1757. July 16, 1757. K.553.
Legatees: Mother Esther and sister Esther. Exec: Mother Esther.
Witnesses: Robert Dryburgh, Jeremiah Elfreth, Daniel Offley.

LAWRENCE, DAVID. Co. of Chester, Pa. Weaver. 5 mo. 18, 1757. Aug. 1, 1757. K.554.
Brother: William. Uncle: Henry Lawrence. Children: Thomas, Ezekiel, Joseph, William and Tace (and unknown child). Beneficiary: Society of Quakers in Haverford Township, Chester County, Pa. Exec: Wife Jane and cousin Daniel Williams (baker). Guardian: Daniel Williams.
Witnesses: Samuel Humphreys, Lewis Davis, Abraham Musgrove.

STOCKWELL, WILLIAM. City of Philadelphia. Shoemaker. July 16, 1757. Aug. 3, 1757. K.557.
Exec. and sole Legatee: Neomi Peers of Philadelphia, widow.
Witnesses: Mathew Biays, Jacob Carver, Philip Veinnheimer.

BANKSON, JACOB, JR. Co. of Philadelphia. Yeoman. Aug. 2, 1757. Aug. 10, 1757. K.557.
Wife: Elinor. Brothers: Andrew, Peter and John. Sister: Deborah. Mother: Elinor. All relatives are legatees. Exec: Brother John and cousin Andrew Bankson (shopkeeper).
Witnesses: Catherine Cox, John Reily.

BAKER, FREDERICK. Norriston Township, Co. of Philadelphia. Farmer. July 22, 1757. Aug. 19, 1757. K.559.
Children: George, Mary, Elizabeth, John, Frederick, Anna, Sarah, Jacob and Susannah. Exec: Wife Mary and son George.
Witnesses: Conrad Stemm, Malchoir Waggoner, Baltzar Stemm.

FREY, JACOB. Hanover, Co. of Philadelphia. March 5, 1751. Aug. 22, 1757. K.562.
Wife: Ease. Children: John, Adamkam, Meriles (Kelsey), Suyse Freyren and Margaret Freyren. Exec. and Overseers: Debrech Bucher, John Schnider.
Witnesses: Christian Sackriter, Sebastian Kechly.

CROSS, JOHN. City of Philadelphia. Innholder. Jan. 10, 1757. Aug. 22, 1757. K.563.
Legatees: Cousin Jean McGee; step-son Joseph Emmite; sister-in-law Jean Wright; negro woman Dane. Exec: William McElwaine, John Wallace, merchants, of Philadelphia.
Witnesses: Gilbert and Sarah Dakeyn.

JANES, ISAAC. Moorland, Co. of Philadelphia. Yeoman. 7 mo. 11, 1757. Sept. 6, 1757. K.564.
Children: William, Levi and Mary. Exec: Wife Mary and William Walmley.
Witnesses: Elizabeth Walton, Thomas Lloyd, Thomas Carrington.

FLOWER, THOMAS. City of Philadelphia. Cooper. Dec. 3, 1755. Sept. 20, 1757. K.565.
Exec. Sole Legatee and Devisee: Brother Henry.
Witnesses: Richard Farmar, William Macune, Paul Isaac Voto.

MORGAN, JESSE. Whitpain, Co. of Philadelphia. 4 mo. 13, 1757. Sept. 14, 1757. L.1.
Wife: Mary. Children: Priscillah, Mary and Dorothy. Brother: Edward. Nephew: Morgan Morgan. Cousins: Owen Hughes, Isaac Hughes, William Morris. Uncles: Benjamin and Edward Hughes. Trustees: Edward Hughes, Edward Morgan, William Morris. Exec: Mary Morgan.
Witnesses: Margaret Morgan (her mark), Ludwick Cook.

GOAD, SOLOMAN. City of London. Mariner. Aug. 16, 1757. Sept. 20, 1757. L.2.
Wife: Barbara. Child: Robert Francis. Nephew: Robert Gibbs [City of London]. Friends: Margaret and Fanny Ashton, Susannah Humphrey, Robert Musguetto. Exec: William Peters, Esq., Thomas Gordon.
Witnesses: Ja. Peller, Richd. Swan, Lumley Woodyear.

BROWNBAUGH, GARRET. Vincent, Co. of Chester, Pa. Yeoman. Aug. 4. 1757. Sept. 23, 1757. L.3.
Wife: Mary. Children: Benjamin, Henry and Kathren. Sons-in-Law: Richard Custar, Frederick Benjamin and Paul Benner. Exec: Benjamin and Mary Brownbaugh.
Witnesses: Johannes Stuanner, Anthony Ace, Rogr. North, Frederick Smith.

BLUM, DOROTHY. Lower Dublin, Co. of Philadelphia. Widdow. May 7, 1756. Sept. 28, 1757. L.5.
Children: Mary Kent and Michael Groover. Grandchild: Meriam Kent. Step-daughter: Sophia Conrad. Step-son: John Graber. Exec: Michael Groover, John Vanhorn, Senr., John Roberts.
Witnesses: Barnard Vandegrift, Benjamin Hufty (his mark), Isaac Ashton, Silas Watts.

BUZBY, THOMAS. Oxford, Co. of Philadelphia. Yeoman. Aug. 31, 1757. Sept. 30, 1757. L.6.
Wife: Mary. Children: Isaac, Abraham, John, Hannah, Abigal, Sarah, Martha and Mary. Exec: Mary, Isaac and Hannah Buzby.
Witnesses: Benjamin Mason, Joseph Griffith, Abram. Leech.

SOBER, SARAH. City of Philadelphia. Widow. Feb. --, 1756. Oct. 3, 1757. L.8.
Children: John and Mary. Grandchildren: Sarah Redman and Ann Redman. Son-in-Law: Dr. John Redman. Exec: Ann Redman, Benjn. Franklin, Richard Peters.
Witnesses: Deborah Franklin, John Morgan.

SHIMER, JACOB. Lower Saucon, Co. of Northampton, Pa. Yeoman. Sept. 10, 1757. Oct. 5, 1757. L.9.
Wife: Elizabeth. Children: Jacob, Conrod, Abraham, Anthony, Elizabeth Vickeson, Mary Shoemaker, Catherine, Sarah, Samuel,

Edward, Peter, Isaac and John. Trustees: Michel Shoemaker, Anthony Larch. Guardian: Elizabeth Shimer. Exec: Elizabeth, Jacob and Conrod Shimer.
Witnesses: Anthony Lerch, John Jones.

MEYER, JACOB. Germantown, Co. of Philadelphia. Yeoman. Aug. 1, 1757. Oct. 8, 1757. L.11.
Wife: Ann. Children: Jacob, Henary and Catherin. Exec: Ann and Henary Meyer.
Witnesses: George Schreiber, John Keyser.

GRAY, GEORGE. Co. of Northampton, Pa. Farmer. Sept. 1, 1757. Oct. 14, 1757. L.13.
Wife: Martha. Children: Esher, Nigell, William, George and John. Exec: Nigell Gray.
Witnesses: James McCalister, Joseph Brown.

GIVEN, MORRIS. Lower Dublin, Co. of Philadelphia. Yeoman. Aug. 8, 1749. Oct. 22, 1757. L.14.
Wife: Anne. Children: John, Morris, Mary and Hannah Jones. Brother-in-Law: Charles Roberts. Exec: Ann Given, Charles Roberts.
Witnesses: George Eaton, Johna. Jones, Step. Jenkins.

MC LEARNE, ROBERT. City of Philadelphia. Jan. 31, 1757. Oct. 26, 1757. L.16.
Hugh McLearne [Co. Donegall, Ireland]. Exec: James McDowell, Nathaniel Graham.
Witnesses: Robert Bailey, Gilbert Dakeyn, Joseph Dunman.

DAVIS, THOMAS. City of Philadelphia. Shopkeeper. Sept. 21, 1757. Oct. 31, 1757. L.17.
Brother: John [Dacre, Great Brittain]. Sisters: Martha Brown [of London], Sarah and Jane. Brothers-in-Law: George and William Dilwyn. Sister-in-Law: Ann Dilwyn. Exec: Jane Davis, Thomas Wharton.
Witnesses: Jonathan Carmalt, David Bacon, Job Bacon.

WALTON, DANIEL, SENR. Byberry, Co. of Philadelphia. 8 mo. 4, 1757. Nov. 5, 1757. L.18.
Wife: Elizabeth. Children: Daniel, Jane and Mercy. Exec: Daniel Walton.

Witnesses: Richard Walton, Daniel Walton, William Walmsley.

SEARLE, JOHN. City of Philadelphia. Mariner. July 1, 1753. Nov. 10, 1757. L.19.
Wife: Mary. Children: Ann McCall, Mary and Elizabeth. Grandchildren: John Searle McCall and children of Ann McCall. Son-in-Law: Samuel McCall, Junr. Brother-in-Law: Edward Hicks. Exec: Samuel McCall, Junr., Edward Hicks.
Witnesses: Sam Carson, Barnard Badger, Robert Clerk.

ADAMS, WILLIAM. Moorland, Co. of Philadelphia. Oct. 10, 1757. Nov. 16, 1757. L.21.
Wife: Sarah. Children: Joseph, Margaret, Jane, Elizabeth, Mary, Sarah, Samuel, William and John. Exec: Samuel Adams.
Witnesses: Samuel Ervin, William Sittleton (his mark), Richard Treat.

DAWSON, JOHN. West Nuttingham, Co. of Chester, Penna. Farmer. Feb. 24, 1756. Nov. 19, 1757. L.23.
Children: Joseph, Samuel, Isaac, Nathan and John. Grandchildren: Children of sons, viz., Samuel, Isaac, Nathan and John Dawson. Daughter-in-Law: Anne Dawson. Exec: Joseph and Anne Dawson.
Witnesses: John Allen, Senr., John Allen, Junr., Elizabeth Kirk (her mark).

RAUSCH, NICOLAUS. Germantown, Co. of Philadelphia. Blew Dyer. Oct. 15, 1751 [1757?]. Nov. 21, 1757. L.25.
Wife: Anna Charlotta. Children: Maria Magdalena, Isaac, Ann Elizabeth, John, Mathias and Nicholas. Exec: Anna Charlotta and Isaac Rausch.
Witnesses: Christn. Jacobus, Jacob Gensell, Philip Henry Rapp.

FITZSIMMONS, WILLIAM. City of Philadelphia. Sept. 17, 1757. Nov. 22, 1757. L.26.
Wife: Honour. Child: Thomas. Exec: James White.
Witnesses: Robt. Harding, John Gass, Jno. Johnson.

DRISSELL, JOHN. Lower Milford, Co. of Bucks, Pa. Yeoman. Feb. 18, 1757. Nov. 22, 1757. L.27.
Wife: Margaret. Children: Ullrich and Abraham. Exec: George Ackerman, Thos. Blackledge.
Witnesses: Christian Clemer, John Drifler, Saml. Foulke.

MOODE, WILLIAM. City of Philadelphia. Cordwainer. July 25, 1757. Nov. 29, 1757. L.28.
Children: Elizabeth, Hannah and Elinor. Exec: Elizabeth, Hannah and Elinor Moode.
Witnesses: William Peters, Jno. Reily, John Kirke.

WARNER, ISAAC. Blockley, Co. of Philadelphia. Yeoman. 11 mo. 10, 1757. Dec. 3, 1757. L.31.
Wife: Jane. Children: Hannah, William, Abraham, Mary, Isaac, Jacob, Anthony and Ann. Cousin: Isaac Warner. Exec: Isaac Warner, James Jones.
Witnesses: Wm. Warner, Richard George, Mary Wynn.

SIDDON, ANN. City of Philadelphia. Mantua Maker. 11 mo. 1, 1757. Dec. 6, 1757. L.32.
Brother: Samuel. Sisters: Sarah and Susannah. Nephew: John Siddon. Niece: Mary Hale. Exec: Susannah Siddon.
Witnesses: Nathaniel Hollande, Anthony Denormandie, Magdalen Brown.

BRENNEMAN, CHRISTIAN. Towamenson, Co. of Philadelphia. Yeoman. Nov. 18, 1757. Dec. 7, 1757. L.33.
Wife: Susannah. Children: Christian, William, Henry, Catherine King, Benjamin, Samuel and Jacob. Exec: Christian and William Brenneman.
Witnesses: Gossen Shrager, Jacob Shoemaker, Andrew Ziegler.

IRVIN, DAVID. Lower Dublin, Co. of Philadelphia. Oct. 31, 1757. Dec. 8, 1757. L.35.
Child: Garret. Grandchild: Elizabeth Ord. Sons-in-Law: Francis Thornton, Jacob Crawford. Cousin: John Irwin. Exec: Garret Irwin, Jacob Crawford.
Witnesses: James Callwall, Silas Watts.

RIMBY, CHRISTOFER. Limerick, Co. of Philadelphia. Nov. 13, 1757. Dec. 14, 1757. L.36.
Children: Christofer and Mary. Exec: George Brooks, David Evans.
Witnesses: Peter Rimby, Francis Hobson.

BAUER, HANS PETER. Upper Sancan, Co. of Northampton, Penna. Yeoman. June 4, 1754. Dec. 15, 1757. L.37.

Exec: Wife Catherine.
Witnesses: Joseph Powell, U. Bomper, Jas. Burnside.

PARSONS, WILLIAM. Easton, Co. of Northampton, Pa. Gentleman. Dec. 15, 1757. Dec. 21, 1757. L.38.
Wife and three Children: No names given, "now living." Sister: Sarah and two children. Late sister Mary and her four(4?) children. "My late dear mother" and (my late) 3 children, viz., "Robert, Susannah and Hannah." Son-in-Law: James Worrall. Nephew: Doctor Stephen Woolley. Nieces: Rebecca Woolley and Elizabeth Cummins. Servant: Elizabeth Kritsman. Poor Scholers, Academy of Philadelphia. Exec: William Coleman and Evan Morgan [of Philadelphia], Timothy Horsfield [of Bethleham].
Witnesses: Da. Henderson, Jost Vollert.

ALLEN, NATHANIEL. City of Philadelphia. Cooper. Nov. 24, 1755. Dec. 22, 1757. L.40.
Children: Nehemiah, John, Nathaniel, Joseph, Mary Richardson and Hanah. Grandchildren: Children of Nathaniel. Niece: Sarah Allen. Joseph and Mary Richardson. Rev. Brockden, William Chancellor. Samuel Morris, Junr. Exec: Nehemiah, John, Nathaniel, Joseph and Hannah Allen.
Codicil: 6 mo. 21, 1757.
Witnesses: John Knowles, Jno. Reily.

PUGH, JOB. Norriton, Co. of Philadelphia. Yeoman. Oct. 10, 1757. Dec. 22, 1757. L.45.
Brothers: Ellis and Thomas. Sister: Elizabeth. Step-daughter: Elizabeth Meredith. Step-children: Phebe, Elizabeth, Nathan, Joseph and Nathan Evans. Granddaughter: Sinai Pugh. Overseers: Joseph Jones, Michael Thomas [of Plymouth], Rowland Evans [of North Wales]. Exec: Hananiah and Michael Pugh.
Witnesses: John Hawksworth, John Roberts, Rowd. Evans.
Codicil: Oct. 11, 1757.
Witnesses: John Hawsksworth, Rowd. Evans.

PENROSE, THOMAS. Wiccacoe, Co. of Philadelphia. Shipwright. Nov. 8, 1757. Dec. 22, 1757. L.47.
Wife: Sarah. Children: Thomas, James, Isaac, Samuel and Jonathan. Exec: Sarah Penrose, Joseph Richardson, Thomas and James Penrose.
Witnesses: Barth: Penrose, Lester Faulkner, Jno. Reily.

DAVIDS, JOSHUA. Radnor, Co. of Chester, Penna. Yeoman. Dec. 5, 1757. Dec. 29, 1757. L.52.
Wife: Elizabeth. Children: No names given. Exec: Elizabeth Davids, Mordecai Morgan.
Witnesses: Lewis Jerman, John Davis, Thomas Thomas.

WYNNE, THOMAS. Blockley, Co. of Philadelphia. Nov. 23, 1751. Dec. 24, 1757. L.54.
Wife: Mary. Children: Thomas, Mary, Sarah, Anne and Lydia. Cousin: James Wynne. Brother-in-Law: Richard George. Exec: Mary Wynne. Asst. Exec: Richard George.
Witnesses: Jesse George, Evan Gerrgo (his mark), Richard George.

FARIES, ROBERT. Merion, Co. of Philadelphia. Yeoman. Nov. 15, 1757. Dec. 28, 1757. L.55.
Wife: Mary. Children: Zachariah, Jane, Margrett, John and Elizabeth. Exec: Mary and Thomas Faries.
Witnesses: Thomas Gordon, James Trueman.

MC CRAY, JAMES. Oxford, Co. of Philadelphia. Yeoman. Oct. 16, 1757. Dec. 28, 1757. L.57.
Wife: Ann. Children: John, Elizabeth Chestnut, Isabel, George, Margaret and James. Exec: Ann and John McCray.
Witnesses: Abraham Leech, Joseph Paul, Philip Mallagan (his mark).

COLLINS, EDWARD. Northern Liberties, City of Philadelphia. Gardener. Feb. 11, 1756. Dec. 30, 1757. L.58.
Wife: Margaret. Children: Richard, William, Elizabeth, Sarah, Margaret and Hannah. Grandchildren: Robert and Abraham Collins. Exec: Margaret Collins, Jacob Levering, Benjamin Bowing.
Witnesses: John Laurence, Towsend White, William Masters, Junr.

PRITCHARD, SARAH. City of Philadelphia. Widow. May 10, 1756. Dec. 31, 1756. L.59.
Nephews: James, Charles, Philip and Thomas Kinsey. Exec: James and Philip Kinsey.
Witnesses: John Bayard, Mary Cluich

WEBSTER, JOHN. Abington, Co. of Philadelphia. Taylor. Nov. 4, 1754. June 19, 1756. L.60

Wife: Ellin. Children: William, John and Martha. Exec: Ellin, William and John Webster.
Witnesses: John Watkins, James Daugherty (his mark), Thomas Rose.

PALTZGROFF, GEORGE. Hannover, Co. of Philadelphia. Blacksmith. May 30, 1757. Aug. 1, 1757. L.62.
Wife: Barbara. Children: Henry, Eva, George, Barbara, Jacob, Mary, Franica, Margaret and Christian. Son-in-Law: Paul Bover. Exec: Barbara Paltzgroff, Jacob Witman.
Witnesses: Valentine Geiger, Philip Faas, Jno. Campbell.

HUTCHINSON, ALICE. City of Philadelphia. Nov. 22, 1757. Feb. 7, 1758. L.64.
Exec: John Cottinger.
Witnesses: Jean Gaillard, Thos. Mallaby, Andw. Farrell.

STANDLEY, MOSES. City of Philadelphia. Merchant. Dec. 7, 1757. Jan. 23, 1758. L.65.
Brother: Valentine and his children, viz., Mary, Charlotte, Susanna and Valentine. Nephews and Nieces: William Standley and children, Richard, Sarah and William. Treasurer: Pennsylvania Hospital. Sister-in-Law: Mary Standley. Friend: Richard Shakelton [of Oxford, New Jersey]. Exec: William Standley, Jacob Shoemaker.
Witnesses: Stephen Paschall, John Hesselius, Robert Ervin.

WELLS, REBECCA, JUNR. City of Philadelphia. Single woman. Aug. 27, 1757. Jan. 23, 1758. L.67.
Mother: Rebecca. Sisters: Ann Collum and Elizabeth. Nephew: William Collum. Niece: Rebecca Wells. Exec: Edward Evans.
Witnesses: Humphrey Robinson, Margt. Ward, Paul Isaac Voto.

ANDERSON, JOHN. City of Philadelphia. Flatman. Dec. 9, 1757. Jan. 26, 1758. L.68.
Mother: Mary Woodside. Brothers: James, Andrew, Jacob and Isaac. Sisters: Anne Pinyard and Mary. Exec: Isaac Anderson, Isaac Jones.
Witnesses: Peter Miller, John Pond.

MERRIFIELD, ROBBARTS. Planter. Late of Island Antigua, now of City of Philadelphia. Jan. 12, 1758. ---.
Wife: Mary.
Codicil.

Children: William, Robbarts and Richard.
Witnesses: Charles Williams, Elizabeth Loury.
N.B. Vide Adm. Bond, Jan. 17, 1758. Administration granted to Charles Williams before Codicil, appended to the Register Genl.

MARTIN, MARY. Cheltenham, Co. of Philadelphia. Widow. 10 mo. 20, 1749/50. Jan. 31, 1758. L.72
Daughter-in-Law: Susannah Martin. Grandchildren: Thomas, Richard and John Martin. Trustees: Daniel Thomas, Joshua Martin. Exec: Susannah Martin.
Witnesses: John Phillips, Toby Leech, Abm. Leech.

EVANS, CATHERINE. City of Philadelphia. Spinster. Jan. 4, 1758. Feb. 1, 1758. L.72.
[Daughter of Robert Evans, late of Merion, decd.] Sisters: Jane Roberts and Ann Tilbury. Brothers: Cadwalader and Thomas. Nephew and Niece: Robert and Catherine Evans. Relation: Elizabeth [widow of Richard Thomas]. Trustees: Anthony Benezet, Isaac Zane. Exec: Owen Jones.
Witnesses: Davis Bassett, Mary Bassett, Jan Siddons.

DAVIS, DAVID. Cohansie, Co. of Cumberland, West Jersey. Nov. 18, 1749/50. Feb. 2, 1758. L.74.
Wife: Sarah. Children: Jonathan, Samuel. Exec: Sarah and Jonathan Davis, Senr. [minister of the Gospel of Cohansie].
Witnesses: Benjn. Mifflin, Richard Ashburn, Hannah Mifflin.

LEWIS, REBECCA. City of Philadelphia. Spinster. Dec. 30, 1757. Feb. 9, 1758. L.73,75.
Sister: Sarah Wharton. Aunt: Esther Dunning. Niece: Rebecca VanLewvanigh. Brother-in-Law: Samuel Wharton.
Witnesses: Thos. Stretch, Abrm. Mitchel, Isaac Stretch.

RANSTED, CALEB. City of Philadelphia. [Late Chester]. Gentleman. Nov. 18, 1755. Sept. 9, 1756. L.76. Proved in Chester.
Wife: Frances. Exec: Frances Ransted.
Witnesses: Eliz. Eyton, Will Dix, Tho. Mesham.

REIMER, FREDERICK. Frederick, Co. of Philadelphia. May 9, 1755. Feb. 11, 1758. L.77.

Wife: Elizabeth. Children: Elizabeth, Salome, Susanna, Barbara, Anna Maria, Cathrine, John Petter, Johannes and Ludwig. Exec: Elizabeth and John Peter Reimer.
Witnesses: Henry Antes, John Philip Leydich.

RUGH, MELCHER. Northern Liberties, City of Philadelphia. Yeoman. Feb. 11, 1758. Feb. 27, 1758. L.79.
Wife: Elizabeth and children. Trustees: William Callender, John Parrock. Exec: Elizabeth Rugh.
Witnesses: George Fontz, George Gayler, Fredrick Hartman.

LINGARD, MARY. City of Philadelphia. Widow. Dec. 19, 1753. Feb. 28, 1758. L.80.
Cousins: Robert Moon, William and Thomas Sitgreaves. Friends: Thomas Gibson, Elizabeth [wife of Abraham Giles]. Exec: William Sitgreaves, Nathaniel Goforth.
Witnesses: Joseph Stretch, John Howard, Paul Isaac Voto.

VANHORN, JOHN, SENR. Lower Dublin, Co. of Philadelphia. Yeoman. Dec. 10, 1757. Feb. 27, 1758. L.81.
Wife: Rebeckah. Children: John, Elenor wife of Josh. Jackson, Jane wife of Barnard Vandegrift, Catherine wife of Jacob Johnson, Halena, Rebeckah, Till and Jean. Grandchildren: John, Crispin and David, sons of daughter Halena, and Susannah, Jane Johnson. Exec: Rebeckah and John Vanhorn.
Witnesses: Joseph Ashton, Thomas Stammers.

KEEN, JOHN. Oxford, Co. of Philadelphia. Yeoman. Jan. 21, 1758. Feb. 28, 1758. L.85.
Children: Margaret wife of Matthew Keen, Matthias, John, Jacob, George, Susannah wife of Edward Millner and Rebeckah wife of Benjamin Engle. Grandchildren: John, Joseph and James Keen, Hannah Leech, Mary and Elizabeth Keen daughters of Elias Keen, decd. Exec: Matthias and Jacob Keen.
Witnesses: Michael Shaw, Jacob Vandegrift, Thomas Stammers.

YENGLING, CHRISTIAN. Worcester, Co. of Philadelphia. Widdower. Jan. 22, 1755. Feb. 28, 1758. L.90.
Children: Modlin, Catharine, Abraham, Susannah, Andrew, Christian, Mary and John. Exec: Jacob Umstead, Peter Husted.

Witnesses: Conrad VanFossen (his mark), Malchior Waggoner, Peter Vanoderson.

BRUNHOLTZ, PETER. City of Philadelphia. Gentleman. June 23, 1757. July 13, 1757. L.91.
Sister: Anne wife of Mr. Groston of Proskew in Gluckeberg. Brother: George. Housekeeper: Kunnigunda Wollfarhie. Lutheran Church of Philadelphia. Friends: Frederick Handschu, Peter Muhlenberg, Christian Beyer. Exec: Henry Kepele, George Huttmer, Senr., Jacob Greff.
Witnesses: Peter Miller, Jacob Greff, Junr.

CUNRADS, JOHN. Creesham, Co. of Philadelphia. Shoemaker. Dec. 13, 1756. March 4, 1758. L.93.
Wife: Ealse. Children: Cornelius, Barbara wife of Sebastian Miller, Margret wife of Jacob Keyser and John. Grandchildren: John, Mary, Ealse and Elizabeth Cunrads. Exec: Cornelius and John Cunrads.
Witnesses: Jacob Fisher, Andrew Barner, Thos. Rose.

WALTON, ELIZABETH. City of Philadelphia. Widow. May 3, 1755. March 7, 1758. L.97.
Children: Rebecca Jervis, Michael and Hannah Evans. Son-in-Law: Jonathan Evans. Grandchildren: Charles, Elizabeth, Mary, John and Samuel Jervis, Mary, William, Joel, Benjamin and John Evans, Elizabeth Walton. Exec: Michael Walton, John Jervis, Jonathan Evans.
Witnesses: William Moode, John Wallace, Jno. Reily.

AX, JOHN. Germantown, Co. of Philadelphia. Sadler. June 1, 1758. March 13, 1758. L.99.
Wife: Elizabeth. Children: George and Ann. Father: John Frederick Ax. Trustee: John Frederick Ax. Exec: Elizabeth Ax, Merchant Malsbey, Senr.
Witnesses: Ludwig Englehart, John Engel, Matthias Keyser.

HAUSE, CHRISTIANA. Germantown, Co. of Philadelphia. Nov. 17, 1757. March 13, 1758. L.101.
Mother: No name. Christana Hesser, Barbary Bickes[?]. Sisters: Catherin Jonson, Mary Nice and Barbary Everman. Nieces: Christiana Jonson, Maly and Betty Jonson. Exec: Frederick Ax.
Witnesses: Ulrick Bodner, Richard Robb.

YEORGER, VIT. Ruscomb Manor, Co. of Berks, Penna. Yeoman. Nov. 11, 1757. March 30, 1758. L.102.
Wife: Sybille. Children: Thomas and Andrew. Son-in-Law: Adam Smell. Exec: Sybille Yeorger, Adam Smell.
Witnesses: George Rock, Adam Swartsback, John Widenhamer, Stephen Huberacker.

GARDNER, JOHN HENRY. Germantown, Co. of Philadelphia. Weaver. Jan. 4, 1758. April 8, 1758. L.104.
Wife: Dorothy. Children: Mary Elizabeth and Henry Frederick. Brother: John. Exec: Dorothy and John Gardner.
Witnesses: Henry Kaller, Christian Lehman.

DODOROW, BERNHARD. New Hanover, Co. of Philadelphia. Yeoman. Jan. 20, 1758. April 12, 1758. L.105.
Wife: Christiana. Children: Philip, Isaac, Jacob, Barnhard, Henry and Elizabeth. Grandchildren: John, Joseph and Mary Neyes. Son-in-Law: George Neyes. Overseers: Philip and John Dodorow. Exec: Bernhard and Isaac Dodorow.
Witnesses: Johannes Zeller, Phillip Haun, Nichs. Bunn.

RAMBO, JOHN. Co. of Philadelphia. Yeoman. March 24, 1758. April 12, 1758. L.108.
Children: Peter, Elizabeth, Ann, Mary, Ealse and Rachel. Guardians: Gunna Rambo, John Pennebacker. Exec: Christian Kouplin, Jacob Humstead.
Witnesses: David Robeson, John Buterwich, Rogr. North.

NITSCHMAN, DAVID. Bethlehem, Co. of Northamton, Prov. of Penna. Carpenter. May 6, 1757. April 26, 1758. L.110.
Children: John and Anna. Grandchild: Ann Johanna Presch. Exec: Gottlieb Spangenberg, Peter Bohler.
Witnesses: Matthew Shropp, Johanes Ettwain, Johannes Bechtel, J. Oncly, George Klein, Timo. Horsfield, Martin Mack.

RAMBO, WILLIAM. Upper Merion, Co. of Philadelphia. March 23, 1758. May 3, 1758. L.112.
Wife: Hannah. Children: Rebecka and Ann. Exec: Hannah Rambo, Rogger North.
Witnesses: Samuel Lane, Henry Priest, Matthias Holsten.

DAVID, JOHN. Limerick, Co. of Philadelphia. Farmer. Aug. 6, 1756. May 8, 1758. L.113.
Children: William, Elisha, Enoch, Mary, John, Elijah and Elinor wife of Jacob Judeheaven. Exec: William David.
Witnesses: Harman Stall (his mark), Mordi. Evans, George Evans.

EVANS, WILLIAM. Limerick, Co. of Philadelphia. Farmer. Nov. 18, 1756. May 8, 1758. L.115.
Wife: No name given. Children: George, Mordecai, John, Owen, Elihue, Ann [widow of Hugh Hillis], Mary wife of George Brooke, Margaret wife of William Hicks and Neomi. Exec: George and John Evans.
Witnesses: William Davis, Elijah Davis, George Evans.

JORDAN, JOHN. Limberick, Co. of Philadelphia. Taylor. March 11, 1754. May 15, 1758. L.118.
Wife: Elizabeth. Children: Francis, Jeremiah, Rachel, Mary and Sarah. Exec: Francis and Elizabeth Jordan.
Witnesses: John Smith, Erasmus Lauer, Rogr. North.

BAKER, PETER. Schippack, Co. of Philadelphia. May 2, 1756. May 15, 1758. L.119.
Wife: Dorothy. Child: Mary. Son-in-Law: Rudolph Harley. Grandchildren: Catherine and Peter Stump, Mary Bechtelsheimer. Exec: Dorothy Baker, Rudolph Harley.
Witnesses: Johannes Kempffer, Michael Baserman.

MIFFLIN, GEORGE. City of Philadelphia. Merchant. Jan. 1, 1755. May 16, 1758. L.121.
Wife: Esther. Children: John and Sarah. Grandchildren: Charles, Thomas and George Mifflin. Exec: John and Sarah Mifflin.
Witnesses: Jno. Bleakley, Jno. Ord, Paul Isaac Voto.

REIFSNYDER, JOHN. New Hannover, Co. of Philadelphia. Freeholder and smith. March 19, 1758. May 26, 1758. L.123.
Wife: Dorothy. Children: John and Sebastian. Exec: Dorothy Reifsnyder, William Hottenstein.
Witnesses: George Hubner, Johannes Frey, Michael Walter.

DAVIES, MARGARET. Upper Dublin, Co. of Philadelphia. Widdow. 5 mo. 16, 1748. June 13, 1758. L.125.

Children: Enoch Morgan, Issachar and Benjamin. Grandchildren: Hannah Martin, Issacher and Margaret Davies, Miriam Lewis, Edward and Margaret Morgan. Friend: Hannah Foulke. Exec: Benjamin Davies.
Witnesses: Edward Foulke, William Foulke, Jno. Evans.

MC OFFEE, DANIEL. Warrington, Co. of Bucks, Pa. Yeoman. March 31, 1757. June 21, 1758. L.127.
Wife: Elizabeth. Children: Daniel, John and Archibald. Exec: Thomas Studdard [of Elizabeth Town, East Jersey], Elizabeth McOffee.
Witnesses: Henry Dunlap, John McMullan (his mark), Mary McMullan (her mark), Archd. McClean.

COUCH, ROBERT. City of Philadelphia. Tavern keeper. July 12, 1758. July 25, 1758. L.128.
Died in attempting to sign. Wife: Margaret. Stepson: James Daily. Friends: Samuel Purdy, Samuel McCreary, Elizabeth Holmes. Exec: Samuel McCreary.
Witnesses at death: Paul Isaac Voto, Henry Carswell, Thos. Newell.

ROOP, JACOB. Creesham, Co. of Philadelphia. Yeoman. July 16, 1758. July 29, 1758. L.131.
Wife: Anna. Children: Mathias and Cathorn. Brothers-in-Law: George Adams, Jacob Heagy. Exec. and Guardians: Anna Roop, George Adams, Jacob Heagy.
Witnesses: John Rex, William Nice, Thos. Rose.

JAMES, THOMAS. Providence, Co.of Philadelphia. Yeoman. April 12, 1758. July 29, 1758. L.133.
Brother: John Edwards. Sister: Ann Edwards. Children: Mary, Margaret, Anne and Isaac (all under age). Guardian: John Bull. Exec: John Edwards.
Witnesses: Thomas James (his mark), Nathan Davis, Elijah Davis.

ANDERSON, ROBERT. City of Philadelphia. Yeoman. July 24, 1758. Aug. 5, 1758. L.134.
Children: Robert, Andrew, William and Thomas. Exec: Thomas Anderson.
Witnesses: Alies Worrell, Sarah Sands, Matthias Keen.

WELLS, REBECCA. City of Philadelphia. Widow. July 31, 1758. Aug. 7, 1758. L.135.
Children: James, Thomas, Elizabeth, Anne and Collum. Grandchild: William Collum. Son-in-Law: James Collum. Exec: Thomas Bourne, Edward Evans.
Witnesses: John Redman, Paul Isaac Voto.

FLEMING, MICHAEL. City of Philadelphia. Jan. 16, 1758. Aug. 15, 1758. L.137.
Exec. and Friends: Patrick and Mary Farguson.
Witnesses: Paul Isaac Voto, Sarah Voto.

WILLIAMS, JANE. City of Philadelphia. Widow. Sept. 2, 1756. Aug. 16, 1758. L.138.
Grandchildren: William, John and Jane Hawkins. Exec: Jacob Shoemaker, Junr., Jacob Dubre.
Witnesses: James Chattin, George Shoemaker.

CAMPBEL, MICHAEL. City of Philadelphia. Dec. 22, 1757. Aug. 18, 1758. L.140.
Friend and Exec: William Cockburn.
Witnesses: George Lee, John Muttoy, Jery. Crowly.

FRANCIS, TENCH. City of Philadelphia. Aug. 4, 1758. Aug. 19, 1758. L.141.
Wife: Elizabeth. Children: Rachel, Turbutt, Philip, Anne, Mary, Elizabeth, Margaret and Tench. Guardian: Elizabeth Francis. Exec: Elizabeth and Tench Francis.
Witnesses: Thos. Cadwallader, Phineas Bond, Peter Howard.
Codicil: Aug. 5, 1758.
Witnesses: George Plim, Peter Howard.

THOMAS, REES, SENR. Merion, Co. of Philadelphia. Aug. 5, 1758. Aug. 19, 1758. L.143.
Children: Aubrey, Leatitia Evans, Hannah, Ann and Rebecka. Exec: David Evans, Hannah Thomas.
Witnesses: Samuel Wells, David Harry, Isaac Davis.

JONES, HUGH. Hatfield, Co. of Philadelphia. Yeoman. April 23, 1758. Aug. 24, 1758. L.145.

Wife: Catharine. Mother: Margaret Griffith. Children: Amos, Mary, Nathan, Jane and Margaret. Cousin: Ellis Pugh. Trustees: Amos Griffith, Joseph Griffith, Rowland Evans. Exec: Catherine and Amos Jones.
Witnesses: Nicholas Gelis, Abram Rutt, John Roberts.

YOCUM, SEVEN (SWEN). Kingsess, Co. of Philadelphia. Yeoman. Feb. 4, 1758. April 28, 1758. L.147.
Children: Peter, James and Andrew. Grandchildren: --- and five others. Exec: Peter Yocum, Neals Jones.
Witnesses: George Sinmier, David Gibson, Mary Gibson.

JONES, EMANUEL. Charlestown, Co. of Chester, Pa. April 30, 1754. Aug. 30, 1758. L.148.
Wife: Jane. Children: David Emanuel and Ann Williams [in Wales, Great Brittain]. Exec: Danal John, Danl. Beaton.
Witnesses: Rich. Sweetman (his mark), Biddey Howard (her mark), Richd. Richison.

HUDDLE, JOSEPH. Moyamensing, Co. of Philadelphia. Aug. 25, 1758. Sept. 6, 1758. L.150.
Wife: Elizabeth. Children: John, Benjamin, William and Joseph. Exec: Joseph and Elizabeth Huddle.
Witnesses: Zach. Nieman, John Barnes.

ENGLEMAN, JEREMIAH LUDWIG. City of Philadelphia. Aug. 25, 1757. Sept. 6, 1758. L.151.
Friend and Exec: Christopher Gravely.
Witnesses: Ant. Lawrance, Bernard Gratz.

BOGERT, JOHN GORGE. Germantown, Co. of Philadelphia. Yeoman. Aug. 23, 1758. Sept. 9, 1758. L.151.
Wife: Barbara. George Rut and Appelona his wife and heirs. Poor of Upper End of Germantown. Exec: Wigerd Miller, John Rex.
Witnesses: John Cunrads, Curnelius Cunrads, Henry Blecher.

CUNRAD, HENRY. Whitpain, Co. of Philadelphia. Yeoman. Sept. 2, 1758. Sept. 12, 1758. L.153.
Children: William, Dennis, John, Peter, Samuel, Benjamin and Joseph. Exec: Joseph and Benjamin Cunrad.
Witnesses: Benjamin Dickinson, Joseph Roberts, James Wood.

COATS, THOMAS. City of Philadelphia. Brickmaker. Aug. 8, 1758. Sept. 14, 1758. L.154.
Wife: Mercey. Father: Thomas. Brother: John. Children: George and Thomas. Sisters: Martha Shead (Shield) and children, Mary Albertson and children, Sarah. Exec: Thomas Say.
Witnesses: Isaac Roberts, Rudman Robeson, Elizabeth Robeson.

HASELL, ANN. City of Philadelphia. Widow. Dec. 21, 1754. Sept. 15, 1758. L.157.
Children: Samuel, Elizabeth, Ann, Jane, Hannah, Sarah and Thomasin. Son-in-Law: Alexander Huston. Sister: Hannah Growdon. Exec: Alexander Huston, Samuel, Elizabeth, Ann, Jane, Hannah, Sarah and Thomasin Hasell.
Witnesses: Nathl. Allen, Philip Syng Junr., John Syng.

BARTLESON, HENRY. Whitemarsh, Co. of Philadelphia. Yeoman. Aug. 14, 1758. Sept. 20, 1758. L.159.
Children: Elizabeth, Sarah, Henry, Sebas, Susanna and Mary Rittenhouse. Son-in-Law: Garret Rittenhouse. Exec: Sebas Bartleson, Jacob Rittenhouse.
Witnesses: Bartle Bartleson, Elizabeth Bartleson, Pat. Menan.

LORD, THEODOROUS. Passyunk, Co. of Philadelphia. Aug. 20, 1758. Sept. 21, 1758. L.160.
Child: Mary. Servant: George Doles. Grandchild: Elinor Lord. Friend: Daniel Williams. Guardian and Trustee: Daniel Williams. Exec: Mary Lord, Daniel Williams.
Witnesses: Charles Jones, Peter Speice (his mark), Joseph Howell.

YARD, GEORGE. City of Philadelphia. Bricklayer. Feb. 21, 1747/8. Sept. 21, 1758. L.163.
Children: William and Elizabeth. Brothers: Benjamin, Joseph and William. Sister: Elizabeth Fox. Nephews and Nieces: Joseph and Elizabeth Fox, Joseph Rhoads, Mary Yard, Mary Putton (Pullen) and Mary daughter of niece Sarah Martin. Exec: Joseph Fox.
Witnesses: Andrew McNare, James Lindley, Meibsam Martin.

SHALLCROSS, JOHN. Oxford, Co. of Philadelphia. Yeoman. 6 mo. 13, 1754. Sept. 21, 1758. L.165.
Wife: Hannah. Sister-in-Law: Catharine Wilmerton. Brother-in-Law: Edward Brooks. Nephews and Nieces: Leonard and Joseph Shallcross,

William, Ann, Ruth, Rebecca and Rachel Shallcross. Kinswoman: Hannah Robinson. Friends: Thomas Wood, Samuel Spencer, Hannah wife of Thomas Dews. Exec: Hannah and Leonard Shallcross.
Witnesses: Joseph Paul, Thos. Rose, Ann Cooper.

RAWLE, ELIZABETH. City of Philadelphia. Single woman. 8 mo. 12, 1758. Sept. 22, 1758. L.169.
Sisters: Jane England and Rebecca Rawle. Cousins: Francis Rawle, Rebecca Cooper and Sarah Rawle. Monthly Meeting of Friends. Exec: Francis Rawle.
Witnesses: P. Soumans, Benjn. Rawle, Mary Mackey.

BALTE, JOHN. Roxbury, Co. of Philadelphia. April 12, 1754. Sept. 23, 1758. L.171.
Wife: Mary Sofia. Child: Jacob. Sons-in-Law: Urban Eshenbrenner, Abraham Krider. Nephew: Conrad Krider. Children of Urban Eshenbrenner. Exec: Mary Sofia Balte, Thomas Looslee Miller.
Witnesses: Daniel Berndeller, Benjamin Levering, John Bowman.

GERHARD, WILLIAM [alias GARRET]. Wicoeo, Co. of Philadelphia. Carter. Sept. 5, 1758. Sept. 25, 1758. L.172.
Wife: Catherine. Children: Christian, Elizabeth, Mathias, William, Mary and Margaret. Exec: Catherine Gerhard, Michael Hahn.
Witnesses: Peter Miller, John Fritz, Jacob Hood.

REES, GWYNN. [Relict of Evan Rees]. Lower Merion, Co. of Philadelphia. Sept. 13, 1758. Sept. 27, 1758. L.174.
Child: Mary. Servant lad: Thomas Webb. Monthly Meeting of Quakers at Merion. Radnor Church in Chester Co. Friends: John Hughes, Esquire of Philadelphia, Evan Davis of Radnor, William Currie and William Godfrey of Tredyrin, Lewis Jones, Edward Williams, Daniel Humphreys. Relatives who may come over from Wales, Great Brittain. Exec: Joshua Humphreys, Daniel Williams, Edward Williams of Blockley.
Witnesses: Willm. Currie, John Fimple, George Fimple.

HARDING, SAMUEL. Wiccacoe, Co. of Philadelphia. Carver. June 2, 1758. Sept. 28, 1758. L.176.
Friends: John and Elizabeth Downey. Exec: Elizabeth Downey.
Witnesses: Robt. Black, Alce Drumbrell.

EDWARDS, SARAH. Stockbridge, Co. of Hampshire, Prov. of Massachusets Bay in New England. Oct. 2, 1758. Oct. 6, 1758. L.177. Dated and signed in Philadelphia, Penna. Children: Sarah Parsons, Mary Dwight, Lucy, Timothy, Susanna, Eunice, Jonathan, Elizabeth and Pierpont. Exec. and Son-in-Law: Timothy Dwight, Esq. [of Northampton Mass:], Timothy Edwards.
Witnesses: Thomas Bourne, Wm. Shippen, Jno. Shippen.

CONNOLY, WILLIAM. City of Philadelphia. Sailmaker. Sept. 23, 1758. Oct. 20, 1758. L.178.
Brothers-in-Law: John Boude, Michael Hillegas, Henry Elves, Junr. Exec: Michl. Hillegas.
Witnesses: Barnaby Barnes, Jacob Winey, Jacob Schreiner.

FREITAG, MARTIN. City of Philadelphia. Sept. 19, 1758. Oct. 20, 1758. L.179.
Wife: ---. Exec. and Guardians: Michael Kreider, Henry Weichsel.
Witnesses: Henry Ress, Anna Barbara Hirsch.

HARRY, ANN. Merion, Co. of Philadelphia. Aug. 23, 1758. Oct. 21, 1758. L.180.
Exec. and Cousin: Jane Wurner.
Witnesses: James Jones, Edwd. Humphreys, Joseph Bonsall.

TREXLER, PETER. Macongy, Co. of Bucks, Penna. Husbandman. Dec. 1744/5. Oct. 21, 1758. L.180.
Wife: Catherine. Children: Peter, John, Jeremiah, Anna, Catherine and Margaret. Exec: Peter Trexler.
Witnesses: Geittie Grimm, George Shamback.

SHELLY, MICHAEL. Lower Milford, Co. of Bucks, Pa. Yeoman. June 14, 1756. Oct. 24, 1758. L.182.
Wife: Barbara. Child: John. Brother: John. Father-in-Law: John Joeder. Exec: John Joeder, John Shelly.
Witnesses: Samuel Landes, Jacob Bidler (his mark), John Kocken.

CART, JOSHUA. Bristol, Co. of Philadelphia. Oct. 7, 1758. Oct. 28, 1758. L.183.
Children: Joseph and Margaret. Brothers: John and Goodson. Exec: John Cart.
Witnesses: Matthew Ingram, Margaret Switzer, L. Batharst.

CUNNINGHAM, GEORGE. City of Philadelphia. Peruke maker. June 23, 1758. Oct. 31, 1758. L.183.
Children: James, Ann, Elizabeth and George. Niece: Margaret Carson. Exec: George Cunningham.
Witnesses: Reuben Forster, Will Clinton, Paul Isaac Voto.

HERMAN, PETER. Northern Liberties, City of Philadelphia. Brewer. Oct. 4, 1758. Dec. 1, 1758. L.186.
Wife: Hannah. Step-brother: William Schmied. Sister: Sibilla Bengel. Brother-in-Law: Nicholas Bengel. Cousin: Peter Kahmer. Exec: Hannah Herman, John Stillwaggon.
Witnesses: Peter Miller, Adam Stricker.

HUMPHREY, ELIZABETH. Guinneth, Co. of Philadelphia. 11 mo. 4, 1758. Dec. 7, 1758. L.187.
Exec: George Gerivch.
Witnesses: Samuel Williams, Rachel Quee.

MILLER, ANDREW. Upper Salford, Co. of Philadelphia. Proved Nov. 2, 1758. L.187.
Wife: Elizabeth. Grandchildren: Children of Anna Mary. Sons-in-Law and Exec: Ulrick Stoller, Frederick Wentz.
Witnesses: John Joseph Roth, Ullrick Hertzel.

FRANCK, PHILIP. Providence, Co. of Philadelphia. Yeoman. Sept. 17, 1758. Nov. 7, 1758. L.189.
Wife: Ann. Children: Jacob and Sebastian. Overseers: Conrad Rubel, George May. Exec: Ann and Sebastian Franck.
Witnesses: Conrad Rubel, George Moyer, Nichos. Bunn.

JONSEN, JACOB. Lower Dublin, Co. of Philadelphia. Sept. 7, 1758. Nov. 8, 1758. L.190.
Wife: Mary. Children: Jacob and others. Brother-in-Law: John Peters. Exec: Mary Jonsen, John Peters, Jacob Jonsen.
Witnesses: Richard Treat, John Jonsen (his mark), Nicolas Painter (his mark).

JONES, DAVID. Radnor, Co of Chester, Penna. 10 mo. 10, 1758. Nov. 11, 1758. L.191.

Wife: Ruth[?]. Children: David, Hannah, Sarah and Ruth. Grandchildren: Anne, David and Margaret [children of daughter Ruth]. Exec: David Jones.
Witnesses: John Moore, Catherine Mills, Anthony Moore.

HALLOWELL, BENJAMIN. Abington, Co. of Philadelphia. Yeoman. Oct. 8, 1758. Nov. 14, 1758. L.192.
Wife: Mary. Children: Benjamin, Mary and Martha Hawkins. Grandchild: Mary Holt. Exec: Benjamin Hallowell, John Lukens.
Witnesses: Thomas Hallowell, James Edmiston, John Barron.

BAYLY, RICHARD. City of Philadelphia. House carpenter. Nov. 5, 1758. Nov. 20, 1758. L.194.
Wife: Elizabeth. Child: John. Cousin: Rebecca Bayly. Exec: Elizabeth Bayly, John Frazer.
Witnesses: Francis Trumble, George Button, Benjamin Fordham.

EVERHARD, JOHN. City of Philadelphia. Butcher. Oct. 19, 1758. Decd. 11, 1758. L.195.
Wife: Dorothy. Children: John, George and David. Brother-in-Law: John Buhler. Exec: George David Seikel, Barthasr. Reser.
Witnesses: Peter Miller, Peter Stierwald, John Philip Shower.

ENGEL, PETER. Shippack, Salford Township, Penna. Nov. 24, 1758. Dec. 22, 1758. L.196.
Brothers: Casper and George. Sisters: Magdalen and Elizabeth. Landlord: Samuel Meyer. Exec: Daniel Preiss, Nicholas Scherenik.
Witnesses: Christian Meyer, Rudolph Hardy.

SUMMER, JOHN GEORGE. Germantown, Co. of Philadelphia. Nov. 15, 1758. Dec. 22, 1758. L.198.
Wife: Cathrine. Brother: John Hesfer. Exec: Cathrine Summer, John Hesfer.
Witnesses: Isaac Will, John Linker.

BULLOCK, GEORGE. City of Philadelphia. Tanner. Dec. 1, 1758. Dec. 26, 1758. L.198.
Wife: Catherine. Children: Joseph, George and Elizabeth Lock. Exec: Catherine Bullock, John Lock, Joseph Howell.
Witnesses: D. Jam: Dore, Jno. Reily.
Codicil: Dec. 1, 1758.

Godson: George Gostolow.
Witnesses: D. Jam: Dore, Jno. Reily.

KAIGHIN, ABIGAIL. Co. of Gloucester, N. Jersey. Widow. Aug. 31, 1758. March 8, 1758. L.200.
Children: Charles and three others. Sister: Hannah Cooper. Exec: William Mode.
Witnesses: Pricilla Ingram, Joseph Hugg, Joseph Harrison.

DAVIES, SAMUEL. City of Philadelphia. Taylor. Dec. 24,1758. Jan. 1, 1759. L.202.
Wife: Martha. Exec: Martha Davies.
Witnesses: Peter de Prefontaine, Samuel Griscom, John Maxwell.

BAKER, JOHN. Kensington, City of Philadelphia. House carpenter. June 10, 1758. Jan. 6, 1759. L.202.
Children: Mary Fare and two children, Isaac, William and Francis. Exec: Henry Dennis.
Witnesses: William Pearson, Nathaniel Richardson, James Hunter.

SWENCK, JACOB. Germantownship, Co. of Philadelphia. Cordwainer. Dec. 9, 1758. Jan. 10, 1759.
Wife: Anne Mary [widow of Hanes Rudy Birge]. Children: Mary, Christina, John, Jacob, Rudy, Henry, Emanuel Birge, Anne Surber and Elizabeth Dottweiler. Exec: Anne Mary Swenck, Charles Widderholt.
Witnesses: John Grotthouse, Michael Millenberger, Christian Lehman.
Codicil: Dec. 28, 1758.
Witnesses: Michael Millenberger, Christian Lehman.

BAKER, JOHN. City of Philadelphia. Shipwright. Oct. 4, 1756. Jan. 14, 1759. L.206.
Child: Sarah. Brother: Joseph. Nephew: John Baker. Exec: Joseph Baker.
Witnesses: Wm. Cooper, Paul Isaac Voto.

GARRET, JACOB. Blockley, Co. of Philadelphia. Yeoman. Dec. 22, 1758. Jan. 16, 1759. L.208.
Child: Margaret. Sister: Magdalena Gardner. Brothers and Exec: John Garret, Joseph Johnson.
Witnesses: Robt. Roberts, Phineas Roberts, David Buderick.
Codicil: Dec. 22, 1758.

Nephew: Morton Garret. Christian Johnson.

BARTHOLOMEW, JOHN. Montgomery, Co. of Philadelphia. Tanner. Jan. 8, 1759. Jan. 22, 1757. L.210.
Wife: Gainor. Children: ---. Brothers: Benjamin and Edward. Brothers-in-Law: Benjamin Davis and Thomas Waters. Friend: David Evans, Deacon of Baptist Church. Trustees and guardians: Edward Bartholomew, Thomas Waters, Joseph Ambler, Junr. Exec: Benjamin Bartholomew, Benjamin Davis.
Witnesses: William Davies, Joseph Griffith, Benjamin Griffith, John Forman.

RUSSELL, NATHANIEL. City of Philadelphia. Mariner. June 13, 1757. Jan. 23, 1759. L.212.
Wife: Mary. Child: Nathaniel in England. Exec: Mary Russell.
Witnesses: Pr. Turner, Paul Isaac Voto.

SHRODE, MATHIAS. City of Philadelphia. Cordwinder. Jan. 21, 1755. Jan. 23, 1759. L.213.
Wife: Mariaoplone. Children: Samuel and Barbary. Exec: Mariaoplone Shrode.
Witnesses: Samuel Neilson, Willm. Dawson.

JAMESON, JOHN. City of Philadelphia. Proved Jan. 24, 1759. L.214.
Wife: Elizabeth. Children: Bety, Mary and Ann. Exec: Elizabeth Jameson.
Witnesses: Benj. Thomas, Joseph Crawford (his mark).

EGE, MICHAEL. City of Philadelphia. Inn holder. Jan. 4, 1759. Jan. 30, 1759. L.214.
Wife: Catherine. Children: George and Michael. Exec: Catherine Ege, Daniel End.
Witnesses: Peter Miller, Christian Snyder, Adam Yoe.

FIELD, TIMOTHY. City of Philadelphia. Oct. 5, 1758. Feb. 5, 1759. L.215.
Exec: Meary Joanes.
Witnesses: John Tyrrell, Edward Duckett.

HUKEY, JACOB. City of Philadelphia. Jan. 31, 1758. Feb. 15, 1759. L.216.
Wife: Catern. Child: Dorothy. Exec: John Trefts, John Everhoot.
Witnesses: Joseph Cox, Johannes Huell.

MIFFLIN, JOHN. City of Philadelphia. Merchant. Feb. 7, 1759. Feb. 26, 1759. L.217.
Wife: Sarah. Children: Thomas and George. Sister: Sarah. Exec: Sarah and Thomas Mifflin, Joseph Saunders.
Witnesses: Jo. Turner, Hugh Roberts, Benjamin Chew.

PLUMLY, SARAH. Widow of George Plumly. City of Philadelphia. Jan. 5, 1759. March 6, 1759. L.219.
Friend and Exec: Mary [wife of John Searson].
Witnesses: Hannah Moore, Rachel Hill, Wm. Sturgeon.

BLILAR, JOHN. Lower Milford, Co. of Bucks, Penna. Yeoman. Jan. 14, 1759. March 6, 1759. L.220.
Wife: Marey. Children: Henrey, Peter, Michael, Catran, and wife of Philip Fuckandal. Exec: Marey Blilar, Mical Fetar.
Witnesses: John Jemison, Valentine Clymer, Jacob Weizlar.

CHAMBERS, DAVID. City of Philadelphia. Stone cutter. Nov. 27, 1756. March 8, 1759. L.221.
Wife: Edith. Children: Mary, David, Easter, William, Joseph and Rebecca. Brother: Alexander. Exec: Edith and Alexander Chambers, Joseph Hall.
Witnesses: Joseph Watkins, Thomas Carteret, John Clifton.

SIBER, JOHN. Co. of Philadelphia. Yeoman. Jan. 8, 1759. March 10, 1759. L.223.
Wife: Barbara. Children: John, Jacob, Frederick, Phillip, Rachel, Rebakha and Sava. Exec: Barbara Siber, Frederick Antis.
Witnesses: John Koplin, Christopher Wice, Peter Herger (his mark).

JACKSON, ANN. City of Philadelphia. Widow. Dec. 16, 1758. March 10, 1759. L.226.
Children: Elizabeth and Jane. Sister: Alice McCauley. Exec: Elizabeth and Jane Jackson.
Witnesses: Thomas Cash, Jno. Reily.

SINGER, CASPER. Hanover, Co. of Philadelphia. March 9, 1759. March 17, 1759. L.227.
Wife: Catherina. Children: Casper, Christina, Hannah, Evah, Cathrina and Susannah. Sons-in-Law: David Keppler, Christopher Hainkle.
Witnesses: Jno. Campbell, Maths. Richard, Michael Walter.

LIVEZEY, THOMAS. Lower Dublin, Co. of Philadelphia. Yeoman. Jan. 13, 1759. March 17, 1759. L.228.
Wife: Mary. Children: Thomas, Sarah, Susannah, Mary, Rachel and Elizabeth. Grandchildren: George and Thomas James. Son-in-Law: John Shoemaker. Exec: John Shoemaker, Thomas Livezey.
Witnesses: Jonathan Livezey, Jonathan Dungan, Michael Younker.

GREENFIELD, GEORGE. Whitemarsh, Co. of Philadelphia. Yeoman. May 5, 1757. March 24, 1759. L.231.
Child: Jesse. Sister: Margaret Idon. Sister-in-Law: Sarah Shepherd. Brother-in-Law: John Shepherd. Exec: John Shepherd of Germantown.
Witnesses: David Reynolds, James Much (his mark), Christ. Lehman.

GILBERT, CATHERINE. Springfield, Co. of Bucks, Pa. Widow of George Gilbert. March 8, 1759. March 24, 1759. L.232.
Brother: Abraham. Children: Catherine, Dorothy Crader and Susanna Coon. Exec: Abraham Crader.
Witnesses: John Beidler, Sebastian Styger, Jacob Beidler (his mark).

FORBES, JOHN. City of Philadelphia. Brigadier General Col. of 17th Reg. of Foot. Feb. 13, 1759. March 24, 1759. L.233.
Brothers: Arthur and Hugh. Cousin and Exec: James Glen, Esquire [Late Governor of Carolina].
Witnesses: Richard Peters, Wm. Russell, James Grant.

HUGH, ROBERT. Gwynedd, Co. of Philadelphia. Jan. 23, 1759. March 24, 1759. L.234.
Children: David, Mary, Jane, William and Ellis. Trustees: Thomas Evans, Evan Jones. Exec: David Hugh.
Witnesses: John Jones, John Jenkins, Evan Jones.

GRIFFITH, HUGH. Gwynedd, Co. of Philadelphia. Yeoman. Nov. 4, 1758. March 26, 1759. L.235.

Child: Margaret. Grandchildren: Hugh Foulke, Hannah and Cadwalader Foulke. Son-in-Law and Exec: Edward and Margaret Foulke.
Witnesses: John Jones, John Evans, Joshua Foulke.

HOLLOWAY, MARY. City of Philadelphia. Widow. March 24, 1759. March 26, 1759. L.237.
Baptist Congregation of Philadelphia. Friends: Mary Borden, Jane wife of John Buckingham, Eleanor and Mary Powell, Margaret Minion, Elizabeth wife of William Sell, Benjamin Loxley, Ann Yerckas. Exec: Benjamin Loxley.
Witnesses: George Wescott, Robert Levers.

BUCKLEY, WILLIAM. City of Philadelphia. Merchant. March 12, 1759. March 28, 1759. L.238.
Wife: Ruth. Children: Phineas, William, Israel, Elizabeth, Rebecca, Elias and Mary. Exec: Ruth Buckley, Ennion Williams of Bristol, Reese Meredith of Philadelphia, Daniel Williams of Philadelphia.
Witnesses: Thos. Cadwalader, Saml. Preston Moore, Jno. Reily.

CUMLY, WALTER. Moreland, Co. of Philadelphia. Yeoman. Oct. 1, 1757. April 3, 1759. L.239.
Wife: Susana. Child: Martha. Brothers: John and Joseph. Nieces and Nephews: Abigal and other children of brothers, John and Joseph Cumly. Exec: Susana Cumly, Abraham and Benjamin Mason.
Witnesses: Robert Tytus (his mark), John Bartold, Joseph Cooper, Hannah Biusby.

BELL, MAGNUS. Signed Aug. 28, 1757. L.241.
Signed on sloop "Dolphin," bound for Jamaica, Hispaniola. Mother: Mirrin. Exec: Charles Lion, mariner.
Witnesses: Richard Thomas, Samuel Morlidge, John Parks.

PRICE, HANNAH. Northern Liberties, City of Philadelphia. March 16, 1759. April 4, 1759. L.241.
Children: John, Hannah Dutton, Sarah Price and Rebecca Carpenter. Grandchildren: John Dutton, Rachel and Hannah Collins. Exec: Hannah Dutton, Sarah Price.
Witnesses: Peter Miller, John Shutter, Abraham Coats.

EATON, URIAH. Montgomery, Co. of Philadelphia. Widow of Joseph Eaton. Feb. 22, 1757. April 9, 1759. L.243.
Children: Isaac, Hannah Doyle and Thomas Humphrey.
Grandchildren: Uriah Doyle, Uriah daughter of Isaac Eaton, Uriah, Elias and Stephen Humphrey. Guardians and Trustees: John Stephen of New Brittain, Isaac James. Exec: Thomas Humphrey, Hannah Doyle.
Witnesses: Isaac James, Sarah Wilgus (her mark), David Stephens.

MOLL, PETER. Hereford, Co. of Birks, Penna. March 19, 1759. April 17, 1759. L.245.
Wife: Magdalena. Brothers and sisters: (No names). First wife's brothers and sisters: (No names). Friends: Juliana Teusher, Abraham Bechtel. Exec: Magdalena Moll.
Witnesses: Valentine Kratz, Christopher Shultze.

BECHTEL, GEORGE. Hereford, Co. of Berks, Penna. March 19, 1759. April 17, 1759. L.246.
Wife: Maria. Children: John and others. Exec: Maria and John Bechtel.
Witnesses: Abraham Bower (his mark), Christopher Shultze.

GENSEL, MATHIAS. City of Philadelphia. Feb. 20, 1759. April 20, 1759. L.248.
Wife: Catherine. Children: John and Charlotte. Stepsons: Nicholas Schreiner and Jacob Schreiner. Exec: Catherine Gensel, Jacob Weiny.
Witnesses: Barnaby Barnes, M. Hillegas, Peter Miller.

STRETCH, ELIZABETH. City of Philadelphia. Feb. 3, 1757. April 23, 1759. L.249.
Brothers: Thomas, Joseph, Isaac and Daniel. Friends: Mary wife of Samuel House, Mary wife of Samuel Howell, Sarah Stretch, Mary daughter of Samuel Stretch, Sarah and Elizabeth Besly, Mary widow of James White. Exec: Thomas and Sarah Stretch.
Witnesses: Daniel Jones, Isaac Greenleafe, Benjamin Reeve.

ECKLES, GEORGE. Moyamensing, City of Philadelphia. Mariner. March 22, 1759. April 27, 1759. L.250.
Wife: Susanna. Child: Susanna. Exec: James Craig, Susanna Eckles.
Witnesses: Walter Burch, Paul Isaac Voto, Mary Faulkner.

MADDOX, JOSHUA. City of Philadelphia. Merchant. July 6, 1758. April 24, 1759. L.251.
Wife: Mary. Children: John and Mary Wallace. Grandchildren: Alexander and Sarah Maddox, Joseph and Sarah Stamper. Exec: Mary Maddox.
Witnesses: John Wilkinson, Jno. Ord, C. Brockden.

RIEFF, GEORGE. Germantown, Co. of Philadelphia. April 7, 1759. April 25, 1759. L.252.
Wife: Caterina. Brothers: Jacob, Peter and Conrad. Sisters: Anna Mary and others. Nephew: Baltis Rieff. Friends: Jacob Shoemaker of Salford, Anna Cobell. Exec: Caterna Riff, Jacob Shoemaker, Simon Siron.
Witnesses: George Adams, Simon Vogelesang, John Bowman.

CURRY, DANIEL. City of Philadelphia. Merchant. April 23, 1759. April 30, 1759. L.254.
Brothers: James and Albert. Sisters: Martha and Mary Hearne. Nephew and Niece: Patrick and Mary Curry. Friends: Thomas Fitzsimmons, William Plumstead, Samuel Carson, Chas. Osbourne, Robert Harding, Mr. Shnyder, Rev. Farmer. Exec: James and Martha Curry, Thomas Fitzsimmons.
Witness: Garett Meade.

REESOR, JOHN. Upper Succon, Co. of Northampton, Penna. Yeoman. March 17, 1759. May 9, 1759. L.255.
Wife: Catharina. Children: David, Abraham, Barbara and Anny. Exec: Philip Geissinger, John Yoder.
Witnesses: John Smith, Jacob Mayer (his mark).

EARNEST, GEORGE. City of Philadelphia. Tavern keeper. April 18, 1759. May 14, 1759. L.256.
Wife: Catren. Children: Valentine, Daniel and Agness. Exec: Catren Earnest.
Witnesses: John Frederick Under (his mark), Jacob Neak (his mark), James Baird.

BOWLING, LUCY. City of Philadelphia. Widow. Aug. 1, 1754. May 16, 1759. L.257.

Children: Ann, wife of John Young. Daughter-in-Law: Hanah Boyd, widow of William Boyd. Grandchildren: Children of William and Philip Boyd, decd. Guardian and Exec: Thomas Say.
Witnesses: Jno. Reily, Jno. Bowen.

EVANS, JOHN. City of Philadelphia. Gentleman. May 2, 1758. May 18, 1759. L.259.
Niece: Amelia Evans. Exec: James Turner, Caleb Parry of Tredyfrun, Co. of Chester.
Witnesses: Joseph Maule, Paul Isaac Voto.

SLAUGHTER, JOHN. Germantown, Co. of Philadelphia. May 12, 1759. May 21, 1759. L.260.
Wife: Catherin. Children: Andrew Campbell, Marey Bertholt and Elizabeth Melenberger. Exec: Christopher Yecle, David Reynolds.
Witnesses: John Shepherd, Charles Hubbs, Martin Green.

WILLS, JOSEPH. City of Philadelphia. Clock maker. Aug. 12, 1748. May 24, 1759. L.261.
Friends: Giles and Grace children of Grace Tucker of South Moulton, Devonshire, Eng., Arent Hassert. Mulatto woman: Margret Peak. Servant: Marge Sophia Gogen. Exec: Thomas Say, Maria Sophia Gogan.
Witness: John Chapman.

GRASSOLD, CHRISTIAN. City of Philadelphia. Taylor. May 4, 1759. May 24, 1759. L.264.
Brother: George Henry. Child: Dorothea. Grandchild: Soloman. Son-in-Law: Michael Haling. Exec: Michael and Dorothea Haling.
Witnesses: Jacob Ehrenzeller, Frederick Hagner, Peter Parish.

LAY, JOHANNES. Germantown, Co. of Philadelphia. May 1, 1749/50. May 26, 1759. L.265.
Poor of the Congregation of his church in Germantown. Friend: Margaretha Boyer. Exec: Alexander Magon of Chestnut Hill, Christopher Sower of Germantown.
Witnesses: Hermanus Keister, Conrad Stam.

MATTHISON, HENRY. City of Philadelphia. Yeoman. Oct. 15, 1755. May 26, 1759. L.266.
Wife: Mary. To Poor persons. Exec: Mary Matthison.

Witnesses: Thos. Tilbury, Alexander Sadler, Christ. Lehman.

OSBOURNE, CHARLES. City of Philadelphia. Druggist. May 12, 1759. June 1, 1759. L.269.
Wife: Elizabeth. Child: Charles. Friends: Elizth. Thompson, William Nicholls. Exec: Phineas Bond, Samuel Carson, Samuel Mifflin.
Witnesses: Joseph Stretch, Frans. Wade, Jno. Reily.
Codicil: May 15, 1759.
Daughter of Sarah Randolph.
Witnesses: Wm. Nicholls, Jno. Reilly.

BALL, TOBIAS. Upper Saccon, Co. of Northumberland. Yeoman. May 5, 1759. June 6, 1759. L.270.
Wife: Appolono. Children: John Philip, Anna Mary, Eve Barbara and Mary Lisbeth. Exec: Appolona Ball, Martin Appelas.
Witnesses: Jacob Kongerere, Philip Buckacre, Peter Knappley.

JARRET, JOHN. Horsham, Co. of Philadelphia. Yeoman. 4 mo. 22, 1759. June 13, 1759. L.272.
Wife: Mary. Child: Hannah Spencer. Grandchild: Mary Kenderdine. Children of Hannah Spencer. John, William, Jonathan and David Jarret. Sons-in-Law: Jacob Spencer, Joseph Kenderdine. Brothers-in-Law: Abram and Joseph Lukens. Trustees: Abraham and Joseph Lukens, Joseph Kenederdine. Exec: John Jarret, Jacob Spencer.
Witnesses: Joseph Lukens, James Paul, John Lukens.

SEWITZ, GEORGE. Upper Saccon, Co. of Northampton. May 24, 1759. June 13, 1759. L.274.
Wife: Barbara. Children: Joseph, Esther, Henry, George, Jacob, Mary and Abraham. Exec: Joseph Sewitz, Henry Weber.
Witnesses: Hans Musselman, Valentine Young.

WEBB, RUTH. City of Philadelphia. Single woman. May 28, 1759. June 18, 1759. L.276.
Brother: Joseph. Sister: Deborah. Friends: Mary Coats, Esther Chase, Alice McCalla, Mary Tagart. Exec: Mary Tagart, Mary Coats.
Witnesses: Ephraim Bonham, Ann Smith (her mark), Paul Isaac Voto.

CRADDOCKE, WILLIAM. City of Philadelphia. May 30, 1759. June 18, 1759. L.277.

Wife: Jane. Brother: Ebenezer. Sister: Mary Odford. Niece: Mary Craddocke. Exec: Evan Morgan, Joseph King, John Baynton.
Witnesses: Wm. Bingham, Blaithwaite Jones, Ephraim Bonham.

THOMAS, HENRY. Lower Milfort, Co. of Bucks, Pa. Cordwinder. Feb. 21, 1758. June 20, 1759. L.278.
Wife: Margaret. Children: Henry, Mary Barbara and Mary Margaret.
Exec: Margret Thomas.
Witnesses: Jacob Martin, Jno. Kooken.
Codicil: April 7, 1759.
Child: Jacob.
Witnesses: Christian Beeler, John Kooken.

MARTIN, JACOB. Lower Millford, Co. of Bucks, Pa. Yeoman. May 28, 1759. June 20, 1759. L.280.
Wife: Anne. Brother: John. Sister: Anne Zetty. Brother-in-Law: Christian Clemer. Friends: Magdalena Oberholtzer. Exec: Anne Martin, Christian Clemer.
Witnesses: Jacob Grofft, John Soudell, John Kooken.
Codicil: May 31, 1759.
Witnesses: John Soudell, John Kooken.

GEORGE, DAVID. Blockley, Co. of Philadelphia. April 25, 1759. June 21, 1759. L.282.
Wife: Margaret. Child: Jesse. Brother: Edward. Son-in-Law: William Lightfoot. Nephew: Jonathan Edwards. Nieces: No names given. Relation: Mary widow of Samuel Walker. Friends: Israel Pemberton and Hugh Roberts in trust for Poor of Village of Langerig, North Wales, Great Brittain and school house in Blockley, Co. of Philadelphia. Trustees: Hugh Roberts, Israel Pemberton. Exec: Jesse George.
Witnesses: Hugh Roberts, Mary Roberts, Peter Weaver.

LYNN, SARAH. City of Philadelphia. Widow. April 23, 1759. June 25, 1759. L.283.
Children: Jeremiah, Sarah amd Hannah. Cousin: Alexander Magee.
Exec: Robert Waln.
Witnesses: Willm. Ranbury, Jno. Reily.

CUNNINGHAM, GEORGE. City of Philadelphia. Peruke maker. May 14, 1759. July 3, 1759. L.284.

Wife: Elizabeth. Children: George and Ann Dorothy. Sisters: Ann and Elizabeth. Cousin: Sarah Cunningham. Friend: Joseph Hall. Poor of the Presbyterian Congregation. Exec: Elizabeth Cunningham. Witnesses: Eden Haydock, Paul Isaac Voto.

LOWNES, JAMES. City of Philadelphia. Yeoman. Feb. 7, 1754. July 9, 1759. L.286.
Children: Joseph, Hannah Allen, Susannah Forester, Mary Phillips and Rebecca Davis. Grandchildren: James, Sarah and Susanna Yarnall, William Phillips, James Lownes, James Forester. Trustees: Nathan Yarnall, Joseph Trotter. Exec: Joseph Lownes, Hannah Allen, Susanna Forester.
Witnesses: Pr. Turner, C. Brockden, Wm. Boddington.

MACKY, JAMES. City of Philadelphia. Merchant. June 27, 1759. July 16, 1759. L.292.
Wife: Elenor. Exec: Elenor Macky, Thomas Bourne.
Witnesses: Owen Roberts, Joseph Eeroyd.

BUDD, GEORGE. City of Philadelphia. Feb. 6, 1759. July 20, 1759. L.293.
Niece and Exec: Deborah Springer.
Witnesses: Paul Isaac Voto, Sarah Voto.

HAMILTON, WILLIAM. City of Philadelphia. June 3, 1759. July 24, 1759. L.294.
Wife: Sarah. Children: (No names). Exec: Sarah Hamilton.
Witnesses: John Johnson, Wm. Murray.

WHALTON, JOSHUA. Buyberry, Co. of Philadelphia. Yeoman. Nov. 3, 1755. July 27, 1759. L.294.
Children: Jonathan, Hannah Sherman, Ann, Casandria, Elizabeth Thomas, Albertson and Joshua. Exec: Joshua Whalton.
Witnesses: Daniel Walton, Isaac Walton, John Floyd.

NAGAL, CARLLE. New Hanover, Co. of Philadelphia. Taylor. July 9, 1759. July 27, 1759. L.296.
Wife: Mary Susan. Children: John and three others. Exec: George Michel Kuntz, Jost Biding.
Witnesses: Frederick Antes, Sebastian Hidleberger, Peter Unker.

BINGHAM, ANN. City of Philadelphia. July 7, 1759. July 30, 1759. L.297.
Child: William. Cousin: Susannah Woolston. Exec: William Bingham.
Witnesses: Samson Levy, Thomas Gregory.

PETERS, HENDRICK. Limerick, Co. of Philadelphia. Farmer. April 18, 1756. July 31, 1759. L.298.
Wife: Bernkin. Children: Warner, Isaac, Alse Miller, Christian Updegraff, Hannah Kendall and Mary Bun. Grandchild: Henry Peters. Exec: Bernkin and Isaac Peters, Nicholas Bun.
Witnesses: Andreas Gresberts, Philip Yost, Antony Miller.

HALLMAN, ANTHONY. Kepack, Co. of Philadelphia. Yeoman. Jan. 25, 1755. Aug. 3, 1759. L.300.
Children: John, Dorothy Heizer, Christian Seffebber, Catherine Kresseman, Mary Salome Perkymer, Barbara Jacobs, Anna Maria Ketchy and Henry. Son-in-Law: John Heizer. Grandchildren: Leonard, Valentine and George Perkymer. Exec: Henry Hallman.
Witnesses: Deter Welchor, Charles Cornelius Rabotcaw.

JONES, HUGH. Mountgomery, Co. of Philadelphia. Tanner. June 23, 1759. August 18, 1759. L.302.
Friends: Elizabeth Davies of Gwynedd, Mary widow of Thomas Evans. Asst. Exec: Evan Jones. Exec: Moses Frable.
Witnesses: John Jones, George Adam Eckart, Evan Jones.

ANDERSON, ARCHIBALD. City of Philadelphia. Brewer. Dec. 28, 1757. Aug. 21, 1759. L.303.
Wife: Mary. Brother: Robert. Nephew: Andw. Anderson. Rev. Mr. Gilbert Tenant for New Presbyterian Church, Susannah Anderson [widow]. Exec: Mary Anderson, Paul Isaac Voto.
Witnesses: Wm. Jackson, Robert Mathews, James James.

JOHNSON, JOHN. City of Philadelphia. Mariner on Ship Britania. Dec. 15, 1757. Aug. 22, 1759. L.305.
Friend and Exec: William Hall.
Witnesses: John Gass, Richard Singleton.

MORGAN, SAMUEL. Radnor, Co. of Chester, Penna. Yeoman. May 31, 1759. Aug. 22, 1759. L.306.

Wife: Magdalen. Children: John, Sarah, Eleanor, Jane, Rachel, Hannah and Ruth. Exec: Magdalen Morgan, Richard Evans.
Witnesses: Evan Thomas, Jasher Roberts, Abel Lewis, James Davis.

STACKHOUSE, JAMES. City of Philadelphia. Plaisterer. Aug. 11, 1759. Aug. 27, 1759. L.308.
Wife: Martha. Children: Hastings, Amos, James, Margaret, Mary and Martha. Exec: Abel James, Martha Stackhouse.
Witnesses: Nathaniel Browne, John Hastings, Saml. Hastings, Paul Isaac Voto.

WHITE, WILLIAM. Bristol, Co. of Philadelphia, Penna. Yeoman. July 25, 1759. Aug. 27, 1759. L.309.
Wife: Anne. Brother: Thomas. Children: Isaac, Samuel, Thomas, Rebecca, Agnes and Mary. Exec: Anne and Thomas White.
Witnesses: Richard Mather, Isaac Cleaver, Christn. Lehman.

KUNTS, GEORGE MICHEL. Fridericks, Co. of Philadelphia. Aug. 10, 1759. Aug. 31, 1759. L.311.
Wife: Eve. Child: Michel. Brother-in-Law: Ludwig Englehart. Exec: Eve Kunts, Ludwig Englehart.
Witnesses: John Phillip Lydick, George Bastian Eigerlberger.

SHALLCROSS, HANNAH. Oxford, Co. of Philadelphia. Widow of John Shallcross. 10 mo. 25, 1758. Sept. 5, 1759. L.312.
John, Hannah, Mary, Elizabeth, Paul and Rebecca [children of kinsman, John Wilmartin], Elizabeth, Mary and Edward [children of cousin Hannah Robeson]. Cousin and Exec: Hannah Robeson. Mary wife of Joseph Shallcross.
Witnesses: Leonard Shallcross, Thomas Rose.

DUNCAN, ROBERT. City of Philadelphia. Taylor. 9 mo. 3, 1759. Sept. 6, 1759. L.314.
Children: Joseph and John. To Poor indigent families. Exec: Mordecai Yarnal, John Jones of Plymouth.
Witnesses: David Bacon, Job Bacon, Alexr. Seaton.

STOLLER, ADAM. City of Philadelphia. Mariner. Aug. 25, 1759. Sept. 6, 1759. L.315.
Mother: Mary Houser of Nazereth, Co. of Northampton, Pa. Sister: Mary Summond. Friends: Mary Jones, Benjamin and Isaac Cathrell,

William and Edith Baynton, William and John Edwards. Exec: Isaac Cathrell, William Baynton.
Witnesses: Anth. Hull, Nathaniel Pettit, Peter Miller.

DEXERNER, DANIEL. City of Philadelphia. Victualer. July 21, 1759. Sept. 8, 1759. L.317.
Wife: Catherine. Son-in-Law: Martin Shring. Exec: Catherine Dexemer.
Witnesses: Henry Bosler, Peter Miller.

SCHUPPINS, JOHN BALTHAZAR. City of Philadelphia. Bookbinder. March 22, 1759. Sept. 11, 1759. L.318.
Housekeeper and Exec: Anna Maria Elizabeth Shuckle.
Witnesses: Samuel Webster, Paul Isaac Voto.

HUDSON, HANNAH. City of Philadelphia. Widow. June 4, 1743/4. Sept. 12, 1759. L.319.
Sister-in-Law: Martha Thomas. Kinswoman: Lydia [wife of Thomas Vernon]. Cousin: Lydia [daughter of Isaac Vernon]. Nephew: Isaac Williams. Friends: David Ogden, Wm. Moode, Mary William [nurse], Sarah Densey, Jane Hatfield. Womans Meeting of Friends in Philadelphia. Exec: Isaac Williams, William Moode.
Witnesses: Mathew Medeerlf, George Clare, Josep Marriate.
Codicil: June 18, 1743.
Lydia wife of Thomas Vernon.
Witnesses: George Clare, Jno. Reily.

ROBERTS, EDWARD. Upper Merion, Co. of Philadelphia. Farmer. July 29, 1759. Sept. 15, 1759. L.321.
Children: Mary, Ann, Sarah Kathrine, John, Margaret and Edward. Brother-in-Law: Mordecai Roberts. Sons-in-Law: Jonathan and Thomas Sturges. Friend: Jonathan Roberts. Trustees: Mordecai Roberts and Joseph Jones [of Plymouth], Robert Jones [of Gulph Mill]. Exec: Ann Roberts, Thomas and Jonathan Sturges.
Witnesses: Jonathan Roberts, Robert Jones.

COOK, ENSWORTH. City of Philadelphia. Innholder. Sept. 12, 1759. Sept. 17, 1759. L.322.
Wife: Sarah. Exec: Sarah Cook.
Witnesses: Anth: Hull, James Plunkett, Sarah Plunkett, Peter Miller.

STROUS, APPOLLONIA. Springfield, Co. of Philadelphia. Widow. Sept. 9, 1759. Sept. 22, 1759. L.323.
Son-in-Law: Adam Sneyder. Grandchildren: Eve Sneyder and Adam Sneyder, Junr. Brother: Jacob Strous. Sisters: Margareth and Magdalena. Exec: Jacob Kuntz, George Ehman.
Witnesses: Dennis Streper (his mark), John George Genner, Henry Junken.

KIRK, JOHN. Abington, Co. of Philadelphia. Yeoman. July 30, 1759. Sept. 24, 1759. L.325.
Wife: Sarah. Children: Rynear, Isaac, Jacob, Sarah, Margret Loofborow, Elizabeth Spencer and Mary Loofborrow. Brothers-in-Law: Peter Tyson and John Lukens.
Witnesses: Derick Tyson, Peter Tyson, John Luken, John Lukens.

FARRELL, JAMES. Son of Richard Farrell, butcher, City of Corke. Mariner on Privateer ship General Amherst from New York, North America. March 15, 1759. Sept. 25, 1759. L.328.
Proved in Philadelphia. Friend: Benjamin Lindnerall. Estate in hands of John Comerford, Francis Goold, Richard Bradshaw, Esq., James Reardon. Exec: Danl. Curry, merchant of Philadelphia, Penna.
Witnesses: Francis Hoffler, John Healy, Josh. Bond.

OBERHOLTZER, JACOB. Upper Salford, Co. of Philadelphia. Yeoman. Jan. 13, 1755. Sept. 26, 1759. L.329.
Wife: Deborah. Children: Mary, Jacob, Catherine, Frederick, John, Abraham and Christian. Son-in-Law: George Frederick. Brother-in-Law: Christian Haldeman. Exec: Deborah Oberholtzer, Christian Haldeman.
Witnesses: Henry Meyer, Jacob Landis, Andrew Zeigler.

RAWLE, REBECCA. City of Philadelphia. Single woman. Sept. 8, 1758. Oct. 4, 1759. L.331.
Niece: Sarah Rawle. Sister: Jane England. Cousins: Francis Rawle and Rebecca Cooper. Exec: Francis Rawle.
Witnesses: Jacob Cooper, Saml. Fisher, John Clark.

WELDON, JOHN. City of Philadelphia. Nov. 5, 1756. Oct. 5, 1759. L.333.
Friend and Exec: Ann Simmons.
Witnesses: Joseph Warner, Jno. Reily.

SCHLEYDORN, HENRY. City of Philadelphia. Merchant. Sept. 6, 1759. Oct. 6, 1759. L.333.
Wife: Elizabeth. Children: John, Eliz. Susannah, Henry and Mary Slaughter. Son-in-Law: Rev. Michael Slaughter. Exec: Elizabeth Schleydorn.
Witnesses: Benjn. Flower, Aquila Jones, Jno. Chevalier.

HARE, ELINOR. City of Philadelphia. Widow. Nov. 9, 1756. Oct. 15, 1759. L.335.
Son-in-Law: William Spafford. Children: Rebecca Spafford, children of Sisters, Sarah Hinsman, Ann Harper and Elizabeth Franklin [all in Bedfordshire, Eng., Great Brittain]. Friend and Exec: John Knowles.
Witnesses: William Turner, James Bailey, Jno. Kirke.
Codicil: Nov. 3, 1757.
Daughter: Rebecca and William Spafford. Friend: Mary Loveday. Brothers of former husband: John, Thomas, Robert and Henry Ellis, all of Hallerton, Leicestershire, England in Great Brittain.
Witnesses: Evan Morgan, William Turner, John Freake.

CROCKET, WALTER. Cheltenham, Co. of Philadelphia. Oct. 14, 1757. Oct. 18, 1759. L.337.
Wife: Christian. Children: Andrew, Robert, John, Mary Mason, Jennet Benner and Walter. Brother-in-Law: James Murray. Exec: Walter Crocket, James Murray.
Witnesses: Joseph Laughlin, John Watkins, Richard Treat.

SALTUS, NORWOOD. City of Philadelphia. Merchant. Oct. 9, 1759. Oct. 18, 1759. L.338.
Wife: Susannah [of Bermuda]. Child: [of Bermuda]. Mother: Hester Forster. Kinsman: The widow Miranda. Friend: Jane wife of John Wood. Sisters: Ruth, Hester, Frances and Margaret. Exec: Francis Many, Judah Foulke.
Witnesses: Ephraim Bonham, Jno. Reily.
Codicil: Oct. 15, 1759.
Son of Joanna.

NEWMAN, WILLIAM. Lower Milford Co. of Bucks, Pa. May 2, 1759. Oct. 24, 1759. L.340.
Wife: Margaret. Son-in-Law: John Edwards. Child: Mary Edwards. Brother-in-Law: Gabriel Clark. Grandchildren: Mary, William and

Margaret Edwards. Friends: William and Margaret Jemison. Exec: John Edwards, Samuel Shaw.
Witnesses: Samuel Clark, Saml. Foulke, John Sigelmire.

HORN, JOHANNES. City of Philadelphia. Joyner. June 25, 1759. Oct. 29, 1759. L.341.
Wife: Gertruyd. Children: Five [no names given]. Guardian and Exec: Gertruyd Horn.
Witnesses: Jacob Miner, L. Weiss.

GREW, THEOPHILUS. City of Philadelphia. Gentleman. Aug. 27, 1759. Oct. 29, 1759. L.342.
Wife: Rebecca. Child: Thomas [at sea]. Exec: Rebecca Grew.
Witnesses: John Cooke, Thos. Duncome, Jno. Reily.

STALY, JOSEPH. Germantown, Co. of Philadelphia. July 24, 1759. Nov. 2, 1759. L.343.
Wife: Fronica. Exec: Fronica Staly, Jacob Teoud.
Witnesses: Jacob Bossord, David Louder, John Bowan.

NEWBERRY, JOHN. Perkyomie, Co. of Philadelphia. Oct. 13, 1758. Nov. 3, 1759. L.344.
Wife: Rebecca. Children: Elizabeth Bean, Ann, Henry, Mary Davies, Rebecca Rees and Mary. Sons-in-Law; David Rees, John Bean.
Grandchild: Isaac Newberry. Exec: John Bean.
Witnesses: Henry Cassel, Henry Cassel Junr., Robert Jones.
Codicil: Oct. 23, 1758.
Grandson: Israel Newberry. Daughter-in-Law: Mary Newberry.
Witnesses: Henry Fritz, Robt. Jones.

POWELL, MARY. City of Philadelphia. Widow of Samuel Powell, merchant. Oct. 28, 1759. Nov. 3, 1759. L.347.
Children: Samuel, Sarah and Abigal Griffiths. Cousins: Mary Hill and Samuel Rhoads. Grandchildren: James and Hester Griffitts, Samuel Griffitts. Brothers: James and Joseph Morris. Sister: Deborah Morris. Friends: Catherine Gregory, Rebecca Harding, Rosanna Smallman, Samuel Robbins, Frederick Gross, Elizabeth Young, Mary Griffitts, Nurse Jackman. Exec: Samuel Powell, Samuel Morris.
Witnesses: Walter Franklin, John Franklin.

GORDON, MARY. City of Philadelphia. Widow. May 1, 1758. Nov. 5, 1759. L.349.
Child: George. Sister: Elizabeth Thornhill. Nieces: Rebecca and Mary Sibbald. Son-in-Law: Thomas Gordon. Grandchildren: Mary and Dorothy Gordon, Martha Morgan. Exec: Thomas and Mary Gordon.
Witnesses: Wm. Curry, Tho. Coombe, Samuel Curry.

NICKERSON, JOHN. Blockley, Co. of Philadelphia. Weaver. July 21, 1759. Nov. 19, 1759. L.350.
Wife: Sarah. Children of sister Mary Hosley, viz., Joseph, Charles, Martha and Mary [in Nottingham, England]. Nephew: John Blankley [Nottingham, England], Joseph Blankley. Cousins: Jacob Blankley, John Thomas and Thomas Nickerson [of England]. Exec: Sarah Nickerson, John Blankley, John Thomas.
Witnesses: Saml. Sellers, David Gibson, Caleb Shreve.

GODSHALKS, JOHN. Hatfield, Co. of Philadelphia. Turner. May 14, 1759. Nov. 30, 1759. L.352.
Wife: Helena. Children: Jacob, Barbara, Elizabeth, Alice, Ann, Catharine, Susanna, Jacob and Magdalena. Dutch Baptist Meeting. Sons-in-Law: Henry Overhols and Peter Hendricks. Grandchildren: Children of daughter Alice, viz., John and Mary Stauffer. Exec: Peter Custer of Worcester, Deelman Kolb of Ballmaster.
Witnesses: John Barkey, Wellen Gaetschalcke, Abraham Heidrick.

FIELD, CHARITY. City of Philadelphia. Single woman. March 21, 1759. Dec. 3, 1759. L.353.
Sister: Hanah Breeze of North or South Carolina. Nieces: Sarah Hart, Margaret Vansant and Elinor Breeze. Granddaughter of Hanah Breeze. Friend: Mary Jones, daughter-in-law of William Clark, Mary Stretch wife of Thos. Stretch, Isaac Stretch. Exec: Thomas and Isaac Stretch.
Witnesses: Joshua Mitchel, Wm. Clark (his mark), Christian Ooll.

UMSTED, JOHN. Limerick, Co. of Philadelphia. Yeoman. Nov. 8, 1759. Dec. 5, 1759. L.355.
Wife: Debora. Children: Herman, John, Mary Vanderslise, Debora Koplin, Susanna Waggener and Eiizabeth. Exec: Debora and Jacob Umstad.
Witnesses: Nichs. Bunn, Nicholas Custer, John Koplin.

ROWAN, JOHN. City of Philadelphia. Brewer. Nov. 22, 1759. Dec. 6, 1759. L.357.
Wife: Margaret. Children: Thomas, John and Ann. Exec: Margaret Rowan, John Meas.
Witnesses: Sharp Delaney, George Keehmel, Jno. Reily.

HOEY, JACOB. Abington, Co. of Philadelphia. Labourer. Nov. 21, 1749. Dec. 7, 1759. L.358.
Brother: William [in Ireland] and John. Sister: Elizabeth. Sisters-in-Law: Eleanor Hoey, Martha Scott. Nephews and nieces: Children of brother Joseph decd., children of sister Elizabeth, viz., Samuel and Marion Patten and two others (no names). Exec: John Hoey.
Witnesses: Sarah Hewit (her mark), Wm. Watkins (his mark), Richard Treat.

LEWIS, EVAN. City of Philadelphia. Distiller. Aug. 26, 1757. Dec. 13, 1759. L.360.
Rev. Mr. William Sturgeon for Poor of Christ's Church. Exec: William Thomas.
Witnesses: Wm. Hollinshead, Paul Isaac Voto, Sarah Voto.

CONROD, BENJAMIN. Whitpain, Co. of Philadelphia. Yeoman. May 7, 1759. Dec. 14, 1759. L.361.
Wife: Margret. Brothers: Peter, Joseph, William, Dennis, John and Samuel. Exec: Margret Conrod.
Witnesses: John Davis, Aaron Davis, John Roberts.

SELLEN, JACOB. Worcester, Co. of Philadelphia. Shopkeeper. Dec. 3, 1759. Dec. 19, 1759. L.362.
Brother: John. Sisters: Barbara Tyson and Elizabeth Vanfossen. Brothers-in-Law: Mathias Tyson and Arnold Vanfossen. Poor of the Mennonist Calais Baptist [at Perkyomie and Skepack]. Exec: Jacob Umstad, Henry Pannebaker Junr.
Witnesses: Christian Younlin, Arnold Zimerman.

JENKINS, CATHERINE. Upper Merian, Co. of Philadelphia. Sept. 28, 1759. Dec. 22, 1759. L.363.
Rev. John Davis of Tredyfrin. Sister: Margaret George. Brother-in-Law: Thomas George. Ministry of the Congregation of Christians, Baptised on profession of Faith in Tredyfrin. Nephews and nieces: Mary, Thomas, Eleanor, William and Elizabeth George. Friends: John

Thomas, George Clifton, Peter and Sarah Thomas, James Smith.
Exec: Thomas George.
Witnesses: Mathias Hotsten, Magdalen Holsten, James Davis.

LEDRACH, ANDREW. Lower Salford, Co. of Philadelphia. Farmer. March 5, 1758. Dec. 28, 1759. L.365.
Wife: Magdalena. Children: Henry, Magdalena Steiner and Esther Oberholtzer. Sons-in-Law: John Steiner and Jacob Oberholtzer.
Exec: Henry Ledrach, John Steiner.
Witnesses: Frederick Altderffer, Christian Huntsberger, Andrew Ziegler.

PEAK, ROBERT. City of Philadelphia. June 8, 1759. Dec. 28, 1759. L.367.
Friend and Exec: Richard Miller.
Witnesses: George Campbell, Danl. Hathorn.

CASSELL, NICHOLAS. City of Philadelphia. Ship joiner. Dec. 26, 1757. Dec. 31, 1759. L.368.
Children: John, Joseph, Susannah Drinker and Mary Corman. Son-in-Law: Edward Drinker. Exec: Edward Drinker, Henry Rigby.
Witnesses: John Drinker, Bradford Roberts, Wm. Cornock.

FLETCHER, GEORGE, ESQUIRE. Fort Edward. Capt. in Lt. Gen'l. Charles Otway's Regt. of Foot. Aug. 3, 1757.
Brothers and sisters: [No names given]. Brother-in-Law: Thomas Benson [of City of Carlisle]. Rev. Mr. Anthony Sharp [of Dear Ham].
Witnesses: Will. Bellew, Richd. Allen, Fo-t Edward.

HAMILTON, ARCHIBALD. Hilltown, Co. of Bucks, Penna. Weaver. Dec. 21, 1759. Jan. 9, 1760. L.370.
Wife: Jane. Children: Jane, Rachel and Mary. Brother-in-Law: Jenkin Evans. Guardians: Morris Morris, Evan Mathias. Exec: Jane Hamilton, Jenken Evans.
Witnesses: Charles Maycock, William Morris, Abraham Morris.

GRIFFIN, GILES JOHN. Late of Kingston, Jamaica, now of City of Philadelphia. Gentleman. Dec. 12, 1759. Jan. 2, 1760. L.371.
Wife: Frances Henrietta. Children: Lucock, Elizabeth, John Poppleton, Samuel Bucklestry and Mary. Brother-in-Law: George

Poppleton. Exec: Frances Henrietta Griffin, Saml. Johnson of Philadelphia, Peter Vallelle, Esquire of St. Thomas, Jamaica.
Witnesses: Joseph Watkins, Cornelius Sturgis, James Watkins.

HORTE, ROBERT. City of Philadelphia. Mariner. Written Jan. 5, 1760. L.373.
Brother: Jacob Verdue Luke. Sisters: Mary and Ann. Uncle: Robert Horte of Spikestown, Barbadoes. N.B. No probate or Ltrs. Test granted the Exec. living in Barbadoes. Exec: Mary and Ann Hoite.
Witnesses: Jas. White, John Bern.

KINTZING, ABRAHAM. City of Philadelphia. Miller. Aug. 13, 1759. Jan. 22, 1760. L.374.
Wife: Margaret [widow and relict of Jacob Herbein]. Children: Abraham and Catherine. Step-daughter: Elizabeth Berker. Exec: Margaret Kintzing.
Witnesses: Mathias Shad, Adam Gouss, L. Weiss.

BRUNNER, ANNA BARBARA. Widow of Phelix Brunner. Upper Milfort, Co. of Northampton, Penna. Jan. 20, 1760. Jan. 28, 1760. L.375.
Grandchildren: Anna, Mary, William, children of Anna Margret Linn, Anna Mary Greesmer, John Adam Willawir, Peter Linn and John Greesmer. Exec: John Adam Willawir.
Witnesses: Henry Miller, Henry Kooken, John Kooken.

BRUNNER, PHELIX. Upper Milfort, Co. of Northampton, Penna. Yeoman. Jan. 14, 1760. Jan. 28, 1760. L.376.
Wife: Anna Barbara. Daughters: Anna Margret Linn, Anna Mary Greesmerner and Anna Mary Willawir. Sons-in-Law: Peter Linn, John Greesmer and Adam Willawir. Exec: John Adam Willawir.
Witnesses: Michl. Keeler, Henry Kooken, Henry Miller, John Kooken.

BREDEN, ROBERT. Upper Dublin, Co. of Philadelphia. July 10, 1759. Jan. 30, 1760. L.378.
Wife: Mary. Children: Elizabeth and Sarah. Sister: Sarah Adams. Presbyterian Congregation at Abington. Cousins: John Adams, Robert Breden. Exec: Mary Breden, Abraham Charlesworth.
Witnesses: George Regan (his mark), Richard Treat, Thomas Hutchinson (his mark).

HITCHCOCK, JOSEPH. City of Philadelphia. House carpenter. Feb. 2, 1760. Feb. 6, 1760. L.380.
Wife: Mary. Children: John and Elizabeth. Exec: Elizabeth and John Hitchcock.
Witnesses: James Davis, Edd. Middleton, Jno. Reily.

THOMPSON, CHRISTOPHER. City of Philadelphia. Brick layer. Feb. 3, 1759. Feb. 6, 1760. L.381.
Child: Sarah Parker. Son-in-Law: Alexander Parker. Grandchildren: Thompson, Samuel, Sarah and Mary Parker. Brothers: John and George [of Yorkshire, Great Brittain], James [of New Castle, Great Brittain]. Sister: Ann Laurence, wife of Thomas Laurence [of St. Dennes, Great lBrittain]. Friends: Anthony Morris, Isaac Zanes, Anthony Benezet. Monthly Meeting of Quakers. Kinsmen: Mary Attmore and Ann Stubbs daughters of Thomas and Mary Stubbs of Co. of Chester, Penna., Christopher Thompson. Exec: Sarah and Thompson Parker, Thomas Say. Perspective Exec: Samuel, Sarah and Mary Parker.
Witnesses: Joseph Watkins Senr., Jno. Knight, Joseph Watkins Junr.

GUNTE, CHRISTIAN. Chestnut Hill, Co. of Philadelphia. May 16, 1755. Feb. 13, 1760. L.384.
Wife: ---. Poor of ye Society and any other denomination. Exec: Christopher Sour Junr., Theobald End.
Witnesses: Jacob Sterner, Mary Ent.

GRISLEY, SAMUEL. City of Philadelphia. Merchant. Dec. 13, 1757. Feb. 12, 1760. L.385.
Nephews: Samuel and Joseph Grisley. Trustees: William Cooper, Samuel Shoemaker. Niece and Exec: Elizabeth Grisley.
Witnesses: John Swift, Saml. Fisher, Joseph Donaldson.

GREDER, JACOB. Benjamen and Schibak, Co. of Philadelphia. Weaver. Jan. 11, 1760. Feb. 19, 1760. L.386.
Wife: Mary. Children: Michael, John, Paul, Barbara, Christian, Jacob, Katharine, Esther and Mary. Friend: John Freed. Exec: John and Paul Greder.
Witnesses: Michael Ziegler, Ludwig Hornung, Andrew Ziegler.

FUCKADOL, JOHN. Springfield, Co. of Bucks, Penna. Labour. Jan. 18, 1760. Feb. 21, 1760. L.390.

Children: ---. Sister: Ketron, wife of Stuffol Shenon. Brother: Filop. Brother-in-Law: Stuffol Shenor. Exec: Michael Tetor, Christian Shup.
Witnesses: Samuel Crago (his mark), Danl. Amorinan.

DAVIS, JOSEPH. City of Philadelphia. Feb. 15, 1760. Feb. 22, 1760. L.391.
Friend and Exec: William McCalla.
Witnesses: William Faries, Jams. Cowpland.

KUSTAR, HERMONUS. Perkiomie, Co. of Philadelphia. Yeoman. Jan. 9, 1760. Feb. 23, 1760. L.394.
Wife: Isabella. Children: Gertrude, Margaret, Modlin, Rebecca, John, Paul and Peter. Grandchildren: Isabella and Barbara Tyson. Sons-in-Law: Henry Umsted, Gesbert Bohrs, Henry Tyson, Henry Pennebaker. Friend: Gertrude Switzer. Exec: Isabella and Peter Kuster, Henry Pennebaker.
Witnesses: Peter Johnson, Dirrick Keyser, Malchior Waggoner.
Codicil: Feb. 1, 1760.
Modlin Tyson.
Witnesses: Dirrick Keyser, Mechior Waggoner.

OVERHOLTZER, MARKS. Coventry, Co. of Chester, Pa. Yeoman. Nov. 21, 1759. Feb. 26, 1760. L.396.
Sister: Elizabeth Kolb. Brothers: Jacob, Henry and Samuel. Friend: Jacob Scheffer. Nephews and nieces: Children of Samuel and Elizabeth. Exec: John Schweitzer, John Sowter.
Witnesses: Andrew Hate (his mark), Anthony Barnhart, Jacob Beery.

WILLARD, ISAAC. Lower Dublin, Co. of Philadelphia. Carpenter. Feb. 21, 1760. Feb. 27, 1760. L.398.
Children: Dorothy Hufty, Thomas, Richard, Isaac and Jesse. Son-in-Law: James Keeney. Exec: John Paul, John Roberts.
Witnesses: John Engle, Robert Webber.

KEMBLE, HEZEKIAH. City of Philadelphia. House carpenter. Proved Feb. 27, 1760. L.399.
Wife: Margaret. Friend: Thomas Kemble. Exec: Margaret Kemble.
Witnesses: Peter Miller, Patk. Craghead, John Gill.

LYNN, HANNAH. City of Philadelphia. Single woman. Jan. 3, 1760. Feb. 4, 1760. L.401.
Brother: Jeremiah. Sister: Sarah. Cousin: Christopher Marshall. Exec: Jeremiah and Sarah Lynn, Christopher Marshall.
Witnesses: Peter Miller, Thos. Boude.

FITZGERALD, WILLIAM. City of Philadelphia. Taylor. Feb. 15, 1760. March 3, 1760. L.402.
Brothers: Richard, Patrick in the County of Cork, Ireland and their children. To poor people. Apprentice John Reardon. Exec: Bryan O'Hara. Thomas England.
Witnesses: Robert Harding, John Middleton.

MOORE, ANTHONY. City of Philadelphia. Blacksmith. April 19, 1754. March 12, 1760. L.403.
Children: Anthony, John, Jane, Rebecca. Exec: Anthony and John Moore, Jonathan Evans.
Witnesses: Henry Barr, Jno. Bowen.

HARMER, JOSHUA. Springfield, Co. of Philadelphia. Yeoman. April 11, 1759. March 15, 1760. L.404.
Wife: Jane. Children: Leah, Elias, Joseph, Benjamin, Oner, Keziah. Exec: Oner Harmer. Trustee: Joseph Morris.
Witnesses: Joseph Ashmead, Thos. Rose, Margaret Rose.

EVANS, BENJAMIN. Limerick, Co. of Philadelphia. Yeoman. March 30, 1759. March 20, 1760. L.407.
Child: Rees. Brothers: Thomas and David. Guardian: George Brooke. Exec: Daniel and Thomas Evans.
Witnesses: William Davis, James Brooke, George Evans.

COATS, JOHN. City of Philadelphia. Brick maker. Dec. 7, 1754. March 20, 1760. L.409.
Children: Warrick, Isaac, Rebecca Shute, Abraham, John, Jane Knox, Sarah Penrose, Mary Dutton and Hannah Dennis. Sons-in-Law: Richard Dewees Penrose and Thomas Shute. Grandchild: George Wright. Trustee: Thomas Say. Exec: All of his children.
Witnesses: Thos. Rodgers, Benj. Leigh, Mattha Veale (her mark).

TUITE, ROBERT. City of Philadelphia. Gentleman. Feb. 1, 1760. March 26, 1760. L.410.
Wife: Mary. Child: Robert. Brother: James [of Maryland] and sisters. Cousin: Nicholas Tuite [of London]. Son-in-Law: Robert Osbourne in Barbadoes and children of wife's former husband, Samuel, James and Cathern Osbourn. Sisters: Elizabeth Kemble, Mary Cahil [in Ireland), Ann McNamara. Exec: Mary Tuite.
Witnesses: John Nixon, William Row, Wm. Peters.

BEEN, JAMES. Worcester, Co. of Philadelphia. Yeoman. Sept. 26, 1759. March 28, 1760. L.413.
Wife: Mary. Children: Thomas, Rebecca, William, Samuel and others. Grandchildren: Mary Stroud and others. Exec: Thomas Been.
Witnesses: Christopher Dresher, Bostian Ring, Melchior Waggoner.

HOVAR, JOHN. Lower Milford, Co. of Bucks, Penna. Cordwinder. Feb. 7, 1760. April 2, 1760. L.414.
Wife: Margrat. Children: Christianah, Barbara, John Junr., Margrat, John Jacob and Felty. Overseers: Christian Willour, Ulrich Spiner. Exec: Margrat Hovan, Philip Heagar.
Witnesses: Ulrich Spiner, Christn. Willour, John Jemison.

JOST, JOHN CONRAD. Limerick, Co. of Philadelphia. March 10, 1760. April 2, 1760. L.415.
Wife: Mary. Children: Frederick, Elizabeth, Edward and others. St. Augustines Church, New Providence. Exec: Mary Jost, Jacob Schrack.
Witnesses: John Fleicher, Bernard Hardt, Wendel Boteshira.

GEORGE, AMY. Radnor, Co. of Chester, Penna. Widow. May 27, 1755. April 5, 1760. L.417.
Children: Richard, John, Jane Evans and Edward. Grandchildren: Amy Evans. Cousin and Exec: Richard George.
Witnesses: Edward Jones, James Miles.

MYER, WILLIAM. Bedminster, Co. of Bucks, Penna. Blacksmith. March 22, 1760. April 8, 1760. L.418.
Wife: Elizabeth. Children: Abraham, Jacob, Henry and Ann. Brothers-in-Law and Exec: Jacob Wismer and Christopher Agney.
Witnesses: Francis Moriarity, William Nash.

WILKINSON, JOHN. City of Philadelphia. Brickmaker. Sept. 6, 1757. April 8, 1760. L.419.
Children: John and Mary Haselton. Grandchildren: John Wilkinson, James, John, Elizabeth and Jane Haselton. Exec: Mary Haselton, William Bingham.
Witnesses: John Wallace, Saml. Johnson.

DIEHL, CHRISTIAN. Covantry, Co. of Chester, Penna. Cordwainer. June 22, 1759. April 11, 1760. L.420.
Wife: Mary Dorothea. Children: Christian and Margareth Elizabeth. Exec: Christian Diehl and Mary Dorothea Diehl.
Witnesses: Michael Syfer, Philip Stong (his mark), Peter Tasher.

PIERCE, THOMAS. City of Philadelphia. April 7, 1760. April 11, 1760. L.422.
Niece and Exec: Mary [wife of John Darke, mariner].
Witnesses: Obediah Aldridge, Samuel Bissell, Robert Levers.

RAIMIG, DANGEL. Bedminster, Co. of Bucks, Pa. March 24, 1760. April 12, 1760. L.423.
Wife: Mary. Children: Susannah, Catarina, Elizabeth and Frederick. Brother: Lorance. Exec: Mary and Lorance Raimig.
Witnesses: Peter Shepherd, Henry Akell.

LEWIS, ESTER. Montgomery, Co. of Philadelphia. June 19, 1758. April 15, 1760. L.424.
Child: Edward. Daughter-in-Law: Hannah Lewis. Sister: Elizabeth [wife of Evan Evans]. Grandchildren: Merian and Ester Lewis, Isechar, Levi, Miriam and Hannah Evans. Cousin: Elizabeth Evans. Friends: Elizabeth and Henry Grammer, Elizabeth [daughter of Isaac Jones. Overseers: Isaac Jones, Benjamin Davids, John Williams. Exec: Edward, Merian and Ester Lewis.
Witnesses: Jonathan Evans, Jane Roberts, Edwd. Roberts.

DILBECK, ISAAC. New Hanover, Co. of Philadelphia. Feb. 21, 1760. April 15, 1760. L.425.
Sister: Mary and children. Exec: Bar iard Dotterer.
Witnesses: Philip Hahn, Elizabeth Dotterer.

MC CURDY, HUGH. Springfield, Co. of Philadelphia. March 8, 1760. April 16, 1760. L.426.

Cousin and Exec: Robert McCurdy.
Witnesses: William Hicks, Wm. Anderson.

FUNK, HENRY. Francony Township, Penna. June 13, 1759. April 25, 1760. L.427.
Children: Esther, John, Henry, Christian, Henry, Abraham, Barbara, Anne, Mary, Fronica and Elizabeth. Poor of Congregation of Menonists. Exec: John and Christian Funk.
Witnesses: Jacob Funck, Jacob Oberholtzer, Benedict German.

CAMPBELL, JOHN. Douglass, Co. of Philadelphia. Feb. 28, 1760. April 26, 1760. L.432.
Wife: Elizabeth. Exec: Elizabeth Campbell, John Potts, Esq., John Hareling Smith.
Witnesses: Maihs. Richard, Michael Walter, Jacob Smith.

FITZRANDOLPH, ISAAC. City of Philadelphia. May 25, 1759. April 29, 1760. L.433.
Brothers: John and James. Exec: John Fitzrandolph.
Witnesses: Peter Miller, L. Weise, Peter Paris.

DELAP, ANN. Moorland, City of Philadelphia. Widow. Jan. 31, 1760. May 3, 1760. L.434.
Daughters: Race Purdy and Mary Cain. Stepson: John Delap. Nephew: William Petterson. Exec: Anthony Yerkes.
Witnesses: Joseph Jeanes, James Patterson (his mark), Joseph Yerkes.

MURRAY, WILLIAM. Moorland, Co. of Philadelphia. Yeoman. Feb. 29, 1760. May 3, 1760. L.435.
Wife: Sarah. Children: Andrew, Hannah, Ruth and William. Exec: James Murray, Joseph Jeanes.
Witnesses: William Masden, David Fulton.

RAMBO, MOUNCE. Kingsess, Co. of Philadelphia. Yeoman. April 5, 1760. May 3, 1760. L.436.
Wife: ---. Children: Ann Lincon, Mary and Swan. Grandchildren: Abraham, Lincon, Catherine Campbell, Morgan Campbell. Exec: Wife and Swan Rambo.
Witnesses: Peter Yocum, Mc. Campbell, Isa. Pearson.

SCHWAGER, PETER. City of Philadelphia. June 8, 1759. May 3, 1760. L.438.
Wife: Magdalena. Children: John, Agnes and Elizabeth. Exec: Magdalena Schwager.
Witnesses: Rudolf Hornecker (his mark), Andrew Lightly.

DOMIG, HENRY. Lower Salford, Co. of Philadelphia. April 13, 1760. May 6, 1760. L.439.
Wife: Anna Margreta. Children: Jacob and John. Exec: Anna Margreta and John and Jacob Domig.
Witnesses: Martin Shauwecker, Nicholas Swenck.

SIEGLE, JOHN CHARLES. Newtown, Co. of Gloucester, New Jersey. Apothecary and Practioner in Physick. May 9, 1759. May 7, 1760. L.440.
Wife: Jacobina. Children: Charles Frederick, John Adam and Ephraim Benedictus.
Exec: Jacobina Siegle.
Witnesses: Joseph Shilpp, Joseph Cooper, Benjn. Cooper.

JONASON, PETER. Kingsessing, Co. of Philadelphia. April 19, 1760. May 7, 1760. L.441.
Wife: Sarah. Children: Abraham, John, Magdalin Holsten and Niels. Son-in-Law: Frederick Holsten. Grandchildren: Mathias, Amy, Peter, Martha and Magdalane Holsten. Exec: Niels and John Jonason.
Witnesses: James Coultas, John Rudolph, John Trapnall, James Bartram.

PRICE, REESE. Merion, Province of Penna. Yeoman. Feb. 29, 1760. May 12, 1760. L.443.
Wife: Ann. Children: John, Edward, Mary Harry, Ellis, Margaret Paschall, Jane and Ellias. Grandchildren: Children of Mary Harry and children of Margaret Paschall. Daughter-in-Law: Mary Price. Exec: Ellias and John Price, John Roberts.
Witnesses: Robert Roberts, John Roberts, John Roberts [carpenter].

BRITTAIN, NATHANIEL. Bybury, Co. of Philadelphia. Yeoman. June 15, 1754. May 13, 1760. L.444.
Wife: Elizabeth. Mother: Mary Garison. Children: John, Elizabeth Derland, Mary Vansandt and Rachel. Sons-in-Law: Nicholas Vansandt and Isaac Belue. Exec: John Brittain, Nicholas Vansandt, Isaac Belue.

Witnesses: John Worthington (his mark), William Walmsley, Sarah Walmsley.

OEHL, NICHOLAS. Upper Hanover, Co. of Philadelphia. April 25, 1760. May 13, 1760. L.446.
Wife: Anna Margaretha. Children: Daniel, Alexander and John, Henry. Exec: Philip Hertzog, Anna Margaretha Oehl.
Witnesses: Henry Miller, John Diebendorffer.

WALTON, CASANDRA. Bybury, Co. of Philadelphia. Dec. 13, 1759. May 17, 1760. L.447.
Sisters: Hannah Sherman and Ann. Brothers: Albertson and Joshua. Exec: Joshua Walton.
Witnesses: Robert Heaton, Jane Wassell.

ALLEN, MARY. City of Philadelphia. Widow. March 10, 1750. May 23, 1760. L.448.
Child: William. Grandchildren: Children of son William. Nieces and Nephews: Rebecca Crapp, Sarah Burd [wife of James], Mary, Sarah, Rebecca and William Paschall. Exec: William Allen. Witnesses: Alexr. Stuart, Nathl. Allen Junr., John Huddele.

EVANS, THOMAS. Gwynedd, Co. of Philadelphia. Inn keeper. March 13, 1760. May 26, 1760. L.449.
Wife: Elizabeth. Children: Owen, Edward, Thomas Junr., Griffith, Mary and John. Grandchild: William Evans. Cousins and Overseers: John Jones, Rowland and Samuel Evans. Exec: Thomas Evans.
Witnesses: Rowd. Evans, Eliezer Williams.
Codicil: May 19, 1760.
Thomas Evans.
Witnesses: Rowd. Evans, Eliezer Williams.

BOHANAN, JAMES. Lower Dublin, Co. of Philadelphia. Yeoman. March 4, 1760. May 26, 1760. L.451.
Wife: Mary. Children: Elizabeth and Jean. Brother: John. Friends: Samuel Dean, Michael Shaw. Exec: Mary Bohanan, Nicholas Randal.
Witnesses: Jacob Keen, Thomas Stammers.

HANDWERCK, HENRY. Frederick, Co. of Philadelphia. Husbandman. April 23, 1760. May 28, 1760. L.453.

Wife: Barbara. Children: Peter and others. Brother: Nicklaus. Exec: Barbara and Nicklaus Handwerck.
Witnesses: Henry Delekamp, Henry Kappes.

COLLATT, JEREMY. Upper Chichester, Co. of Chester, Penna. May 21, 1760. May 29, 1760. L.454.
Wife: Mary. Children: Rachel and Mary. Grandchildren: William, James and Joseph Collatt, John Linwell. Brother: Joseph. Sister: Jane. Exec: Mary Collatt, Edward Linwell.
Witnesses: James Lone, John Lone, Jas. Allen.

HOFFMAN, JACOB. Lower Salford, Co. of Philadelphia. Yeoman. April 7, 1760. May 20, 1760. L.456.
Wife: Barbara. Children: Henry, Jacob, Frederick, Fronica, Anna Barbara, Elizabeth, Catherine, Susannah and Christina. Sons-in-Law: Michael Yew, Philip Stong. Exec: Barbara Hoffman, Michael Yew, Philip Stong.
Witnesses: Henry Woohrman, Abraham Heiderich.

JOHNSON, NICHOLAS. Lower Salford, Co. of Philadelphia. Yeoman. May 9, 1760. May 30, 1760. L.458.
Wife: Magdalena. Children: Magdalena, John and Jacob. Exec: Magdalena Johnson, Christian Moyer.
Witnesses: Rudolph Harly, John Jansen, Jacob Kropp (his mark).

GRAY, MARY. Kingsess, Co. of Philadelphia. Widow. Sept. 29, 1759. June 2, 1760. L.459.
Children: George, Elizabeth Coultas and Mary James. Grandchildren: May wife of John Withy, George and Susannah Syng, Thomas and Joseph James, George Gray. Great grandson: James Withy. Sons-in-Law: Thomas James, James Coultas. Daughter-in-Law: Mary Gray. Brother-in-Law: Samuel Gray. Friend: Hannah James. Exec: George Gray, James and Elizabeth Coultas.
Witnesses: Jno. Sibbald, James James, Richd. Sewell.

RILIE, WILLIAM. Charlestown, Co. of Chester. Yeoman. May 2, 1760. June 11, 1760. L.462.
Wife: Susannah. Children: John, William, Mary, Phebe and Susannah. Exec: Susannah Rilie, Rogert Hunt.
Witnesses: Zachariah Rogers, Jonathan Davis, James Williams.

EBERHARD, JOSEPH. Upper Milford, Co. of Northampton, Penna. Yeoman. Nov. 3, 1759. June 16, 1760. L.463.
Wife: Catherine. Children: Michael, Joseph, Jacob, John, Peter, Abraham, Veronica, Elizabeth and Barbara. Grandchildren: Ann Margaret and Joseph Horneker. Exec: Michael and Joseph Eberhard.
Witnesses: Felix Bunner, Michael Kayler, John Kooken.

NEITZCHOELTZER, JACOB. City of Philadelphia. May 5, 1760. June 16, 1760. L.467.
Wife: Sibilla. Children: John Michael, Jacob, Anne Catherine and others. Henry Frederick Eshback, John Miller, Charles Naglees' children.
Witnesses: Jacob Bernhardt, Godfrey Langebein.

YOACUM, ANN. Kingsess, Co. of Philadelphia. Widow. Sept. 28, 1755. June 21, 1760. L.468.
Children: Christian Lascum and Peter. Son-in-Law: William Lascum. Grandchildren: Benjamin, Peter and Ann Lascum, Deborah, Ann, Peter and Abraham Yoacum. Exec: Peter Yoacum, Isaac Pearson.
Witnesses: Joseph Fordham, Thomas Pearson, Britta Campbell.

HARRISON, JOHN. City of Philadelphia. April 24, 1760. June 30, 1760. L.470.
Wife: Susannah. Children: Joseph and William. Exec: Susannah Harrison.
Witnesses: Robert Wright, Wm. Boyer.

GRABER, ANDREW. Upper Hanover, Co. of Philadelphia. Yeoman. March 10, 1760. July 1, 1760. L.470.
Wife: Gertraut. Children: Ulrick, Andrew and Philip. Step-daughters: Anna Margaretha and Anna Christina. Exec: Gertraut and Andrew Graber.
Witnesses: Wendall Wiand, Johannes Martin, Jacob Dingeil.

JACOB, SAMUEL. City of Philadelphia. Shop keeper. April 7, 1752. July 4, 1760. L.474.
Wife: Mary. Children: Thomas, Mary and Ann Gillingham. Son-in-Law: John Gillingham. Exec: Mary Jacob, Abel James.
Witnesses: Judah Foulke, David Palmer, Jno. Groves.

GRAY, GEORGE. City of Philadelphia. Brewer. August 1, 1758. July 10, 1760. L.474.
Wife: Marcey. Children: Joseph, William, John, George, Mary, Elizabeth, Marcey and Hannah. Brother-in-Law: John Warner. Cousin: George Gray. Exec: Marcey Gray, John Warner, George Gray.
Witnesses: Archd. Hillhouse, Isaac Stretch, Jno. Reily.
Codicil: Sept. 15, 1759.
Daughter Sarah Gray and another child expected.
Witnesses: John Maydwell, Gurnay Wall, Martha Weall.
Codicil: March 29, 1760.
Exec: Samuel Morris Junr.
Witnesses: Thomas Warner, Jno. Middleton.

STANTER, CASPER. Lancaster. Hussar. July 2, 1758. July 15, 1760. L.477.
Mr. Schneider Catholick, Pastor. Friends and Exec: Michael Wisel, Christopher Magol.
Witnesses: Abra Myer, Nicholas Schiendlman, Mary Eventzmann.

PORTER, JOHN. Moyamensing, Co. of Philadelphia. April 11, 1759. July 19, 1760. L.478.
Wife: Mary. Children: Lydia, Sarah and John. Exec: Mary Porter, Andrew Read, Charles Pettit.
Witnesses: John Woodside, John Church, Joseph White.

JONES, JENKIN. City of Philadelphia. Minister of the Gospel. Sept. 14, 1759. July 18, 1760. L.480.
Brother: David. Sisters: Jaen and Elizabeth Rees. Children: [No names given]. Nephews and Nieces: John Jones, Mary Rees and children of sister Jaen. Elders of the Baptist Congregation. Wife's Sons-in-Law and Exec: Barnaby Barns and Stephen Wats.
Witnesses: James Hunter, John Stanaland, Joseph Powell.

HUBRICKS, JOSEPH. City of Philadelphia. Nov. 21, 1758. July 23, 1760. L.481.
Friend and Exec: George Hawkins.
Witness: Alexr. Campbell.

BENSON, JOHN. City of Philadelphia. Baker. Oct. 9, 1754. July 25, 1760. L.482.

Wife: Mary. Children: Alice Forster and Mary. Brothers: Andrew and Robert. Brother-in-Law: Matthew Wright. Nephews and Nieces: Children of Robert Benson, children of Matthew Wright, children of Margaret Littler, children of Elizabeth Tasker. Sisters: Margaret Littler and Elizabeth Tasker [in England]. Trustess: Thomas Cumming, Jeremiah Elfreth. Exec: Mary Benson.
Witnesses: Joseph Stretch, John Jones Junr., Paul Isaac Voto.

BRANSON, WILLIAM. City of Philadelphia. Merchant. June 1, 1760. Aug. 2, 1760. L.485.
Child: Elizabeth Lardner. Father: [No name given]. Son-in-Law: Lynford Lardner. Grandchildren: Frances, Hannah, William and John Lardner, Samuel, Mary and Hannah Flower, Branson, George, William, Samuel and Benjamin Van Leer, William Branson, Mary Hockley.
Exec: Lynford Lardner.
Witnesses: Jacob Winey, Mc. Hillegass, Paul Isaac Voto, Josh. Cannon.

COPE, HENRY. City of Philadelphia. Mariner. March 20, 1760. Aug. 4, 1760. L.491.
Friend and Exec: Rachel Brown.
Witnesses: John Wright, John Williams, Rebecca Henry.

JONES, DAVID. Hanover, Co. of Philadelphia. Yeoman. Feb. 6, 1760. Aug. 4, 1760. L.492.
Wife: Elinor. Children: David, John, William, Margret, Rachel and Mary. Sons-in-Law: Adam Ash, Joshua Scoott and Bastian Franks.
Exec: Elinor and David Jones.
Witnesses: Henry Culston, Henry Nieman, George Evans.

HELFENSTON, NICKLES. Lower Dublin, Co. of Philadelphia. Yeoman. April 5, 1760. Aug. 7, 1760. L.493.
Wife: Eve Elizabeth. Children: Nickles, Susannah, Earnst, Harman, Daniel, Christina, Margaret and Richard. Exec: Eve Elizabeth and Nickles Helfenston.
Witnesses: John Vanhorn, Jacob Duffield, Jno. Bartolet.

MEFFORD, ANDREW. Coventry, Chester Co., Penna. Yeoman. May 31, 1760. Aug. 13, 1760. L.495.
Wife: Macdelan. Children: Margaret Dawer, John and Casper. Exec: Macdelan and John Mefford.
Witnesses: Jacob Light, Charles Heckman.

MC CRAY, WILLIAM. City of Philadelphia. Joyner. Aug. 5, 1760. Aug. 30, 1760. L.496.
Brothers: Robert, James, Samuel and John. Sisters: Martha, Ann and Jane. Friend: Archibald Askins. Exec: Robert McCray, James Harvey.
Witnesses: Thomas Watson, Jno. Middleton.

NUTT, ANNA. Coventry, Co. of Chester, Penna. Widow and relict of Samuel Nutt. Inn Master. May 2, 1744/5. Oct. 30, 1760. L.497.
Children: Rebecca, Grace and Anna. Sister: Hester Hockley. Sons-in-Law: Rebert Grace and John Potts. Grandchildren: Anna Nutt, Samuel, Anna, Rebecca, Ruth, Mary, and Martha Savage. Overseers of Philadelphia Baptist Meeting. Friends: Thomas Rutter, Ann Hockley.
Exec: John Potts.
Witnesses: Marcus Hullings, William Bird, Thos. Yorke.

CRAWFORD, JOSHUA. City of Philadelphia, late of Monmouth, Eastern division of New Jersey. Sadler. Aug. 14, 1759. Aug. 19, 1760. L.500.
Brothers: Richard, William and Job. Sisters: Elizabeth and Lidia.
Exec: Richard and William Crawford.
Witnesses: Jonathan Carmalt, Isaac Paschall, Joseph Jacobs, Paul Isaac Voto.

STONEMETZ, JOHN. Northern Liberties, Co. of Philadelphia. Inn holder. Aug. 13, 1760. Aug. 20, 1760. L.501.
Wife: Mary. Children: Regina, Mary and Margaret. Exec: Mary Stonemetz.
Witnesses: Barnard Lawerswyler, John Lort, George Shaaf.

RICHARDS, SAMUEL. Tredyfrin, Co. of Chester, Penna. Yeoman. July 13, 1760. Aug. 23, 1760. L.502.
Wife: Elizabeth. Children: Rowland, Catherin, Lewis and Samuel.
Trustees: Joseph Jones of Plymouth, Edward Jones of Radnor. Exec: Elizabeth and Samuel Richards.
Witnesses: David Havard, Danl. Walker, Joseph Walker.

HOGERMUED, MATHIAS ADAM. Germantown, Co. of Philadelphia. July 8, 1760. Aug. 23, 1760. L.504.
Wife: Catherine. Children: John, Mathias, Jacob, Anne, Catherine and Barbara. Exec: John and Mathias Hogermued.

Witnesses: Peter Smith, Simon Hoglesing, John Bowman.

MC SPARRAN, JOHN. City of Philadelphia. Aug. 15, 1760. Aug. 26, 1760. L.505.
One child. Brothers: Archibald and Joseph. Exec: Archibald McSparran.
Witnesses: Sara Brudey (her mark), Wm. Murray.

BRINGHURST, ANNA. Germantown, Co. of Philadelphia. Widow of George Bringhurst. Aug. 6, 1760. Aug. 26, 1760. L.506.
Children: John, George, Samuel and William. Grandchildren: Elizabeth, Anna, Mary and George Palmer. Son-in-Law: George Palmer. Exec: John and George Bringhurst, George Palmer.
Witnesses: William Ashmead, Deby Wright, Thos. Rose.

THOMAS, ROBERT. Lower Dublin, Co. of Philadelphia. Miller. Aug. 12, 1760. Sept. 1, 1760. L.508.
Wife: Martha. Children: Robert, Joseph, Richard and Elisha. Son-in-Law: Thomas Austin. Daughter-in-Law: Mary Thomas. Grandchildren: Robert, Joseph and Richard and Thomas Austin, Mary and Jacob Thomas. Exec: Martha, Robert and Elisha Thomas.
Witnesses: Thomas Street, Peter Eaton, Evan Thomas.

SCULL, ROBERT. City of Philadelphia. Gentleman. Aug. 27, 1760. Sept. 1, 1760. L.509.
Child: John. Cousin: Eleanor Scull. Brothers and Sisters: [No names]. Brother-in-Law: John Lukens. Exec: John Lukens, John Biddle.
Witnesses: Joseph Ogden, James Steel, Robert Levers.

LOCHLIN, JOSEPH. Lower Dublin, Co. of Philadelphia. Stone mason. Nov. 7, 1758. Sept. 2, 1760. L.510.
Children: Jacob, Samuel and Martha. Brother-in-Law: Jacob Hufty. Exec: Jacob Hufty, Robert Thomas Senr.
Witnesses: Joseph Shallcross, John Ashton, Thomas Stammers.

BARTH, JACOB. Colebrook Deal, Co. of Bucks. Carebinder. April 9, 1760. Sept. 3, 1760. L.513.
Wife: Dorothea. Children: John, Martin, Jacob and Michael. Exec: Dorothea Barth.
Witnesses: Andrew Miller, Michael Schatz, John Martin Rupp.

BOHRS, GESBERT. Worcester, Co. of Philadelphia. Weaver. Aug. 2, 1760. Sept. 3, 1760. L.514.
Wife: Margereth. Children: Eddi, Arnold, Peter, Hendrick and Catharina. Son-in-Law: Gerreld Godshalk. Exec: Gerreld Godshalk, Peter Kustar.
Witnesses: Dielman Kolb, Derrick Keyser, Michael Waggoner.

MC CULLOUGH, JAMES. City of Philadelphia. Merchant. Aug. 18, 1759. Sept. 12,1760. L.516.
Wife: Rachel. Children: Mary, Sarah, Rachel and Ann. Brother: Hugh. Contributors of Pennsylvania Hospital. Poor children of Presbyterian Meeting House, 3rd and Arch Sts. Exec: Jacob Duche, Hugh McCullough.
Witnesses: John Baldwin, William Peters, Jno. Reily.

REBOLD, JACOB. Germantown, Co. of Philadelphia. Stocken weaver. Aug. 26, 1760. Sept. 13, 1760. L.519.
Wife: Barbara. Children: Jacob, Judith, Bizia, Magdalen, Anna, Maria, Mary, Daniel and Hartman. Father-in-Law: Hartman Adam. Guardians and Exec: Barbara Rebold, Hartman Adam, John Deelusang.
Witnesses: Thos. Rose, Jacob Coleman, Jean Dedier.

DAVIS, MARGARET. City of Philadelphia. Feme [Ferne?] sole trader. Sept. 13, 1760. Sept. 22, 1760. L.521.
Child: Margaret. Son-in-Law: Walter Smith. Exec: Buckridge Sims, Doctor John Redman.
Witnesses: Wm. Peters, James Holdan, Susannah Sormain.

HEYSLER, GEORGE. Germantown, Co. of Philadelphia. Sept. 6, 1760. Sept. 24, 1760. L.523.
Wife: Mary. Children: Susana and William. Exec: Mary Heysler, Nicholas Rittenhouse.
Witnesses: J. B. Poeninghousen, William Van Aken, John Bowman.

THOMAS, ISAAC. Cheltenham, Co. of Philadelphia. Mason. Sept. 21, 1760. Sept. 27, 1760. L.524.
Brothers: Jacob, John and Nathan. Sisters: Ann, Mary, Sarah, Margeret and Hannah. Brothers-in-Law: Benjamin Morris, Mathias Keen, William Button and John White. Exec: Jacob Thomas.
Witnesses: Daniel Rositer, Ann Thomas, Thos. Rose.

FISHER, HERMAN. Upper Hanover, Co. of Philadelphia. Yeoman. July 18, 1760. Sept. 30, 1760. L.526.
Wife: Margareth. Children: Jacob, John, George, Herman, Wendell, Anna Mary, Catharina, Barbara, Margareth, Sophia and Christiana. Exec: Margareth and Jacob Fisher, John Mock.
Witnesses: Wendal Wiand, David Shultze, Christopher Zeigler.

TABER, JOHN. City of Philadelphia. Taylor. June 26, 1760. Sept. 30, 1760. L.531.
Wife: Rebecca. Children: Edward, John, Benjamin and Samuel Bolton. Exec: Rebecca Taber.
Witnesses: John Harper, Evan Morgan, Paul Isaac Voto.

REDWITZER, CATHERINE. Plymouth, Co. of Philadelphia. Widow. Dec. 15, 1759. Oct. 4, 1760. L.532.
Children: Sarah Wagstaff and Elizabeth Caughlin. Son-in-Law: James Wagstaff. Negro woman: Moll. Exec: Simon Syron, Thomas Rose, James Stroud.
Witnesses: Joseph Jones, James Wood, John Morris.

WALN, JOSEPH. Norriton, Co. of Philadelphia. March 5, 1759. Oct. 13, 1760. L.536.
Wife: Susanna. Brothers: Nicholas, Richard and Robert. Sisters: Susanna Lewis, Ann Marys and Mary Brown. Nephews and nieces: Richard and Nicholas Waln, William Lewis, Jesse and Joseph Waln, Sarah, Ann and Mary Waln. Father-in-Law: James Paul. Negro man: Solomon. Exec: James Paul, Richard and Robert Waln.
Witnesses: Peter Thomas, Josiah Wood, Israel Jacobs.

ATTWOODD, MARY. City of Philadelphia. Widow. Nov. 12, 1758. Oct. 20, 1760. L.538.
Child: Mary Pennery. Exec: John Okely [of Bethleham, Co. of Northampton].
Witnesses: Jacob Franck, Matthias Shade, Christopher Myrtelus.

WEGLY, GEORGE. Lower Salford, Co. of Philadelphia. Sept. 25, 1760. Oct. 21, 1760. L.539.
Wife: [No name given]. Children: Abraham, Anne Mary, Elizabeth, Catherine, George, Margaret and John. Son-in-Law: Frederick Gable. Exec: George Schamback, Leonard Berkheimer.
Witnesses: Conrad Gerkes, Adam Staut, Andrew Zeigler.

ROBERTS, ROBERT. Gwynedd, Co. of Philadelphia. Carpenter. Aug. 14, 1760. Oct. 29, 1760. L.541.
Wife: Sarah. Children: Ellin, Cadwalader, Joseph, Ann Mary and Hannah. Brother-in-Law: Edward Ambler. Cousins and Guardians: John and Eldad Roberts.
Witnesses: Samuel Evans, George Maris.

JANSEN, DIRK. Germantown, Co. of Philadelphia. Yeoman. Jan. 11, 1755. Nov. 1, 1760. L.542.
Children: John, Richard, Ann, Catherine and Rebecca. Son-in-Law: Thomas Nedrow. Grandchildren: Dirk and Daniel Lukens, Mary Reser, Hannah Spencer and Rebecca Lukens. Overseers of the Meeting of Friends. Exec: Richard, Catherine and Rebecca Jansen.
Witnesses: Christian Warner, John Bowman, John Knor.

JOHNSON, JOHN. Upper Dublin, Co. of Philadelphia. Oct. 19. 1760. Nov. 1, 1760. L.547.
Wife: Marget. Children: John and Ann. Brother: William. Guardian: William Johnson. Exec: Marget Johnson.
Witnesses: John Fitzwater, Isaac Knight.

JOURDAN, JOHN. City of Philadelphia. Sept. 22, 1744/5. Nov. 1, 1760. L.548.
Nephews and Nieces: John and Elizabeth Willcocks, Alexander and Elizabeth Willcocks. Exec: John Willcocks Senr. and Elizabeth Willcocks.
Witnesses: George McCall, John Yeates.
Codicil: July 10, 1760.
Witnesses: Thomas Barclay, Samuel Gillaspey.

GRIFFITH, ABRAHAM. Rockhill, Co. of Bucks, Penna. Cordwainer. May 25, 1760. Nov. 30, 1760. L.550.
Wife: Hannah. Children: Isaac, Abraham, Jonathan and Mary Morgan. Grandchildren: Hannah Bucor, Samuel and Sarah Griffith, Isaac Beshire. Exec: Isaac Griffith.
Witnesses: John Dennis, Kezia Dennis, Deborah Morgan (her mark).

OVERHOLT, JACOB. Plumsted, Co. of Bucks, Penna. Yeoman. June 28, 1760. Nov. 7, 1760. L.552.
Wife: Barbere. Children: Jacob, Abraham, Magdalin Landis, Anna Kolp, Elizabeth Kolp, Mary Bebehiver, Hester Packman, Barbara

Rosenberger and Sarah Landis. Sons-in-Law: David and Tillman Kolp, Daniel Bebehiver, Henry Rusenberger, Rodolf Landis, George Packman and Abraham Landis. Exec: Jacob Overholt, Abram Landis.
Witnesses: Frederick Saul, Dise Tisnman.

SUTTON, GEORGE. June 19, 1759. Nov. 12, 1760. M.1.
Legatees: Mother, (Name not given) and Nieces, Alice and Ann. Exec: Brother William.
Witnesses: Paul Isaac Voto, Aulay McAulay.

CARLILE, JOHN. Aug. 14, 1760. Nov. 12, 1760. M.1.
Exec. and sole Legatee: Wife Elisabeth.
Witnesses: John Jackson, James Stuart.

HALL, JOSEPH. City of Philadelphia. Joyner. Oct. 10, 1760. Nov. 19, 1760. M.3.
Beneficiaries: "The poor of the congregation to which I belong." Exec: Wife Ann and Thomas Charlton.
Witnesses: Joseph Pursell, Paul Isaac and Sarah Voto.

BREESON, JAMES. May 26, 1760. Nov. 27, 1760. M.3.
Legatees: Mother Mary, brothers Edward and Hugh. Exec: John Jones.
Witnesses: Andrew Stewart, Paul Isaac Voto.

WOOD, JAMES. Plimouth, Co. of Philadelphia. Yeoman. Oct. 31,1760. Dec. 1, 1760. M.4.
Children: Margaret (Lawrence), Hannah, Elizabeth, James, John and Daws. Exec: Wife Catherine.
Witnesses: Jacob Roberts, Richard Jackson, Thos. Rose.

WILLIAMS, ROLAND. March 19, 1760. Dec. 2, 1760. M.5.
Exec. and sole Legatee: Mary Pemford.
Witness: Samuel Uppowen.

FITZWATER, GEORGE. Upper Dublin, Co. of Philadelphia. 8 mo. 14, 1760. Dec. 3, 1760. M.6.
Children: Joseph, Martha, Thomas, Abel, Mary, Ruth and Elizabeth. Exec: Son Joseph.
Witnesses: Peter and Nathan Clever, John Fitzwater.

CARROLL, PATRICK. City of Philadelphia. Sept. 26, 1760. Dec. 6, 1760. M.8.
Legatees: Brother William, sisters Mary, Catherine and Grace. Exec: William Hussey of Philadelphia.
Witnesses: John Power, Thos. Keefe.

THOMAS, OWEN. Co. of Chester, Penna. Yeoman. Sept. 29, 1760. Dec. 6, 1760. M.8.
Wife: Elanor. Children: Morris, Elizabeth, Rachel, Mary, David, Sarah and Owen. Grandchildren: Joseph, Elizabeth and Elanor Alison, (names of others not given). Sons-in-Law: Joseph Thomas, Richard Jury, Abner Evans and Oliver Alison. Exec: Son Owen.
Witnesses: Jno. McFarland, Owen Williams (his mark), Morgan Morgan (his mark).

BUCKSON, JOHN. Co. of Philadelphia. Yeoman. April 10, 1755. Dec. 12, 1760. M.11.
Exec. and sole Legatee: Wife Abigal.
Witnesses: Zecharia Davis, Richard Moore.

NICKSON, RACHEL. City of Philadelphia. Widow. Aug. 9, 1750. Dec. 17, 1760. M.12.
Daughter-in-Law: Rebecca Smith. Cousins: Joseph Rakestraw's widow and children (names not given). Kinsmen: James Chattham and John Bissell. All of the above are legatees together with Phebe Morris in trust for the Monthly Meeting of Women Friends, Philadelphia. Exec: Cousins Henry Warrington of New Jersey (yeoman), Samuel Bissell, Philadelphia, (carpenter) and Hannah Bissell.
Witnesses: Joseph Marriott, Zachariah Barr, Samuel Lewis.

NASH, WILLIAM. Co. of Bucks, Penna. Nov. 18, 1760. Dec. 23, 1760. M.13.
Children: By first wife, Elsie (wife of Wm. Tyson), Ann (wife of Joseph Tyson), Katherine (wife of Benj. Hendricks); by 2nd wife, William, Madeline (wife of Jacob Frets), Barbara (Frets) and Martin Overhold; by 3rd wife, Mary, Elizabeth, Joseph and Abraham. Exec: Wife: Angnes and Wm.Tyson.
Witnesses: Abraham Schwartz, Joseph Nash.

STEINMETZ, DANIEL. City of Philadelphia. Shopkeeper. May 6, 1760. Dec. 23, 1760. M.14.

Children: Daniel, Anna Maria, Jacob, John, Elizabeth, Catherine, Susannah and Margaret. Exec: Wife Ann Maria and sons Daniel and John.
Witnesses: Peter Miller, Jno. Parrish, Daniel Rees.

ROBERTS, AARON. Narriton, Co. of Philadelphia. Yeoman. Nov. 11, 1760. Dec. 24, 1760. M.17.
Parents: Aaron and Sarah. Brothers: Moses and Joseph, Legatees. Overseer: Michael Pugh. Exec: Brother Moses.
Witnesses: Michael Pugh, John Bell.

DIXON, ROBERT. City of Philadelphia. Tavernkeeper. Nov. 7, 1760. Dec. 26, 1760. M.19.
Wife: Sarah. Child: Sarah. Exec: Brother-in-Law Joseph Ogden and cousin Thomas Sheppard.
Witnesses: Jonathan Durell, Robert Flemming.

DOAN, DANIEL. City of Philadelphia. Nov. 29, 1760. Dec. 27, 1760. M.20.
Children: Deborah, Mary and Thomas. Exec: Wife Sarah.
Witnesses: Joseph Doan, Henry Shade, John Ross.

HARRINGTON, EDWARD. City of Philadelphia. Carpenter. Nov. 30, 1760. Dec. 29, 1760. M.21.
Legatees: Nephew Timothy Harrington Jr. of Cashell, Ire., Robert Harding, Philadelphia, and contingent legacies to friends Rev. Geo. Hunter (Charles Co., Md.) and Rev. John Lewis (Cecil Co., Md.). Exec: Wife Abigail.
Witnesses: Joseph Cauffman, William Gallagher, John Walsh.

THOMAS, TIMOTHY. Abington, Co. of Philadelphia. Dec. 2, 1760. Jan. 6, 1761. M.23.
Wife: Elizabeth. Children: Abednego, Mary and others, names not given. Exec: Brethern Joshua Thomas and Richard Treat.
Witnesses: Jas. Caldwell, Hugh Caldwell, Malachi Treat.

LLOYD, SAMUEL. City of Philadelphia. Merchant. 12 mo. 23, 1760. Jan. 4, 1761. M.25.
Mother: Sarah. Grandmother: Martha Roberts. Brother: Robert. Sister: Martha. All are legatees, except George Roberts. Exec: Mother and Geo. Roberts.

Witnesses: George Owen, Isaac Parrish, Hugh Roberts.

WOOD, JOHN. City of Philadelphia. Watchmaker. July 15, 1760. Jan. 16, 1761. M.25.
Exec. and Children: John, Mary and Elizabeth.
Witnesses: Thos. Charlton, John Reily, Martha Dowdney.

LEE, BENJAMIN. City of Philadelphia. Sadler. Oct. 17, 1760. Jan. 17, 1761. M.28.
Children: Joseph and Sarah (wife of Geo. Kidd). Exec: Son and Son-in-Law.
Witnesses: Peter Miller, Thos. Preston.

DIEHL, MAGDALEN. Northern Liberties, City of Philadelphia. Widow. March 3, 1761. March 17, 1761. M.29.
Children: George and Rachel (names of grandchildren not given).
Beneficiaries: Rev. Parson Conrad Steiner and The Dutch Reformed (Calvin) Church of Philadelphia. Exec: William Clampffer.
Witnesses: Adam Streiker, Conrad Leboldt, Henry Steinmetz.

TILL, JOHN. City of Philadelphia. Sept. 23, 1760. Jan. 19, 1761. M.30.
Children: John, Thomas and William. Sons-in-Law: William Carter and Robert Patterson. Exec: Wife Brightwood and Capt. Walter Goodman.
Witnesses: James West, Robert Hendrickson.

MILLER, ELIZABETH. City of Philadelphia. Widow of Thomas. June 24, 1760. Jan. 27, 1761. M. 32.
Brothers: Peter and Thomas. Beneficiaries: Grandchildren, Theodore, Elizabeth, Mary, Grace and Ann Stagg; nephew John Hutton; cousins Peter and James (sons of brother Peter Patton); children of cousins Elizabeth Garrett; Peter Hatton (and wife), a son of brother Thomas; Hannah wife of Joseph Lownds; sister Jane (widow of brother Thomas); nephews Thomas, Joseph and Peter (sons of Thomas); Nathan son of Joseph Wild, late of Ireland; Israel Pemberton and John Regnell in trust for the Friends Monthly Meeting of Philadelphia.
Exec: Nephew Thomas Hatton and Charles Jones.
Witnesses: Andrew McNair, Pluncket Fleeson, Samuel Howell.
Codicil: No date.
Signed in presence of same witnesses.

ASH, HENRY. City of Philadelphia. Mariner. Nov. 22, 1759. Jan. 28, 1761. M.35.
Children: Names not given. Exec: Wife Rebecca and Abel James (merchant).
Witnesses: Peter Miller, Caspar Weister, George James.

KNIGHT, JOHN. City of Philadelphia. Baker. Jan. 5, 1761. Jan. 29, 1761. M.36.
Children: Charles, John and Rachel. Exec: Wife Elizabeth.
Witnesses: Benj. Davis, Joseph Thornhill, Austin Bartholomew.

MASTERS, WILLIAM, ESQUIRE. City of Philadelphia. Proved Jan. 30, 1761. M.38.
Wife: Mary. Children: William (mother Winefred Robeson), Mary, Sarah and Rachel. Guardians and Exec: Wife, Benjamin Franklin, Joseph Fox, Joseph Gallaway, Esquires.
Witnesses: Townsend White, William Henry, Emannel Josiah.

MC CARTY, CHARLES. Co. of Bucks, Penna. Lawyer. March 28, 1760. Jan. 31, 1761. M.39.
Children: Jane and Daniel. Exec: Wife, Rebecca.
Witnesses: Paul Isaac Voto, Sarah Voto.

HALCOMB (HOLCOMB), MARY. City of Philadelphia. Widow. Jan. 23, 1761. Feb. 4, 1761. M.40.
Children: Rebecca (Garrignes), Mary (Walton), Susannah (Vandeering), Sophia, Elizabeth (Hallowell), Hannah (Jones) and Sarah (Lewis). Grandchildren: Mary and Martha Hallowell; Mary Hellings; Mary and Rachel Garrignes; Tacy Vandeering; Jacob Halcomb; Jacob Garrignes, Joseph Hallowell; Jacob Gills; Charles and John Vandeering; Jacob, Jesse, Isaac and Thomas Walton. All of above named are legatees, together with Susannah and Mary, daughters of Joshua Morris. Exec. and Trustees: Sons-in-Law Joseph Hallowell and John Vandeering.
Witnesses: Samuel Hurford, Sarah and Richard Waggstaffe.
Codicil: Jan. 26, 1761.
Witnesses: Mary Care, Hannah Oldfield.

JERRARD, RICHARD. City of Philadelphia. Wheelwright. June 15, 1761. Feb. 5, 1761. M.43.
Son: John. Exec: Wife Mary.

Witnesses: James Macky, Jas. Benbridge, Paul Isaac Voto.

MORTON, GEORGE. City of Philadelphia. Gentleman. Jan. 22, 1761. Feb. 6, 1761. M.45.
Wife: Sarah. Son: George. Exec: Samuel Tucker and Joseph Philips of Trenton, N.J., merchants.
Witnesses: Edward and Anne Croston, John Middleton.

VENSEN, JONATHAN. City of Philadelphia. Shipwright. Jan. 28, 1760. Feb. 9, 1761. M.46.
Exec. and sole Legatee: Friend James Berrimans of Philadelphia, shipwright.
Witnesses: John Manchant, Wm. White, Paul Isaac Voto.

RICE, WILLIAM. City of Philadelphia. Shipwright. Jan. 19, 1761. Feb. 10, 1761. M.47.
Sons: John, William, Joseph and Thomas. Father-in-Law: John Norris. Exec: Wife Rebekah and son John.
Witnesses: William Pearson, Hugh Thompson, Griffie Vaughan.

COMLY, JOHN. City of Philadelphia. Yeoman. Nov. 26, 1760. Feb. 14, 1761. M.49.
Children: Abraham, Abigail, Isaac, Jacob, John, Mary and Susannah. Exec: Wife Hannah and sons Isaac and Jacob.
Witnesses: Benj. Mason, Abigail Comly Junr. (her mark), Edward Richey.

SMITH, FREDERICK. Co. of Philadelphia. Dec. 10, 1759. Feb. 18, 1761. M.50.
Children: John, Jacob, Frederick, Nelly and Valentine. Exec: Wife Mary and Henry Pawling, of Providence, Esq.
Witnesses: Christian Recoup, Peter Bunn, Philip Fitzsimons.

POWELL, JOSEPH. Co. of Chester, Penna. March 31, 1760. Feb. 19, 1761. M.51.
Wife: Name not given. Children: John, Joseph and daughters names not given. Grandchildren: Benjamin and Samuel Powell. Sons-in-Law: Peter Worral, David Sharpless, Thomas Pearson. Daughter-in-Law: Susannah Powell. Overseers: John Morris, Henry Lawrence. Exec: Sons John and Joseph.
Witnesses: Henry Lawrence, Junr., Joel Willis, Abraham Thomas.

MOORE, ALEXANDER. City of Philadelphia. Peruke maker. Feb. 16, 1761. Feb. 24, 1761. M.52.
Legatees: Two daughters of brother Chichester Moore; niece Jane (daughter of late sister Jane Campbell); brother-in-law Alexander Campbell; sister Ann Thompson and her son Alexander; nephew David Campbell; kinsmen Peter (son of Wm. Roth), James Mallaby; wife's relation James (son of Jas. Willson Senr.); Rev. Wm. Macclednacham of Philadelphia; friend David Hall Junr. (son of David); brother Chichester Moore. Exec: Wife Mary, Thomas Charlton and Jno. Bleakly, shop keepers.
Witnesses: Thos. Rogers, Wm. Scott, John Reily.

JERVIS, THOMAS. Co. of Philadelphia. Sept. 11, 1760. Feb. 25, 1761. M.54.
Exec: Wife Elizabeth and cousin and legatee Jervis James.
Witnesses: Jos. Reynolds, Simon Stewert, Jacob Whittman.

DUTTON, ISAAC. Kensington, Co. of Philadelphia. Oct. 9, 1760. March 2, 1761. M.55.
Children: Elizabeth and Sarah. Children-in-Law: George, Lidia and Mary Wright. Exec: Wife Mary, Abram Coates and Henry Dennis.
Witnesses: Joseph Lynn, Wm. Pearson, Henry Dennis.

BLACK, ROBERT. City of Philadelphia. Cabinet maker. Nov. 28, 1760. March 3, 1761. M.57.
Exec: Wife Sarah and friend James Black, merchant, (legatee).
Witnesses: Colen Johnston, Wm. Muir, Moses Ghiselin.
Codicil: No date.
Witnesses: Wm. Spyde, William Young.

EAVE, ELIZABETH. Helverstone, Lower Dublin, Co. of Philadelphia. Widow. Nov. 3, 1760. March 4, 1761. M.58.
Children: Margaret, Christe, Daniel, Harman, Nicholis, Susannah Crest and Richard. Exec: Sons Harman and Nicolis.
Witnesses: Michael and Elizabeth Grover, John Vanhery.

ENGERS, ABRAHAM. Co. of Chester, Penna. Bachelor. Jan. 14, 1761. March 6, 1761. M.60.
Brothers: Yost and Jacob. Nieces: Magdalena, Mary and Ann Engers (daughters of Yost); Esther and Francis (children of Jacob). Exec: Andrew Hate.

Witnesses: Bernhard Smith, Jacob Beery.

ARBUCKLE, JAMES. Northern Liberties, Co. of Philadelphia. Shop keeper. Dec. 12, 1760. March 10, 1761. M.61.
Wife: Rachel. Children: Grace (wife of Jonathan Thomas), Hannah (wife of Jno. Vanhorn), Thomas Hilborne and Mary Paul (first wife's children). Exec: Said sons-in-law.
Witnesses: Thomas Barton, Samuel Noble, Paul Isaac Voto.

BARRY, EDWARD. Nov. 12, 1756. March 19, 1761. M.64.
Exec. and sole Legatee: Elizabeth Hohn.
Witnesses: Anthony Armbruster, Stephen Fourage.

SMITH, BERNHARD. Co. of Chester, Penna. Feb. 22, 1761. March 20, 1761. M.64.
Exec: Wife, Mary and Valentine Kelly.
Witnesses: Andrew Hate (his mark), Abraham Grob.

ENGLE, CASPER. Coventry, Co. of Chester, Penna. Shoemaker. Oct. 14, 1760. March 24, 1761. M.66.
Sister: Magdalen. Children: Elizabeth and David. Exec: Wife Elizabeth.
Witnesses: Jacob Grumbacker, Martin Urner.

GERBER, JACOB. City of Philadelphia. Stay maker. Feb. 21, 1761. March 26, 1761. M.67.
Children: Charles, Mary and Bettsey (and unknown child). Exec: Wife Mary and brother-in-law Isaac Rouch.
Witnesses: John Kearsley, Christian Schibeler.

MOYER, CASPER. Harford, Co. of Berks, Penna. May 10, 1760. March 31, 1761. M.68.
Wife: Elizabatha. Son: Isaac. Stepchildren: John, Daniel, Abraham and Ann Buop, whose father was Conrad Buop. Exec: Brothers-in-law Abraham Stover and Baltzar Zimmerman.
Witnesses: Henry Stover, Casper Bowman.

ANDREWS, MARY. City of Philadelphia. June 10, 1757. April 2, 1761. M.70.
Legatees: George and Jane Brintnall (issue of niece Esther); William Peters (son of Wm. Peters, Esquire), issue of niece Mary; niece Esther

Brintnall, widow; Mordecai son of brother Mordecai Andrews; Peter and Isaac (children of of brother Edward Andrews); Minister and Church Wardens of Christ Church, Philadelphia; also the poor of said church; niece Mary Andrews; niece Sarah Jewell; niece Rebecca Robinson and three children; Sarah daughter of Capt. Thos. Lloyd; William Peters Senr. and his wife Mary; Richard (son of William Peters); friend Love (wife of Abram Vinenig); niece Denny Oliver, widow; friends Ann Pidgeon of Trenton, N.J. and her sister Catherine Pierce of Burlington, N.J.; Sarah (wife of nephew Alexander Parker); Alexander Parker and Sarah, his wife, and children (names not given); friend Ezekell Shepherd (joiner); friend Benj. Price (Attorney-at-Law); Evan Morgan (cooper); friend Ann Rundle; the Pennsylvania Hospital; nephew Nehemiah Andrews; friend Sarah Griscomb, spinster; friend Barbara Grant, widow; Mrs. Moore (wife of Wm. Moore of Moore Hall, Chester Co., Esquire); Henry Jenkinson (clerk to Wm. Peters Senr.); great niece Mary (daughter of Mary Peters). Exec: William Peters Senr., Benjamin Price, Evan Morgan.
Witnesses: Abraham Mason, Wm. West, Daniel Rundle.
Codicil: Dec. 22, 1758.
Witnesses: Daniel and Ann Rundle.

SMITH, JOHN. Co. of Chester, Penna. Feb. 6, 1761. April 3, 1761. M.82.
Children: Valentine, Gertroud and Mary Elizabeth. Exec: Wife Elizabeth and brother Valentine.
Witnesses: John Henge, John Sneider.

ROBESON, WILLIAM. Plymouth Township, Co. of Philadelphia. Tailor. 7 mo. 27, 1744. April 4, 1761. M.83.
Wife: Gaynor. Brothers: James and Philip and their children (legatees) of Lankershire, England. Half-brother: Robert. Exec: Joseph Jones, Edward Stroud.
Witnesses: Saml. Davis, Jno. Bell, Jonathan Jones.

BOWEN, JOHN. Co. of Philadelphia. Laborer. March 18, 1761. April 4, 1761. M.85.
Exec. and Legatees: Sister-in-law Elizabeth (widow of brother Thomas) and her children (names not given); Cattrin Jones (widow of Peter) and Peter Evans.
Witnesses: Robert Jones, Jacob Williams, John Barry.

HANS (HOUSE), HERONIMAS. Co. of Philadelphia. Yeoman. Oct. 21, 1760. April 10, 1761. M.86.
Wife: Margaret. Legatees: Grandchildren: George, Heronimas, Valentine, Henry, Elizabeth Grate, Anna Marrll and Ann Elizabeth, also the Church of Providence, Limerick Township. Exec: John Cappler, Valentine Stanemetz.
Witnesses: Valentine Kelly (his mark), Henry Kelly, Henry Vanderslice.

CUPP, DANIEL. Co. of Philadelphia. Weaver. April 2, 1761. April 13, 1761. M.89.
Wife: Magdalena. Children: Mary and Daniel. Exec: John Martin.
Witnesses: Jacob Copler, Philip Sheisnaberger, Archibald McClean Jr.

EVANS, GEORGE. Co. of Philadelphia. Yeoman. March 8, 1761. April 15, 1761. M.90.
Children: George, Mary (wife of Enoch Evan), James, Hannah, William and Samuel. Beneficiary: Christian Shead (servant). Exec: Wife Elizabeth and son George.
Witnesses: George Brooke, George and David Evans.

EVANS, MARY. Limerick Township, Co. of Philadelphia. Widow of Owen. Signed Sept. 10, 1758. M.93.
Legatees: Ann (wife of Edward Lane), Mary (wife of James Brooke), Gwenefred (wife of John Umstat), Jane, David, Thomas and Benjamin.
Grandson: Rees Evans. Exec: Son David and Edward Lane.
Witnesses: George Brooke, Jacob Hoven, George Evans.
Codicil: Feb. 26, 1760.
Witnesses: Same names.

BROOKE, GEORGE. Co. of Philadelphia. Yeoman. March 28, 1761. April 15, 1761. M.95.
Legatees: Step sisters Mary Hoven, Ann Uptergrave, Rachel and Elizabeth Lanchaster, Abagail Attlip and Hannah Hollam; step-brother John Barlow; Abraham (son of Abraham Uptegrave); Mary (daughter of Evan David, blacksmith); the Friends Meeting of New Providence; John, George, Mary, Ann, William and Mathias (children of brother William Brooke); Anna, William, Ann, Thomas, Elinor, Rees, George and Mathew (children of brother Mathias Brooke); and brothers William and Mathias. Exec: Wife (name not given), brother Mathias and brother-in-law George Evans.

Witnesses: Rose Manlesby, David Evans, Israel Jacobs.

CAMPBELL, DAVID. Late of New Castle, Del. Peruke maker. March 2, 1761. April 24, 1761. M.98.
Son: David. Exec: Brother Edward Campbell of Philadelphia.
Witnesses: Thos. Rodgers, William Scott, Henry Bromet.

COATES, MOSES. Co. of Chester. April 14, 1761. April 25, 1761. M.99.
Wife: Name not given. Children: Elizabeth, Moses, Benjamin, Aaron and Thomas. Grandchildren: Susannah and Priscilla Madenhall, Elizabeth (daughter of Moses Coates, Junr.). Exec: Moses Coates, Junr.
Witnesses: Joseph Griffith, George Skofield, Jonathan Coates.

RAMBO, KATHERINE. Kingsess, Co. of Philadelphia. Widow of Mounts. March 23, 1761. May 2, 1761. M.100.
Father: Swan Boon. Children: Swan, Mary and Ann. Grandchildren: Katherine and Margaret Campbell. Exec: Son Swan and Thomas Thomas.
Witnesses: Peter Yocom, John Trapnall.

HOLT, JOSHUA. Co. of Philadelphia. Yeoman. Aug. 8, 1761. May 5, 1761. M.101.
Children: Benjamin, Mordicai, Joshua, Susannah, Rebecca, Sarah (Walton), Ann (Parry) and Mary (Morris). Grandchildren: Sarah Walton, Hannah Parry and Sarah Holt. Son-in-Law: James Morris. Exec: Joshua Holt and John Lukens.
Witnesses: Thomas Barns, William Lukens, Wm. Lukens, Junr.

MC CALL, SAMUEL, SENR. City of Philadelphia. Merchant. April 25, 1761. May 5, 1761. M.103.
Wife: Ann. Children: Ann, Isabell, Catherine, Margaret, Elinor and Mary. Exec: Wife, Archibald McCall and Joseph Swift.
Witnesses: William Henry, Benjamin Chew, Alexander Stuart.

ROBINSON, GANOR. Plymoth, Co. of Philadelphia. Widow. April 29, 1761. May 6, 1761. M.105.
Beneficiaries: Ellis Hugh, Joshua Richards, Margaret Jackson, Jacob John and Robert Roberts, Henry Cunrod, Joshua Dickinson and Plymoth Meeting. Exec: Joseph Jones.

Witnesses: James Stroud, Joseph Dickinson.

JOHNSON, MARY. City of Philadelphia. Widow of Samuel. Oct. 15, 1760. May 15, 1761. M.106.
Legatees: Brother Thomas Burch, wife and children (names not given); James Trumble and his wife (Christian names not given); friends Elizabeth Carrah, Jane Clennen and Anna Bell. Exec: Thos. Burch, Thomas Lawrence of Philadelphia.
Witnesses: Christopher Ludwick, Henry Duff, Paul Isaac Voto.
Codicil: No date.
By its terms the following additional legatees are named: nephews Thos., Cheadle, John, Benjamin, William and Francis Burch and nieces Mary (Hullet), Kiza (Cock), Sarah and Ann Burch. Upon the death of Thos. Burch, nephew Cheadle Burch is to succeed him as Exec.

THOMAS, JOHN. Chiltenham, Co. of Philadelphia. Yeoman. April 19, 1761. May 19, 1761. M.108.
Children: John, Elizabeth and Elioner. Sister: Edith Hough.
Beneficiaries: The Baptist Society and the Germantown School.
Guardians: Brother-in-law Joseph Hart and Isaac Hough. Exec: Said brother-in-law.
Witnesses: Jacob Benner, Isaac Leech, Olimpas Jodon.

HENRY, JACOB. City of Philadelphia. Merchant. April 14, 1760. May 21, 1761. M.111.
Legatees: Mother Frumatt Henry; brothers Solomon, Philip and Jonathan Henry (merchant, London); cousins Bernard and Michael Gratz (of Philadelphia), merchants; sister Tracey (wife of Isaac Prager); nieces Getlah, Deborah and Grace; the Jews Burying Ground of Philadelphia; the Synagogue in Longendorff in Upper Silesia; and Exec. David Franks and Mathias Bush of Philadelphia, merchants.
Witnesses: Peter Sonmans, William Bradford.

ABERCROMBIE, JAMES. City of Philadelphia. Mariner. Dec. 11, 1758. May 21, 1761. M.113.
Wife: Margaret. Son: James. Brother: David. Sister: Jannet.
Legatees: Contingent upon the death of son James, friend John (son of Alex Stedman). Exec: Charles and Alexander Stedman, Samuel McCall.
Witnesses: Robert Harper, Johannes Geo. Waine.

SYNG, PHILIP. City of Philadelphia. Silversmith. Sept. 25, 1760. May 22, 1761. M.114.
Sisters and Brother, Legatees: Abigail, Esther, Elizabeth, Martha, Joseph, Hannah, Ann, Mary, Christiana and Sarah. Exec: Father, Philip.
Witnesses: Susannah Humphreys, Thomas Sparrow, Jacob Read.

FERRIS, JOHN. City of Philadelphia. Cooper. March 16, 1761. May 26, 1761. M.115.
Child: Rachel. Exec: Wife Esther.
Witnesses: Thomas Marshall, Robert Craig, Richard Tyson.

COLLIER, MARY. Upper Dublin, Co. of Philadelphia. May 16, 1761. May 27, 1761. M.116.
Children: Thomas, Elizabeth (Hart), and Mary (Daniel).
Grandchildren: Mary Ward and William Vincent. Exec: Son Thomas.
Witnesses: Robert Heaton, John Paul and Magdaline Clarke (her mark).

CRAIGMILES, ANDREW. City of Philadelphia. Seaman. June 14, 1759. June 10, 1761. M.117.
Legatees: Sister Margaret (of Ireland), friend Robert Conn. Exec: Friend Robert Conn.
Witnesses: Wm. Oliphant, John Green.

LYCAN, HANCE. Co. of Philadelphia. Yeoman. May 29, 1761. June 15, 1761. M.118.
Children: Mary and Andrew. Exec: Wife Margaret and son Andrew.
Witnesses: John Hufty, Silas Crispin, Thomas Stammers.

RAWLE, FRANCIS. City of Philadelphia. Merchant. June 5, 1761. June 15, 1761. M.119.
Wife: Rebecca. Children: Anna, William and Margaret (and unknown child). Legatees: Cousin Sarah (daughter of Uncle Francis Rawle); Aunt Jane England; friend Samuel Shoemaker, merchant. Exec: Wife, Samuel Shoemaker and Joshua Howell.
Witnesses: James Cooper, Jos. Galloway, Samuel Rhoads, Junr.

JESSOP, ROBERT. City of Philadelphia. Merchant. June 5, 1761. June 17, 1761. M.121.

Sole legatee: Brother Francis Jessop of Dublin, Ire., merchant. Exec: James Eddy, Philadelphia, merchant.
Witnesses: Christopher Marshall, Wm. Harvey, James Freeland.

PAUL, JAMES. Abington, Co. of Philadelphia. Yeoman. 12 mo. 8, 1760. June 23, 1761. M.122.
Children: Robert, John, Jacob, Susannah, Hannah, Margaret (Edge) and Ann (Knight). Brother-in-Law: Robert Jones. Father-in-Law: Morris Morris. Exec: Wife Sarah and sons Robert and John.
Witnesses: Thomas Fletcher, Moses Leckerd, Jno. Luken.
Codicil: 12 mo. 11, 1760.
Witnesses: Same.

STRETTELL, ROBERT. City of Philadelphia. Merchant. June 21, 1750. June 26, 1761. M.127.
Children: Amos, John, Frances and Ann. Legatees: Sister-in-law Frances Chamberlin; kinsmen Thos. Rooke; son-in-law Isaac Jones; the exec. for charitable uses. Exec: Wife Chilotesia and son Amos.
Witnesses: William Jeron, Thos. Lloyd, Mark Kuhl, Junr.
Codicil: Aug. 22, 1750.
Witnesses: Chas. Brockden, Mary Lisle, Peter Miller, Junr.

DOTWEILER, HANS. Co. of Philadelphia. Weaver. Dec. 17, 1750. June 26, 1761. M.130.
Wife: Susannah. Children: Henry, Jacob, John, Joseph, Anna, Mary and Susannah. Exec: Sons Jacob and John.
Witnesses: Paul Fret, Henry and Isaac Kolb, Robt. Jones.

RESER, BERNHARD. Co. of Philadelphia. Yeoman. Oct. 18, 1760. June 27, 1760. M.133.
Wife: Elizabeth. Children: Magdalene, Elizabeth, John, Battas and Sophia. Exec: Son Battas, Jno. Jones and Thos. Rose.
Witnesses: Wm. Wilson, Joseph North, Nathan Thomas.

JOHNSON, JOSEPH. City of Philadelphia. Tin plate worker. June 2, 1761. June 30, 1761. M.137.
Wife: Martha. Children: Lydia and Joseph. Exec: Wife, brother-in-law Samuel Sansom and kinsman John Drinker.
Witnesses: Hezekiah Williams, Abraham Mitchell, Paul Isaac Voto.

HALL, SAMUEL. City of Philadelphia. Bricklayer. June 15,1761. July 6,1761. M.139.
Children: Samuel and Edward. Exec: Wife Mary and Joseph Fox, Philadelphia.
Witnesses: Henry and Joseph Hollen.

MUSHETT, JOHN. Cumberland, Co. of Philadelphia. Innkeeper. Oct. 12, 1754. July 13, 1761. M.140.
Wife: Margaret. Children: Jane (wife of Joseph McFarran), William and Arsball. Exec: Son William and Col. Benjamin Chambers.
Witnesses: Jno. Reily, John Bowen, Thomas Coombe.

JONES, JOHN. City of Philadelphia. Cordwainer. Dec. 26, 1760. July 13, 1761. M.141.
Father-in-Law: Charles Finney. Legatees: Henry Hall (of Mansfield, N.J.) and his children; Parnell Gibbs, grandson of said Henry Hall; five children of Samuel Finney, to wit: Charles, Rebecca, Joseph, Mary and Rachel; John and Mary Searson; sister-in-law Elizabeth Tod; friends Ann Redman; Elizabeth Lloyd; Ann wife of Capt. Alexander Sage; Samuel Garrigues (Philadelphia, peruke maker) and his wife; Joshua Richey, of Philadelphia, cordwainer; Anthony Benezet; John Jones, Philadelphia, brickmaker; John Guest and wife Elizabeth; Nathaniel Evans, son of Edward Evans; the Penna. Hospital; the overseers and trustees of the Philadelphia public school; and to his five slaves their freedom and annuities. Exec: Israel and James Pemberton, Joseph Fox, merchants of Philadelphia. Witnesses: John Hallowell, Christopher Marshall, Jno. Reily.

EVANS, ELLENOR. Former husband Griffith Evans. Upper Merion, Co. of Philadelphia. Widow. Jan. 23, 1758. July 18, 1761. M.149.
Child: Elizabeth (wife of David Stephens). Grandchildren: Morris and Eleanor. Exec: Henry Paulin, Thos. Watters, James David.
Witnesses: John and Abigail Brickson (her mark), Jno. Moore.
Codicil: April 16, 1761.
Witnesses: Danl. Walker, David Francis.

ROBERTS, ANN. Gwynead, Co. of Philadelphia. Widow. Aug. 2, 1760. July 25, 1761. M.151.
Children: Ann (wife of Owen Evans), Evan and Robert.
Grandchildren: Isaiah, Elizabeth and Joan Evans; Tacy and Phebe

(children of Wm. Roberts). Trustees: Cousins Rowland and John Evans, also Witnesses. Exec: Sons Robert and Evan and Owen Evans.

ROBERTS, EVAN. Gwynead, Co. of Philadelphia. Yeoman. 5 mo. 24, 1750. July 25, 1761. M.153.
Children: David, Robert, Ellis, William and Grace. Trustees: John Roberts, William Foulke. Exec: Wife Jane and son William.
Witnesses: John Jones, Thomas (his mark) and Rowland Evans.
Codicil: 8 mo. 6, 1752.
Witnesses: Rowland Evans, Edward Evans.

NILE, TOBIAS. City of Philadelphia. Corker [Cooker?]. Jan. 26, 1759. July 27, 1761. M.155.
Children: Names not given. Exec: Wife Alice.
Witnesses: Thomas Chilow, Wm. Perkins.

KING, JOHN. Co. of Philadelphia. Joyner. June 1, 1761. Aug. 1, 1767. M.156.
Children: John and Mary. Brothers: Michael and George. Exec: Wife Margareth and father-in-law Joseph Smith. Exec. and Guardians: Brother George and brother-in-law Henry Smith.
Witnesses: George Merchel, Abraham Hedrick.

TITUS, SAMUEL. Co. of Philadelphia. Yeoman. 4 mo. 15, 1761. Aug. 1, 1761. M.159.
Parents: Salis and Sarah. Sister: Pheby Perry. Nieces [*sic*]: Silas, Thomas and Sarah. Exec: Mother and Uncle Thomas Townsend.
Witnesses: William Walmsley, James Thornton, Jno. Townsend.

ROTH, GEORGE. June 20, 1761. Aug. 1, 1761. M.160.
Wife: Mary. Son: Lewis. Exec: Thomas Grumling.
Witnesses: Henry Grumling, Thomas Grumling.

KREIDER, MICHAEL. Co. of Philadelphia. Blacksmith. July 7, 1761. Aug. 1, 1761. M.161.
Children: John, Abraham, Daniel, Jacob, Catherine, Magdalena and David. Beneficiaries: Conrad Knepper, for the benefit of the poor of Hatfield Township, Pa. Exec: Wife Catherine and son John.
Witnesses: Henry Ress, Abraham Heiderick.

MARSHALL, THOMAS. City of Philadelphia. Cooper. May 27, 1761. Aug. 10, 1761. M.163.
Child: Deborah. Exec: Wife Ann.
Witnesses: William Isaac, Richard Tyson, Peter Thompson.

HERWICK, JOHN. Co. of Bucks, Penna. Oct. 15, 1753. Aug. 11, 1761. M.164.
Children: Catherine (wife of Michael Heider), Paul, Jacob, Nicholas and Mary (Mire). Exec: Sons Jacob and Nicholas.
Witnesses: George Hickerman, John Redrock.

POTTS, JOSHUA. Mooreland, Co. of Philadelphia. Yeoman. Sept. 19, 1757. Aug. 11, 1761. M.165.
Brothers: Nathaniel and William. Children: Thomas, Mary, Anne, Abigail, Rebecca and Hannah. Guardians: Brother William and father-in-law Joseph Borden. Exec: Wife Ann and Joseph Hart.
Witnesses: David Rees, William Hancock, Benjamin Griffith.

SEEHLER, JOHN. Co. of Philadelphia. Yeoman. June 20, 1761. Aug. 12, 1761. M.168.
Children: John, Jacob, Andreas and Abraham (names of daughters not given). Exec: Wife Ann Maria and son Abraham.
Witnesses: Wyand Pennybaker, Christopher Schultz.

LINN, PETER. Co. of Montgomery, Penna. Yeoman. April 21, 1761. Aug. 18, 1761. M.170.
Father-in-Law: Felix Brumer. Children: Anne, Mary (wife of John Adam), William, Peter, John, Dewald, Felix, Ann Margareth and Elizabeth. Exec: Wife Anne Margareth and son Felix.
Witnesses: John Riswick, Andrew Beyer (his mark), David Shultze.

MOWRE, JACOB. Co. of Philadelphia. Yeoman. June 26, 1761. Aug. 18, 1761. M.173.
Children: Peter, Andrew, Jacob, Frederick, Margareth (wife of Paul Rothermel), Veronica (wife of John Shill), Sophia (2nd wife of Paul Rothermel), Barbara (wife of Isaac Berts), Ann, Mary and Catherina. Exec: Wife Sophia and son Andrew.
Witnesses: Conrad Wannemacher (his mark), Jacob Wannemacher, David Shultze.

WEST, CHARLES. City of Philadelphia. Shipwright. Aug. 5, 1761. Aug. 24, 1761. M.177.
Children: James, Charles, Mary (wife of Danl. Cooper), Thomas and Prudence (Warner). Exec: Wife Sarah and sons James and Charles.
Witnesses: Michael Hulings, Paul Isaac Voto, Thomas Gilbert.

COLLINS, MARGARETT. City of Philadelphia. Widow. Oct. 23, 1758. Aug. 25, 1761. M.185.
Children: Sarah and Hannah (wife of Benj. Bowen). Exec: Daughter Sarah.
Witnesses: Cadwallader Evans, John Knight, Robert Owen.

REES, DANIEL. City of Philadelphia. Yeoman. March 26, 1759. Aug. 26, 1761. M.186.
Wife: Ann. Children: Daniel, Thomas, Abel, Elizabeth (Ward), Mary and Evan. Exec: Son Daniel.
Witnesses: John Edwards, Michael Bowre, Israel Jacobs.

JUSTICE, CHARLES. City of Philadelphia. Feb. 14, 1761. Sept. 10, 1761. M.188.
Son: Charles. A contingent bequest is made to a Swede School at Wicaco in said Co. Exec: Wife Rebecca and John Justice.
Witnesses: Mary Robinson, Thos. Thomas.

SULTSER, ANTHONY. Germantown, Co. of Philadelphia. Aug. 29, 1761. Sept. 22, 1761. M.189.
Exec: Wife Barbara.
Witnesses: William Spera, Jno. Adams, Conrad Good.

ELLIS, EVAN. Gwynead, Co. of Philadelphia. Aug. 24, 1761. Sept. 24, 1761. M.190.
Sisters: Margaret, Jane, Elinor (Jones) and Douce (Williams). Nephews: Evan Jones and Evan Williams (of Wales), Humphrey Jones. Nieces: Jane (daughter of John Humphry of Wales) and Margaret (daughter of sister Jane, surname not given). Overseers: Amos Griffith, Robert Ellis, David Pugh. Exec: Humphrey Jones.
Witnesses: Rowland Edwards, John Davis, Evan Jones.

JENKINS, STEPHEN. Co. of Philadelphia. Yeoman. April 3, 1759. Sept. 28, 1761. M.191.

Children: Phineas, Stephen, Sarah (Tyson), Abigail (Hugh), William and Charles. Grandchildren: Mary, Abigail and Hannah (daughters of Stephen); Abigail Tyson; William (son of Charles). Legatee: Ann Carr. Exec: Son Charles and daughter-in-law Mary Jenkins.
Witnesses: Robert Combs, Job Combs, John Scott.

USHER, ROBERT. Sept. 29, 1761. Oct. 2, 1761. M.193.
Mother: Ann. Brothers: Edward, John (of London, Eng.) and Abraham. Niece: Anne (daughter of Abraham). Sisters: Ann, Elizabeth, Margaret and Jane. Cousin: Martha Usher. Legatees: Thomas Charlton, Henry Usher, Waring Wolfenden. Exec: Thomas Charlton, William West, John Shee.
Witnesses: Randle Mitchell, Lettice Charlton.

TAYLOR, HENRY. Co. of Bucks, Penna. Yeoman. June 8, 1761. Oct. 2, 1761. M.195.
Wife: Elizabeth. Children: Abraham, Samuel, Henry, Jacob, Frena, Susanna, Mary Ann and Elizabeth. Exec: Adam Goodwalds, Christian Shelly, Casper Yeoder.
Witnesses: Peter Seggon, Ulrick Dreshell, Samuel Foulke.

HUFTY, JACOB. Co. of Philadelphia. Yeoman. Oct. 2, 1761. Oct. 6, 1761. M.197.
Legatees: Brothers David and Charles; sister Martha; cousin Jacob Laughlin; friend Patrick Neal; Alice Griffith (house keeper) and her daughter, Alice. Exec: Jacob Laughlin, Silas Watts.
Witnesses: Wm. Roberts, Junr., Meirlag, Patrick O'Neal.

VANDERSLICE, MARTHA. Co. of Philadelphia. Widow of Anthony. Sept. 14, 1761. Oct. 6, 1761. M.200.
Children: Henry, Anthony, Ann (wife of Harmen Umstad), Catherine (wife of Warner Petters) and Eva (wife of Isaac Petters). Exec: John Penebaker and son-in-law Harmen Umstad.
Witnesses: John Kroplin, Michael Snider.

FRICK, CONRAD. Germantown, Co. of Philadelphia. Sept. 10, 1761. Oct. 7, 1761. M.202.
Children: John, Philip, Barbara and Frederick. Grandchild: John Frick. Exec: Son Philip and cousin Theobald Endt.
Witnesses: John Bowman, Chas. Widerholt, Jacob Bossert.

BANNISTER, EDWARD. Co. of Philadelphia. Sept. 21, 1761. Oct. 7, 1761. M.203.
Legatees: His children (names not given) and Abraham Dawes. Exec: Abraham Dawes.
Witnesses: Samuel Morris, William Anderson, John Stephens.

FITZWATER, THOMAS. Whippain, Co. of Philadelphia. Yeoman. Sept. 24, 1761. Oct. 14, 1761. M.205.
Children: Thomas, John, William, Mary, Martha, Catherine, Deborah, Joseph and Jeremiah. Exec: Wife Rosannah and son Thomas.
Witnesses: William Dehaven, Frederick Kern, Jno. Robinson.

HOOT, JACOB. City of Philadelphia. Yeoman. Sept. 16, 1761. Oct. 13, 1761. M.206.
Legatees: Children of sister Elizabeth (names not given). Exec: Wife Margaret.
Witnesses: Robert Porter, Thomas Smith.

KNORR, GEORGE. Germantown, Co. of Philadelphia. Oct. 4, 1761. Oct. 19, 1761. M.207.
Children: John, Jacob, David, Mathias, Mary (Smith) and Catherine. Exec: Wife Hannah and sons John and Jacob.
Witnesses: Richard Johnson, Baltas Boehm, John Bowman.

SHALTER, BALTHASON. Co. of Philadelphia. Nov. 24, 1759. Oct. 27, 1761. M.208.
Legatees: Francis B. Shalter (nephew), niece Eva Margarith Kurz; cousin Ludwig Englehard; and the poor of Frederick Township. Exec: Nephew Francis B. Shalter.
Witnesses: Peter Herbel, Thomas Lincoln.

MC CLAMONT, WILLIAM. Co. of Philadelphia. Yeoman. April 29, 1748. Oct. 29, 1761. M.209.
Children: Elizabeth, Margaret, Jennet and John. Exec: Son John and brother John McGlathry.
Witnesses: Hugh Berry, Henry McGlathry.

ASHETON, MARGARET. Co. of Philadelphia. Spinster. Aug. 5, 1761. Oct. 30, 1761. M.210.

Legatees: Brother Ralph; sister Francis; Aunt Rebecca Goad of London, widow; brother-in-law Jas. Humphreys; and the Pennsylvania Hospital. Exec: Mother Susannah.
Witnesses: Jas. Stephens, Jno. Baldwin, John Reily.

WILSON, JOHN. May 10, 1760. Oct. 26, 1761. M.212.
Exec. and sole Legatee: Wife Mary.
Witnesses: Henry and Jas. Hollen.

MURDOCH, WILLIAM. City of Philadelphia. Tailor. Sept. 24, 1761. Nov. 3, 1761. M.212.
Exec: Wife Mary and sons William and Samuel.
Witnesses: William Maclenachan, Richard Farmer, Jno. Reily.

KIRK, MARY. Co. of Chester, Penna. Oct. 13, 1761. Nov. 14, 1761. M.213.
Beneficiaries: Brother Humphreys' children; sister Rachel's children; brother Sublinus Ellis and his children, Jane, Elizabeth and Humphrey; sisters-in-law Phebe and Mary Ellis; brother Jeremiah's sons, to wit: Jesse, Jonathan and David. Exec: Brother Jeremiah and nephew Jesse Ellis.
Witnesses: James Dougherty, Daniel Williams.

FOREMAN, PHILIP. Co. of Chester, Penna. Mason. Oct. 26, 1761. Nov. 14, 1761. M.214.
Exec: Wife Elizabeth, brother-in-law George Bissel and Jno. Price, of Lower Merion (names of children not given).
Witnesses: Jeremiah Ellis, Claire Johnson, Lewis Scothorn.

KOLB, MARTIN. Co. of Philadelphia. Yeoman. June 12, 1749. Nov. 17, 1761. M.215.
Children: Isaac, Dielman, Magdalena (Bechtell), Cornelia (Detwiler), Sarah (Ruttenhasen), Mary (Fried) and Hannah. Exec: Wife Magdalena and son Dielman.
Witnesses: Andrew and Michael Zeigler, Jacob Greider.

HASTINGS, SAMUEL. City of Philadelphia. Shipwright. July 21, 1761. Nov. 18, 1761. M.217.
Wife: Susannah. Children: Martha, Elizabeth and Samuel. Exec: Son Samuel and son-in-law John Head.
Witnesses: Thomas Bound, Samuel Bownel, Paul Isaac Voto.

MC ILVAINE, DAVID. City of Philadelphia. Merchant. June 25, 1761. Nov. 23, 1761. M.218.
Father-in-Law: Alexander Graydon, Esquire. Legatees: Sister Ann (of Scotland); nephew William McIlvain and brother William. Exec: Wife Elizabeth and brother William.
Witnesses: Robert Cross, William Sword, William Murray.

BRITTAIN, ELIZABETH. Co. of Philadelphia. Widow. Nov. 17, 1761. Dec. 1, 1761. M.221.
Children: Nathaniel, Rachel (wife of Frederick Fitzer), Martha (wife of Daniel Gregory of New Jersey) and Sarah (wife of John Stiles of North Carolina). Exec: Frederick Fitzer.
Witnesses: William Brittain, Thomas Whitton, John Watts.
Codicil: Nov. 17,1761.
Additional legatees are the heirs of son William.
Witnesses: Same.

DONAT, GEORGE. Co. of Philadelphia. Nov. 23, 1761. Dec. 10, 1761. M.222.
Children: George, John, Christian, Andrew, Margaret and Catherine. Exec: Wife Catherine and sons George and Christian.
Witnesses: Geo. Eman, Wm. Anderson, David Shonee.

WARNER, SWEN. City of Philadelphia. Cordwainer. July 2, 1759. Dec. 11, 1761. M.224.
Wife: Sarah. Children: Joseph and Elizabeth Syng. Exec: Son Joseph, Philip Syng, Joseph Stretch and Joseph Morris.
Witnesses: James Graisburry, William Craig, William Colladay.

NICHOLSON, WILLIAM. City of Philadelphia. Inn holder. Dec. 6, 1761. Dec. 14, 1761. M.225.
Legatees: Ann Nicholson (relationship not stated); Jane Bromley; Martin Ashbourn; John Jenkins; two sisters and their children (names not given); Henry Kepley; John, son of Charles Williams. Exec: Wife Grace and Henry Kepley in America; and in Ireland, Rev. Henry Clark and Jos. Bromley.
Witnesses: Edward Marefield, John Odenheimer, Anthony Wright.

PRIMMER, RICHARD. City of Philadelphia. Yeoman. May 5, 1761. Dec. 28, 1761. M.227.

Legatees: Geo. Aveston; Henry Duff (of Philadelphia, inn holder) and Ann his wife; negro Violet. Exec: Henry Duff.
Witnesses: Martin Ashbourn, Geo. Barthalomew, Paul Isaac Voto.

SPRING, RICHARD. Co. of Bucks, Penna. Feb. 4, 1751. Dec. 28, 1761. M.227.
Sole Beneficiary: The Penna. Hospital. Exec: Hugh Roberts of Philadelphia.
Witnesses: Thomas Bond, Charles Ryan.

BRYAN, THOMAS. City of Philadelphia. Mariner. Sept. 21, 1744. Oct. 21, 1761. M.228.
Exec: Wife Elizabeth.
Witnesses: Gabriel Wilkinson, Peter Stelle.

JONES, JOHN. Co. of Philadelphia. Yeoman. Sept. 2, 1761. Dec. 16, 1761. M.230.
Children: Mary (wife of Edward Walker), Jonathan, Benjamin, Elijah, Jacob, Joshua, Elizabeth and Ann. Brother-in-Law: Peter Gilbert. Legatees, Guardians and Trustees: Samuel Erwin and Daniel Longstretch. Exec: Son Jonathan.
Witnesses: Chas. Garrison, Mathew Barnes, Danl. Thomas.

MILLER, GODFREY. Co. of Bucks, Penna. Yeoman. Nov. 12, 1761. Dec. 23, 1761. M.233.
Daughter: Susannah. Grandchildren: Jacob, William and Philip Miller. Exec: Wife Agnes and Jacob Biser.
Witnesses: Frederick Conrad, Simon Butler, Henry Wyerman.

MUIR, WILLIAM. City of Philadelphia. Bookbinder. Nov. 4, 1761. Jan. 2, 1762. M.234.
Legatees: Sister Mary; Mrs. Rogers (wife of Thos. Rogers); Jas. Black, wife and daughter Hannah; negro Dina. Exec: William Sword and James McGronger.
Witnesses: Joseph Baker, Joseph Claypool, Paul Isaac Voto.

MASSEY, WIGHT. City of Philadelphia. Baker. Nov. 3, 1761. Feb. 2, 1762. M.236.
Wife: Elanor. Late wife Elizabeth. Children: Charles, Thomas, Elizabeth, Ebenezer and Samuel. Exec: Cousin Samuel Oldman of Philadelphia and said Elizabeth and Samuel.

Witnesses: Joseph King, John Knowles, William Wishart.

HOLSTEN, ANDREW. Upper Merion, Co. of Philadelphia. Inn keeper. Dec. 27, 1761. Feb. 3, 1762. M.240.
Children: Peter, Martha, Emy and Magdalen. Exec: Thomas George and son Peter.
Witnesses: John Eastburne, George George.

GRIFFIN, THOMAS. Co. of Bucks, Penna. Cordwainer. Oct. 3, 1761. Feb. 6, 1762. M.242.
Legatees: Brother William; Peter Peterson Vanhorn; Amos Griffiths; Jonathan Drake, Junr.; Elizabeth Evans; Evan and Isaac Jones, cordwainer; Penna. Hospital; the freeholders of Montgomery Co. for a public school. Exec: Isaac and Evan Jones.
Witnesses: John Adamson, Evan Jones, John Roberts.

BERGER, JOST. Co. of Philadelphia. Jan. 18, 1762. Feb. 10, 1762. M.244.
Wife: Margaret. Unknown child. God-son and Daughter: John Jost Keppel and Margaret Julius. Exec. and Witnesses: Lawrence Keppel, Frederick Saur.

GOGENOUR, HENRY. Co. of Chester, Penna. Miller. Jan. 2, 1762. Feb. 12, 1762. M.245.
Children: George and Elizabeth. Beneficiaries: The poor of Coventry, Chester Co., Penna. Exec: Son George.
Witnesses: John Switzar, Andrew Hath, Martin Urner.

HOCKLEY, HENRY. Co. of Chester, Penna. March 18, 1761. Feb. 12, 1762. M.247 [?].
Children: James, Thomas, Abigail (wife of John Patrick) and Ruth. Grandchildren: Ruth, Henry and Nancy Teaf. Exec: Wife Hester and sons.
Witnesses: Thomas and John Potts, Junr., Hugh Williams.

NICE, ANTHONY. Co. of Philadelphia. Yeoman. Jan. 2, 1761. Feb. 19, 1762. M.249.
Wife: Mary. Children: John, George, Richard (alias Jesse) and William. Exec: Sons John and George.
Witnesses: Peter Miller, Stephens Williams, Joseph Cauffman.

DAVIS, RICHARD. Hatfield, Co. of Philadelphia. Jan. 22, 1762. Feb. 20, 1762. M.250.
Sole beneficiary: The Township of Hatfield for the establishment of a public school. Overseers: Thomas Davis, John Wright. Exec: John Jenkins.
Witnesses: Walter Howell, Humphrey Bate, Hugh Tay.

VANDEGRIFT, ELIZABETH. Lower Dublin, Co. of Philadelphia. Widow. Jan. 27, 1762. March 5, 1762. M.252.
Brother: Josiah. Sister: Martha. Son: George. Niece: Martha. Exec: Jonathan Thomas.
Witnesses: Josiah Matlack, Robt. Heaton.

COOKE, ISAAC. Gwynead, Co. of Philadelphia. Yeoman. Nov. 8, 1756. March 6, 1762. M.253.
Legatees: Evan and his four sisters (names not given), children of John Evans.
Witnesses: Rowland Evans, John Hauk.

WEST, JAMES. Co. of Philadelphia. Shipwright. Sept. 27, 1761. March 8, 1762. M.254.
Wife: Name not given. [Mary Cooper] Children: Charles, James, William and Sarah. Exec: Brother Charles, Daniel and William Cooper (yeoman).
Witnesses: Michael Hullings, John Gilbert, Senr., Paul Isaac Voto.

POHLL, PETER. Limerick Township, Co. of Philadelphia. Feb. 18, 1762. March 9, 1762. M.258.
Son: Thomas. Step-son: Vollentine Hause. Exec: Wife Anna Elizabeth and Abraham Paull.
Witnesses: Christopher Grist, Michael Bastin.

JAMES, PHILIP. Co. of Philadelphia. Sept. 28, 1761. March 15, 1762. M.260.
Sole legatee: Wife Jane. Exec: Robert Martin, Robert Coulton.
Witnesses: Robert Wallis, Robert Hall, William Saston.

HINCHMAN, ISAAC. City of Philadelphia. Merchant. Feb. 11, 1762. March 30, 1762. M.261.
Children: Sarah, Mary and Michael. Overseer: Benjamin Morgan. Exec: Wife Littis and brother James.

Witnesses: John Gilbert, Brian Wilkinson, Thomas Gilbert, Paul Isaac Voto.

COX, RICHARD. Co. of Chester. Husbandman. Nov. 17, 1757. March 31, 1762. M.263.
Wife: Mary. Children: Joseph, Benjamin, Sarah (Burson), Elizabeth (wife of Wm. Paye), Mary (wife of Jonathan Potts) and John. Grandchild: Hannah Burson. Exec: Sons Joseph and Benjamin.
Witnesses: John, Enoch and Hannah Meredith.

FUSSELL, SOLOMON. City of Philadelphia. Merchant. Feb. 24, 1762. April 3, 1762. M.265.
Wife: Mary. Children: Elizabeth, William, Barbara, Jacob, Susannah and Sarah. Mother-in-Law: Barbara Cony. Exec: Joshua Fisher and Stephen Collins of Philadelphia (merchants) and John Burrough, Junr., of N.J.
Witnesses: Paul Isaac Voto, Caleb Atmore, Daniel Jones.
Codicil: Feb. 26, 1762.
Wherein step-daughter Elizabeth Wilson is made a legatee.
Witnesses: Same.

ROBERTS, MARY. Abington, Co. of Philadelphia. Widow. 1 mo. 9, 1756. April 5, 1762. M.266.
Son: John, names of other children not given. Sons-in-Law: Phineas Jenkins and William Jenkins. Grandchildren: Sarah, Abraham, Mary, Margaret and Isaac Cadwalader, Mary Bowers.
Witnesses: John Pemberton, John Brock, Charles Roberts.

JONES, CADWALADER. Gwynead, Co. of Philadelphia. Yeoman. March 26, 1762. April 7, 1762. M.267.
Children: Ann, John, Rachel, Martha and Jane. Trustees: Nephews Phineas and Joseph Griffith. Exec: Son-in-law Jno. Lukins and son John.
Witnesses: Owen and Samuel Evans, Daniel Williams.

DUBRE, JAMES (DANIEL?). Moorland, Co. of Philadelphia. 2 mo. 23, 1762. April 10, 1762. M.269.
Children: Benjamin, Jacob, Hannah, Esther, Mary, Sarah, James, William, Rachel, Joseph and John. Exec: Wife Rachel and Thos. Hallowell, Senr.
Witnesses: John Meglaughlin, Abraham Lukens, Thomas Hallowell.

LEECH, THOMAS. City of Philadelphia. Gentleman. March 23, 1762. April 12, 1760. M.270.
Children: Thomas, William and Hester (Kollock). Exec: Sons Thomas and William.
Witnesses: James Stephens, William Peters, Jno. Reily.
Codicil: March 23, 1762.

ROBERTS, ROBERT. Co. of Philadelphia. Oct. 25, 1761. April 17, 1762. M.273.
Children: Edward, Samuel, Ann (wife of John Robinson), Elizabeth, Elanor and Hannah. Grandson: David Lloyd. Exec: Brothers Joseph and Edward and cousin John Roberts.
Witnesses: Hugh Roberts, David Davis Conrad.

ROBERTS, SARAH. Norriton, Co. of Philadelphia. Widow. Sept. 26, 1761. April 19, 1762. M.274.
Father: John Longworthy. Children: Moses and Joseph. Overseers: John Bell, Michael Pugh. Exec: Son Moses.
Witnesses: Michael Pugh, Richard Miles.

ZUBLER, JOHN. City of Philadelphia. Inn holder. Jan. 6, 1762. April 20, 1762. M.275.
Wife: Susannah. Children: John, Margaret and George. Exec. and guardians: Wife and Daniel Etter (inn holder).
Witnesses: Peter Miller, William Coates.

EDELMAN, PETER. City of Philadelphia. Tavern keeper. Jan. 28, 1762. April 20, 1762. M.276.
Children: George and Elizabeth. Exec: Wife Christian.
Witnesses: Mathias Startz, Andrew Liburt.

PHIPPS, JOHN. Co. of Philadelphia. Yeoman. 7 mo. 22, 1757. April 20, 1762. M.276.
Children: John, Joseph, Thomas, Ann, Sarah, Susanna, Mary, Lydia and Hannah. Grandchildren: Isaac, Peter, John and Margaret (children of Thomas Phipps). Trustees: Joshua Morris (of Abington) and Thomas Rose (of Germantown). Exec: Wife Elizabeth.
Witnesses: Phineas Jenkins, John Roberts, Isaac Cleaver, James Mitten.

SCHREINER, WILLIAM. City of Philadelphia. Tailor. March 27, 1762. April 22, 1762. M.280.
Children: Elizabeth and Mary. Exec. and Guardian: Wife Elizabeth.
Witnesses: John William Hoffman, Frederick Hagner, Lewis Weiss.

MILLER, NICHOLAS. Co. of Philadelphia. Farmer. March 20, 1762. April 24, 1762. M.281.
Child: Nicholas. Exec: Wife Elizabeth, Jacob Cropp and Cassimer Messimer.
Witnesses: George and Martin Bentle.

LUDWICK, JOHAN. Aeho[?], Co. of Philadelphia. Jan. 14, 1762. April 24, 1762. M.283.
Uncle: John George Weidner. Children: Names not given. Exec: Wife Catherina and William Shonler.
Witnesses: Peter Marsteller, Philip Yost.

VALENTINE, THOMAS. Co. of Chester, Penna. Feb. 16, 1762. April 27, 1762. M.284.
Children: Thomas, William, John, Rachel and Mary. Brother: Jonathan. Exec: Wife Rebecca.
Witnesses: Mechl. and George Buchanan, Jno. Vallentine.

YEACKLE, ABRAHAM. Co. of Philadelphia. Aug. 17, 1761. April 28, 1762. M.285.
Wife: Maria. Children: John, Balthaser, Susannah (wife of Abraham Weegner), Rosina (wife of Casper Seibt) and Elizabeth.
Witnesses: George and Christopher Shultz.

JUSTICE, CHRISTIAN. City of Philadelphia. Widow. Dec. 7, 1750. April 30, 1762. M.287.
Children: John, Peter, Mounce, Gunner, Ann, Christian and Bidget.
Grandchildren: Richard, William, Christian and Hester (children of Bidget, surname not given). Exec: Daughters Ann and Christian.
Witnesses: Francis Garrigues, William Palmel, Mathias Bias.

MARDON, THOMAS. Co. of Philadelphia. April 26, 1762. May 3, 1762. M.288.
Children: Rachel, Mary, Sarah (wife of Jonathan Wilson) and Jacob.
Exec: Son John.
Witnesses: Richard, Daniel and Joseph Walton.

BOORE, DAVID. City of Philadelphia. March. 8, 1762. May 4, 1762. M.289.
Children: Thomas and Mary. Exec: Wife Mary.
Witnesses: Wm. Oliphant, Samuel Johnson, Lawrence Boore.

BATE (BALE), GEORGE. Dec. 2, 1760. May 4, 1762. M.290.
Exec. and sole Legatee: William Forrest.
Witnesses: William Johnson, William Salsbury, Thos. Booth.

KNIGHT, JOSEPH. Co. of Philadelphia. Yeoman. 2 mo. 7, 1754. May 6, 1762. M.291.
Wife: Abigail. Children: Mary and Giles. Grandchildren: Joseph, Giles, Mary, Susannah, Abigail, Rebecca, Elizabeth Knight; and Lydia, daughter of James Thornton. Exec: Son Giles.
Witnesses: Thomas Knight (his mark), William Baker, Eve Weaver (her mark).

BECKER, HENRY. Nov. 18, 1761. May 12, 1762. M.293.
Exec: Brother Bastian and sister Gertraut, who with brother Jacob and sister Elizabeth are sole legatees.
Witnesses: Jacob and Mary Coleman.

HYAT, MARGARET. City of Philadelphia. Widow of John. April 30, 1761. May 13, 1762. M.294.
Nieces and Legatees: Margaret and Francis (children of brother Ralph Ashton), and Susannah (daughter of niece Susannah Humphreys).
Exec: Notary James Humphreys and niece Margaret.
Witnesses: Catherine Ellis, Edmund Physick and Richard Hockley.

HODNET, JEFFERY. Co. of Philadelphia. Yeoman. March 26, 1762. May 22, 1762. M.295.
Children: James and Jeffery. Legatee: Frances Recraft of Carbery, County Cork, Ireland, Gentleman. Exec: Wife Elizabeth.
Witnesses: Joseph Sims, Henry Muag.

REES, DAVID. Co. of Philadelphia. May 12, 1762. May 24, 1762. M.297.
Children: David, Rachel, Rebecca and Euphenia. Exec: Wife Margaret and upon her death, Rachel (daughter) and Richard Treat succeed.
Witnesses: Jacob and James Tompkins, Jas. Waterman.

HUFFTY, ANN. Co. of Philadelphia. April 5, 1762. May 27, 1762. M.299.
Children: Sarah (Carter), Mary (Shaw), David, Ann (Fisher), Rachel (Dewees) and Jacob. Grandchild: Mary (daughter of Henry Dewees)
Exec: Henry Dewees.
Witnesses: William and Joseph Johnson, William Barge.

TUNIS, ANTHONY. Co. of Philadelphia. Yeoman. Feb. 6, 1762. May 29, 1762. M.300.
Wife: Mary. Children: Joseph, Abraham (trustee), Elinor (Cooke), Alse (Lees), Hannah (Ribor) and Bethsheba. Grandchildren: Elinor, Anthony and Mary Cooke; Agnes, Catherine, Tunis, Phebe and Elizabeth Lees. Son-in-Law: Evan Griffith. Exec: Son Joseph.
Witnesses: John Price, Richard George, Michael Gashler.

JENKINS, JOHN. City of Philadelphia. Scrivener. March 16, 1762. April 26, 1762. M.303.
Wife: Unity. Children: John, Ann, Mary, George, Richard and William. Exec: Wife, Joseph Gallaway and David James Dove.
Witnesses: John Sawer, Alexander Bensted.

JENNY, JEAN ELIZABETH. City of Philadelphia. Widow. Jan. 11, 1762. Jan. 13, 1762. M.305.
Sole Legatee: Relation Mary Vollean. Exec: Rev. Mr. Geo. Craig.
Witnesses: Jno. Rose, Jno. Keasbey.

ARMITT, JOHN. City of Philadelphia. 8 mo. 8, 1758. June 1, 1762. M.307.
Brother: Stephen. Legatees: Children of said Stephen, John, Richard, Samuel, Sarah, Ann and Mary Armitt; cousin Sarah (wife of Isaac Garrigue); Mary and Elizabeth (children of cousin Joseph Armitt); cousins Sophia Fielding and John Armitt. Exec: Wife Mary.
Witnesses: Jacob Lewis, Joseph King.

DUCHE, ANTHONY. City of Philadelphia. Potter. May 2, 1761. June 1, 1762. M.309.
Children: Ann, Anthony, Jacob and Andrew. Grandchildren: Ann Mears, James and Andrew Duche. Exec: Daughter Ann.
Witnesses: William Falconer, Hugh Hodge and Paul Isaac Voto.

BURCKHART, PHILIP. April 19, 1762. June 2, 1762. M.311.

Children: Philip, Daniel, William, Jacob, Michael, Ann, Mary Elizabeth, Maria, Frederica, Nicholas, Margaret Dorothea and unknown child. Exec: Wife Barbara.
Witnesses: John Gamber, Junr., William Clampffer.

BIKLER, PETER. April 21, 1762. June 4, 1762. M.312.
Children: Magdalen, Christian, David and Elizabeth. Exec: Wife Elizabeth and son Christian.
Witnesses: Christian Clemer, Michael Musselman.

MILLER, JOHN. Co. of Philadelphia. Freeholder. Oct. 30, 1761. June 4, 1762. M.312.
Son: Jacob and other children, names not given. Exec: Wife Ann Maria and son-in-law Hermanus Newman.
Witnesses: Nicholas Jekes (his mark), Michael Walter.

HOAKEN, JOHN. Co. of Bucks, Penna. Aug. 6, 1760. June 14, 1762. M.314.
Children: Peter, Gertraut and John. Grandchild: Mary Breght. Exec: Wife Gertraut and son John.
Witnesses: Francis Michael Bishop, Yost Artman, Samuel Lantes.

KING, GEORGE. Co. of Philadelphia. May 4, 1761. June 21, 1762. M.315.
Children: Samuel, John and Catherin. Exec: Wife Catherin and Christopher Ottinger.
Witnesses: Peter Adams, John Ottinger, William Anderson.

WAMBOLD, ADAM. Co. of Chester, Penna. May 27, 1762. June 23, 1762. M.316.
Wife: Catherine. Children: Frederick, Elizabeth, Mary, Catherine, Ludwick, Elias, Peter, Magdalena, Adam and George. Exec: John Gross.
Witnesses: Jacob Beery, John Martin, Godfred Dovenhover.

POUND, MARY. City of Philadelphia. Widow. April 16, 1754. June 26, 1762. M.317.
Child: Mary (wife of Joseph Wood). Grandchildren: Sarah, Elizabeth, Ann, Joseph, Robert, Thomas and Josiah Wood. Great-granddaughter: Mary Doyle. Exec. and Guardian: Thomas Say, Philadelphia, merchant.

Witnesses: Joseph Catham, John Elton, Jos. Pemberton.
Codicil: [No date.]
Witnesses: Samuel Head and Blair McClenachan, who testify that it was signed about eight weeks before date of probate.

BASHLER, HENRY. City of Philadelphia. Inn holder. Nov. 30, 1761. July 13, 1761. M.320.
Legatees and Devisees: Charlotte Walther (wife's granddaughter); school of the German Reformed Church of Philadelphia; step-son Henry Walther of Lancaster, Pa., miller; step-daughter Catherine (wife of Conrad Shultz); Daniel Bashler, laborer and Elizabeth Bashler of Lancaster; nephew George Bashler. A contingent bequest is made to the "reformed school house at Philadelphia." Exec: Wife Mary, Wm. Clampffer and Philip Behm, who, with Conrad Shutz are also Trustees.
Witnesses: Richard Robers, Lewis Weiss.

OTTINGER, WILLIAM. Co. of Philadelphia. May 30, 1762. Aug. 6, 1762. M.325.
Children: Susannah, Mary, Margaret, Elizabeth and Christopher.
Exec: Wife Hannah and William Streeper.
Witnesses: Ullery Vackerly, Andrew Why, David Reynolds.

ROBERTS, AQUILA. City of Philadelphia. Sail maker. July 17, 1762. Aug. 6, 1762. M.326.
Wife: Mary. Children: Mary, Ann and John. Sister: Ann Roger (of New York). Exec: Brother Samuel, cousin Owen Jones of Philadelphia (merchant), and Joseph Moulder (sail maker).
Witnesses: Patrick Tomius, Jas. Stephens, Jno. Reily.

BADGER, BERNARD. New York. Mariner. Feb. 8, 1753. Sept. 6, 1762. M.329.
Exec. and sole Legatee: Wife Susannah.
Witnesses: Mary and Ann Riche, Whitehead Hicks.

WATSON, LUKE. March 18, 1758. Aug. 6, 1762. M.330.
Exec. and sole Legatee: Margaret Warnick (relationship not stated).
Witnesses: Paul Isaac and Sarah Voto.

FAULKNER, WILLIAM. City of Philadelphia. Mariner. June 25, 1762. Aug. 9, 1762. M.331.
Children: William, Francis and James. Exec: Wife Susannah.

Witnesses: Daniel Jones, Joseph Ogden, Elizabeth Dorman.

SUTTON, JOHN. Dec. 26, 1757. Aug. 10, 1762. M.332.
Beneficiaries: Father and mother John and Sarah and brother Peter.
Exec: Thomas Bonde.
Witnesses: Jeremiah Smith, William Moulder.

HUDSON, WILLIAM. City of Philadelphia. Tanner. April 27, 1762. Aug. 10, 1762. M.333.
Father: Evans. Children: Samuel, Rachel, Elizabeth (Morris), Sarah (Langdale), Mary, Jane, Susannah, Rachel (Jory) and Hannah. Exec: Samuel, Mary and Susannah.
Witnesses: Wm. Pyewell, Samuel Bettle, Junr., Peter Miller.

SEITZ, ANDREW. City of Philadelphia. Stocking weaver. July 5, 1762. Aug. 17, 1762. M.340.
Mother: Elizabeth. Exec: Wife Cleophia and Henry Welfling.
Witnesses: Henry Welfling, Philip Shridt, Jno. Goodshurs.

VERNON, GEORGE. Sept. 11, 1761. Aug. 13, 1762. M.341.
Exec. and sole Legatee: Jacob Huber.
Witnesses: L. Weiss, Peter Miller, John McPherson, Henry Robinson.

BROOKE, JAMES. Co. of Philadelphia. Yeoman. June 9, 1762. Aug. 19, 1762. M.342.
Children: Elizabeth (Loyd), Martha, Samuel, David and John. Exec: Wife Hannah and son Joseph.
Witnesses: Jeremiah Jordan, Jacob Frick, Jos. Millard.

NELSON, JOHN. New York. Aug. 23, 1762. Aug. 27, 1762. M.346.
Mother: Frances. Sisters and Legatees: Sarah and Margaret. Exec: Jno. Sears, Senr., Jno. Sears, Junr.
Witnesses: Thomas Clark, Esther Sayer, Paul Isaac Voto.

STIVER, FREDERICK. Aug. 18, 1762. Aug. 27, 1762. M.347.
Exec. and sole Legatee: Brother Jno. Girgeson.
Witnesses: Paul Isaac Voto, Perer Dehaven, Christian Derrick.

CARPENTER, SAMUEL. City of Philadelphia. Merchant. Jan. 20, 1760. Sept. 2, 1762. M.348.

Legatees: Ann Josiah, the wife of Emanual Josiah; Robt. and James sons of the above; and brother Joshua. Exec: Ann Josiah.
Witnesses: Wm. Bradford, Jno. Knowle, Thos. Cuthbert.

POWELL, SAMUEL. City of Philadelphia. Brass founder. Feb. 28, 1753. Sept. 16, 1762. M.349.
Legatees: Brother and sisters, names not given. Exec: Wife Martha.
Witnesses: John Coats, Jas. Kinsay.

CHURCH, JOHN. City of Philadelphia. Wharf builder. Sept. 8, 1762. Sept. 23, 1762. M.351.
Children: Samuel, John, Thomas, Sheppard and unknown child.
Brother: William. Sister: Mary McCall. Legatee: Negro Cato. Exec: Wife Mary and Jos. Watkins, Junr.
Witnesses: James Payne, John Weir, Thomas Davis.
Codicil: Same date.
Witnesses: Same.

MOORE, JAMES. City of Philadelphia. Tallow chandler. Aug. 25, 1762. Sept. 23, 1762. M.352.
Son: Thomas. Step-children: Lucia, Thomas and Abigail. Legatee: Francis Davis. Exec: Wife Ann and son Thomas.
Witnesses: Saml. Gillaspey, Daniel Offley, Paul Isaac Voto.

BLIZARD, CONWAY. City of Philadelphia. Yeoman. Sept. 22, 1762. Sept. 26, 1762. M.354.
Legatees: Brother George of Ballinderry, Antrim County, gentleman; cousin Nancy Blizard. Exec: Joseph Blyth and Andrew Steuart of Philadelphia.
Witnesses: Thos. England, Elizabeth Boulding, Mary Blyth (her mark).

RUTTER, SOLOMAN. City of Philadelphia. Ship wright. Sept. 28, 1762. Oct. 5, 1762. M.355.
Nephew and sole Legatee: Thomas Rutter. Exec: Edward Tew, Andrew Donaldson.
Witnesses: Jonathan Hanson, Anthony Duche, Junr., Lawrence Boore.

EVANS, JOHN. Gwynead, Co. of Philadelphia. Bachelor. 4 mo. 1, 1762. Sept. 26, 1762. M.356.
Legatees: Sister Elizabeth Richards; nephews Rowland and Samuel Richards; sister-in-law Elizabeth Evans and her daughter Mary;

nephews Thomas, Edward, Griffith and John Evans. Relatives not legatees: Brother Thomas and nephew Owen Evans. Exec: Nephew John.
Witnesses: Jno. Evans, Joshua Foulke.

ROBERTS, MORDICAI. Co. of Chester, Penna. 3 mo. 10, 1762. Oct. 6, 1762. M.358.
Children: Mordicai, John, Sarah and Ann. Exec: George and Owen Evans.
Witnesses: James Pugh, Mary Roberts, Simon Meredith.

MURRAY, WILLIAM. City of Philadelphia. Merchant. Sept. 23, 1762. Sept. 28, 1762. M.359.
Children: Agnes, George and unknown child. Exec: Wife Jane, brother John, Abraham Usher and Randle Mitchel (merchants).
Witnesses: John Mease, James Sloan.

YEAKEY, JOHN. March 20, 1751. Oct. 5,1762. M.361.
Wife: Anna Margaret. Children: Evan, Katherine, Mary Katherine, Yonlianna and Susannah.
Witnesses: Peter Hybey (his mark), Simeon Meatzeser, Henry Christ.

MC CALL, SAMUEL. City of Philadelphia. Merchant. June 1, 1762. Oct. 4, 1762. M.363.
Wife: Mary. Children: John Searle, Ann, Mary, George, Eleanor Margaret and Catherine. Exec: Brother Archibald, brother-in-law Joseph Swift and son John Searle.
Witnesses: Jas. Moore, Samuel Gillaspey, Jno. Murray.

CALDWELL, DAVID. City of Philadelphia. Merchant. Sept. 20, 1762. Oct. 7, 1762. M.365.
Parents: David and Margaret. Brothers: Samuel and John. Children: John, Elizabeth and unknown child. Exec: Wife Grace, John Mease, William Allison and brother Samuel.
Witnesses: Samuel Purviance, Junr., Thos. Galbreath, Paul Isaac Voto.

MC CREREY, SAMUEL. City of Philadelphia. Wigge maker. March 22, 1762. Oct. 7, 1762. M.367.
Legatees: Nephew Wm. Carlisle (shoemaker); Jemimea Nowland and her daughter Betsy; friend Clement Biddle; brother Hugh and his son. Exec: Staniss Foord and Jno. Biddle.

Witnesses: Charles Moore (hatter), John Read.

DICAS, MARY. City of Philadelphia. Widow. Nov. 17, 1761. Oct.9, 1762. M.369.
Sons-in-Law: Henry and John Shute. Exec: Son Thomas.
Witnesses: Thos. Charlton, Paul Isaac Voto.

BARTHOLOMEW, MARY. Co. of Philadelphia. Widow, relict of John. July 18, 1760. Oct. 7, 1762. M.370 and 372.
Children: Ann (Waters), Elizabeth (Davis), Rachel (Davis), Edward, Andrew, Joseph, Mary (Thomas), John, Thomas and Austin.
Grandchildren: Elizabeth (wife of Patrick Anderson); Hannah Davis; John, Joseph and Mary Bartholomew (children of son Andrew);Benjamin, John, Hannah and Rachel (children of son Joseph); Mary (daughter of Isaac Davis); Benjamin and Catherine (children of son John). Trustees: Jno. Jones, carpenter, David Evans, Isaac James, Humphrey Bate, Joseph Griffith. Exec: Son Edward and son-in-law Benjamin Davis.
Witnesses: John Davis, William Murray, Benjamin Griffith.
Codicil: March 26, 1762.
Legatee: Sister Sarah Perry. Co-Exec: Austin.
Witnesses: Isaac Coates, Jno. McNellins.

EDWARDS, THOMAS. City of Philadelphia. Yeoman. April 20, 1761. Oct. 22, 1762. M.374.
Grandchildren: Alexander, John and Joseph Edwards (names of parents not given). Exec: Wife Mary and son-in-law Richard Finney.
Witnesses: Jacob Hall, Joseph Paull, Catherine Needler (her mark).

MORGAN, BENJAMIN. City of Philadelphia. Mariner. Feb. 15, 1762. Oct. 21, 1762. M.375.
Brother: Evan. Sisters: Mary and Hannah. Nephews: John Austin and William Morgan. Niece: Mary Gordon. Cousin: Mary Morgan. All of above are legatees, also one other brother, name not given.
Exec: Evan Morgan, William Ball.
Witnesses: William Collins, Robert Willis, Jno. Pickworth.

GOODSHURES, JOHN. Color maker. Sept. 22, 1762. Oct. 19, 1762. M.376.
Son: John Jacob. Exec: Wife Maria Barbara.
Witnesses: Ubrick Yeakley, Rudolph Huber.

MC KELHENEY, JOHN. Co. of Chester, Penna. Yeoman. Feb. 26, 1762. Oct. 21, 1762. M.377.
Brother: John, Junr. Son: William. Exec: Jacob Harsbarger and Nicholas Terefas.
Witnesses: Jos. McCurtain, Joseph Skeen, Jane Skeen (her mark).

STARR, RACHEL. Charles Township, Penna. Widow. Feb. 7, 1762. Oct. 22, 1762. M.378.
Children: Joseph, John, James, Moses and Rachel. Daughters-in-Law: Rebecca and Hannah. Son-in-Law: Richardson. Grand daughters: Rebecca, Joseph Junr., James, Samuel, Isaac, Mary and Rachel (children of son Joseph); John, James, Thomas and Mary (children of son John and Sarah Starr); Rachel and Hannah (children of son James); Elizabeth, James and Rachel (children of daughter Rachel Williams); and children of son Moses, whose names are not given.
Exec: Sons Joseph and James.
Witnesses: William Lewis, James Hancock, Wm. Fussill, Jonathan Coats.

PHILLIPS, JOHN. City of Philadelphia. Merchant. March 30, 1762. Oct. 19, 1762. M.380.
Children: John and Margaret (wife of Anthony Stocker).
Grandchildren: Anne, Mary and John Clement Stocker. Trustee: Chas. Stedman. Exec: Son John.
Witnesses: Wm. West, Thomas Gilbert, David Caldwell.
Codicil: July 20, 1762.
Witnesses: Same.

WILLIAMS, STEPHEN. City of Philadelphia. Gentleman. Sept. 7, 1761. May 1, 1762. M.383.
Wife: Sarah Ann. Son: Stephen. Legatees: Rev. Mr. Stephen Roe of London, Eng.; Penna. Hospital; two sons of Daniel Williams of Philadelphia; (relationsip and names not stated); Moses Annis; Andrew Hodge; Andrew Read; Trinity and St. Peters Churches, Philadelphia.
Exec: Andrew Read, Andrew Hodge and Daniel Williams.
Witnesses: Thompson Parker, Benjamin Price.

JEYKELL, MARGARET. City of Philadelphia. Widow. Sept. 18, 1762. Oct. 24, 1762. M.305.
Children: Francina (Hicks), Margaret and John. Exec: Son John.
Witnesses: Henry Lisle, Jas. Blair, Jno. Reily.

WAAGENSEIL, CHRISTOPHER. Co. of Philadelphia. Yeoman. June 13, 1760. Oct. 27, 1762. M.387.
Children: John, Anna Maria (wife of John Dirr) and Elizabeth Catherina (wife of David Haag). Exec: Wife Anna Christiana.
Witnesses: John Martin, Frederick Limbach, David Shultz.

FOULKE, THOMAS. Co. of Philadelphia. Yeoman. June 11, 1751. Oct. 24, 1762. M.389.
Wife: Gwyn. Children: William, Edward, Elinor, Sarah (wife of William Jones) and Susannah (wife of Rowland Evans). Sister: Gwyn Edwards. Exec: Son William.
Witnesses: Abram David, John Roberts, Jacob Edge.

SCULL, NICHOLAS. City of Philadelphia. Surveyor. Aug. 24,1761. Oct. 19, 1762. M.392.
Children: Nicholas, John, Jasper, Mary (Biddle), Abigail (Biddle) and James. Grandchildren: William and Mary (heirs of son Edward, deceased). Exec: Son James and Mary Biddle.
Witnesses: John Ross, Alex. Huston.

GAMBER, JOHN. City of Philadelphia. Cooper. Oct. 2, 1762. Oct. 27, 1762. M.394.
Children: John and Anne Mary (wife of Nicholas Schreiner). Exec: Wife Ann and son John.
Witnesses: Peter Miller, Earnest Kurtz.

BOURKE, ANNE. City of Philadelphia, late of Kent Co., Md. Spinster. Oct. 18, 1762. Oct. 30, 1762. M.395.
Beneficiaries: Sister-in-law Sarah Bourke; brothers William and Walter; sister Bridget and her children of Killalla, Ire.; friends Ann David and Emond Bourke. Exec: Daniel Clark of Philadelphia, merchant, Lewis Droomgoole of Kent Co., Md.
Witnesses: Elizabeth Hatton, Edmund Nikell, William Gallaghar.

BARKLEY, JAMES. City of Philadelphia. Shop keeper. Oct. 7, 1762. Nov. 1, 1762. M.397.
Legatees: Nieces Mary Menaugh and Mary Bayly; nephew James Poge; and children of brothers Hugh and John (names not given).
Exec: Wife Mary, John Bleakely and Robert Bayly.
Witnesses: Jno. Gass, James McLaughlin, Paul Isaac Voto.

PIERS, MANUEL. Nov. 28, 1758. Nov. 1, 1762. M.398.
Legatees: Friend Robert Hall and to him in trust for "two poor widows." Exec: Friend Robert Hall.
Witnesses: Thomas Robeson, Andrew Burr, James Spavold, James Tybert.

JUDAH, ABRAHAM. City of Philadelphia. Merchant. Oct. 23, 1762. Nov. 11, 1762. M.399.
Wife: Bridget. Children: Rebecca, Ann, William, Sarah, David and Hannah. Brother: Benjamin. Exec: Redmond Conynham, Jno. Wilcox, Maxfield Nesbitt.
Witnesses: Robt. Lewton, Benj. Judah, Jean Cholmers.

DOBINS, JOSEPH. City of Philadelphia. Victular. Sept. 13, 1762. Oct. 27, 1762. M.401.
Children: Joseph, Elizabeth, Rebecca, Catherine and Mary Ann. Exec: Wife Rebecca and Mathew Johns.
Witnesses: Jacob Bankson, Rose Wilson (her mark), Wm. Thomas.

GRAHMS, MARY. Co. of Cecil, Md. Widow of John. Dec. 19, 1747. Nov. 20, 1762. M.403.
Children: Catherine, William and Robert. Exec: Brother George Currey of Chester Co., Penna.
Witnesses: Jas. Dickson, Robt. Currey, Hugh Muckelroy (his mark).

DOHR, TYELLIAS. Co. of Philadelphia. Locksmith. July 10, 1761. Nov. 6, 1762. M.405.
Legatees: Baltas Riser, Senr. and his wife Mary; Baltas Riser, Junr., heirs at law (names not given). Exec: Christopher Sower and Thomas Rose.
Witnesses: Joseph Ashmead, Jas. Dilworth, Isaac Boudeman.

PIKE, JOSEPH. City of Cork, Ireland. Merchant. Nov. 25, 1727. Feb. 18, 1729. M.407.
Proved before the Prerogative court in Ireland and in Philadelphia. Children: Samuel, Richard (of London), Mary, Elizabeth, Ann, Rachel (Beale) and Benjamin. Beneficiaries: Servant Robert Arnell and his wife; Benj. Holme; Francis Griffith Senr.; Elizabeth Peace; John and Martha Dober; James and Mary Dennis; the poor of the people called Quakers, either in Cork, Ireland or elsewhere; the poor of the Church of England of Cork; John Little; the poor beggars of Cork; Elizabeth

Jacob of Waterford; John Gibbs of the County of Tiperary; Samuel (son of brother Joseph Hoare); cousin Rich. Allen; brother Richard's children (names not given); cousin Richard Pike and wife; cousins Ebenezar Pike, Rebecca Randle, Abigail Coole and Mary Neat of Chippinham; overseers of Will hereafter named; toward the building of a new Meeting House (place not stated); Jas. Wilson; cousins Rychyeat Coole and Sarah Wall of Bristol; Charles Howell and Nicholas Harris. Overseers: Jos. Hoare, Richard Pike and John Dennis. Exec: Widow Elizabeth and son Samuel.
Witnesses: Daniel Engain, William Simmins, Robert Wallis.

PIKE, ELIZABETH. Sunday's Will in North Liberties, City of Cork, Ireland. Widow. May 24, 1733. May 14, 1741. M.415.
Proved before the Surrogate of Cork, Ireland. Children: Richard, Mary (wife of Thos. Beale, of Cork, merchant), Rachel (Beale), Ann (Strangman), Elizabeth (wife of Joshua Beale) and Benjamin. Grandchildren: Joshua, Joseph, Mary and Sarah (children of Joshua and Elizabeth Beale); Joshua (son of Thos. Beale). Cousins and Legatees: Mary Neat, Sarah Wall, Abigail Coole, Martha Dobbs, Elizabeth Pease, Francis Knight, Richard Allen, Mary Pike; nephew William; nieces Ann, Susannah and Rachel (children of brother Richard); Elizabeth Hutchenson; cousins Mary and Ann Erberry; the poor of the Meeting of Cork; Margaret Day and Ann Carrel. Exec: Son Richard.
Witnesses: Frederick Rogers, Richard Dealy, Michael Mead.
Codicil: July 31, 1733.

PIKE, RICHARD. Stake Newington, Co. of Middlesex, Eng. Sept. 2, 1752. April 5, 1755. M.418.
Proved before the Prerogative Court of Canterburry, Eng. Legatees: Kinsmen Samuel Hoare and Nathaniel Newberry, merchants of London; nieces Rachel Strangman and Sarah Beale (daughter of Joshusa Beale); nephews Joseph and Samuel Strangman; Joshua and Joseph (sons of Joshua Beale); Samuel Beale (son of sister Rachel); Sarah Foster; Mary Edes. Exec: Kinsmen Samuel Hoare and Nathaniel Newberry.
Witnesses: Denis Beck, William Braund, Wm. Russell.

FERGUERSON, CHARLES. Army. April 25, 1759. Nov. 26, 1762. M.419.

Sole Legatee: Brother Alexander. Exec: Hugh Forbes of Philadelphia.
Witnesses: Thos. Parker, Mary Hallowell.

CAMPBELL, THOMAS. City of Philadelphia. Merchant. Oct. 11, 1762. Nov. 26, 1762. M.420.
Children: Peter and Sarah. Brothers: John (of Liverpool, Eng.) and Brynn of Ireland. Legatees: Alice Harper; Margaret Abercrombie, widow; servant Catherine Money; kinswoman Margaret Campbell, tayloress; the Penna. Hospital; the college in Philadelphia; negro Tom; and also Exec: Stephen Carmick, merchant, Dr. Richard Farmer and Benj. Price, Attorney-at-Law.
Witnesses: Plunket Flesson, Anthony Siddon.

BLACK, ROBERT. May 20, 1762. Nov. 30, 1762. M.423.
Sole Legatee: Mother Rose Black, County Antrim, Ire. Exec: William McMullin.
Witnesses: Robt. Scott, Samuel Ross, John McMullin.

MC DONALD, JOHN. May 5, 1762. Nov. 26, 1762. M.424.
Exec. and sole Legatee: Michael McIntire.
Witness: George Taylor.

BONTON, JOHN DANIEL. City of Philadelphia. Baker. April 13, 1759. Nov. 24, 1762. M.425.
Wife: Name not given. Children: Frederick, Geo., Willhelmena (Udree) and Jacob. Exec: Wife, son Geo. and son-in-law Jacob Udree.
Witnesses: Mathias Abel, Paul Isaac Voto.

TROUT, BALTZAR. City of Philadelphia. Reed worker. Nov. 1, 1762. Dec. 1, 1762. M.427.
Child: Mary. Exec: Wife Barbara and brother-in-law Nicholas Rittenhouse.
Witnesses: Christopher Brust, Peter Smith, Christian Lehman.

SCHANDEY, NICHOLAS. Co. of Philadelphia. Paper maker. Aug. 15, 1762. Dec. 1, 1762. M.429.
Children: Jacob, Henry, Ursalah and Mary. Exec: Wife Susannah and Henry Dewees.
Witnesses: Nathan Sheppard, John Bernard Mayer, William Levering.

PICKIN, JOSEPH. May 5, 1762. Dec. 3, 1762. M.431.
Legatees: Brothers-in-law John and Wm. Parker; contingent bequest to his Exec: Henry Crosley.
Witnesses: James Delancy, Paul Isaac Voto.

HOOD, THOMAS. City of Philadelphia. Yeoman. Nov. 14, 1762. Dec. 6, 1762. M.432.
Children: James, Jonathan, Joseph, Sarah and Thomas. Exec: Wife Rebecca and George Palmer.
Witnesses: Joseph Garret, Stephen Paschal, Mary Peart.

BOYCE, JOSEPH. Sept. 28, 1762. Dec. 4, 1762. M.434.
Sole Legatee: Andrew More. Exec: John Winter.
Witnesses: Ralph Marshall, Robert Lumsden.

VERCO, THOMAS. May 3, 1762. Dec. 6, 1762. M.435.
Exec. and sole Legatee: Wife Mary and Thos. Harper.
Witnesses: John Creson, Jas. Hunter.

MC GONEGALL, JOHN. May 4, 1762. Dec. 8, 1762. M.436.
Exec. and sole Legatee: John Neil.
Witnesses: William Scott, Patrick Fegan.

GARDER, WILLIAM. City of Philadelphia. Physician. Nov. 25, 1762. Dec. 9, 1762. M.437.
Legatees: Sisters Elizabeth (wife of Samuel Green, barber), Sarah Green of Litchfield, Eng. and Sarah Coughlin of Philadelphia. Exec: Sarah Coughlin and John Middleton of Philadelphia, conveyancer.
Witnesses: Solomon Wilson, Evan Williams, Elizabeth Coughlin.

MC NAMARRA, CHRISTOPHER. Mariner. May 2, 1762. Dec. 8, 1762. M.438.
Exec. and sole Legatee: John Duncan (tobacconist) of Philadelphia.
Witness: Elias Cole.

THOMAS, JOHN. Merion, Co. of Philadelphia. Oct. 24, 1762. Dec. 7, 1762. M.440.
Children: Jesse and Abele. Trustees: Brothers-in-law Robert, Israel and John Roberts. Exec: Wife and sons (name of wife not given).
Witnesses: John Kite, Owen and John Roberts.

SNYDER, JOHN. Dublin, Co. of Philadelphia. Sept. 10, 1762. Dec. 8, 1762. M.441.
Wife: Plantine. Children: Geo. Adam and Catherine (wife of Jacob Reife, Junr.). Exec: Son and son-in-law.
Witnesses: John Trump, Daniel Rhinehalt.

SHRIBER, CASPER. Chestnut Hill, Co. of Philadelphia. Hatter. Nov. 29, 1762. Dec. 11, 1762. M.442.
Children: Geo., John, Nathaniel, Susannah, Juliana, Amelia and Philipina. Exec: Wife Catherine and son-in-law Philip Weaver.
Witnesses: Andrew Campbell, Martin Houser, Geo. Shriber.

MARSHALL, JOSEPH. City of Philadelphia. Bricklayer. Nov. 27, 1762. Dec. 11, 1762. M.444.
Wife: Rachel. Children: Ralph, George, Joseph, Hannah, John and Jacob. Beneficiaries: Mother Mary and sisters (names not given); the Penna. Hospital. Exec: Daniel Offley, Joseph King, Isaac Zane, Christopher Marshall.
Witnesses: Joseph Ledrn, Elizabeth Marshall, Robert Whyte, Henry Burnett.

SCOTT, WILLIAM. May 5, 1762. Dec. 11, 1762. M.447.
Exec. and sole Legatee: John Coughran.
Witnesses: Jno. Magonigle, John Makiltrick (his mark), Patrick Fegan.

BARKY, JNO. WOOLERY. Salford, Co. of Philadelphia. Yeoman. Nov. 9, 1762. Dec. 11, 1762. M.448.
Wife: Mary. Children: Michael, John, Samuel, Mary, Thomas, Salome, Isaac, Elizabeth, Christian, Abraham and Fronica. Exec: Sons John and Michael.
Witnesses: Andrew Ziegler, Henry Ledraugh, Abraham Clemens.

CARESON, ANDREW. Seaman. Nov. 10, 1762. Dec. 13, 1762. M.451.
Legatees: Daniel Collins and Thomas Careson (mariners); Jeremiah Shay. Exec: Daniel Collins.
Witnesses: George Taylor, James Wilson, James Pearson.

GRAFF, SIMON. New Hannover, Co. of Philadelphia. Freeholder. Nov. 23, 1762. Dec. 18, 1762. M.452.

Children: Son John and "a parcel of small children" (names not given). Exec: Wife Margareth.
Witnesses: Michael Walter, Adam Liebegut.

EVANS, SARAH. Spinster. July 14, 1762. Dec. 21, 1762. M.454.
Legatees: Sister Sidney Howell; nieces Sidney and Rebecca and nephew David (children of brother Evan Evans); grandniece Rebecca (daughter of Joseph and Sidney Howell). Exec: Cousin Owen Jones and Jos. Howell.
Witnesses: Cadwallader Evans, Geo. Roberts, Susanna Jones.

POWELL, DAVID. City of Philadelphia, late of Antigua. Blacksmith. Dec. 18, 1762. Dec. 23, 1762. M.455.
Legatee: Cousin David Powell (son of Howell Powell of South Wales). Exec: Wife Mary.
Witnesses: Francis Sewer, Philip Thomas, L. Bathhurst.

GEDDES, WILLIAM. May 5, 1762. Dec. 23, 1762. M.457.
Legatees: Nephew Henry Stephenson; sisters Margaret Hamilton and Sarah Latimer (wife of James). Exec: James Latimer.
Witnesses: Paul Isaac Voto, Archibald Wallace.

ENGLE, BENJAMIN. Co. of Philadelphia. Tanner. Oct. 8, 1762. Dec. 31, 1762. M.458.
Children: Charles and Ann. Father: Paul. Legatees: John Jones, Richard Johnson in trust for the Union School of Germantown. Exec: Wife Rebecca, brother Paul and brother-in-law Leonard Stoneburner.
Witnesses: Peter Smith, Christian Lehman, Thomas Rose.

ROBESON, PETER. Mariner. Oct. 10, 1762. Dec. 27, 1762. M.462.
Sole legatee: Brother George. Exec: William Appleby (housekeeper, Philadelphia), Barney McCloskey.
Witnesses: John Lawson, Reuben Emerson, Mathew Dunlap.

HAMILTON, JOHN. Seaman. Aug. 8, 1762. Jan. 3, 1763. M.462.
Beneficiaries: Seamen of ship "Francis," names not given. Exec: Thos. Osburn and John Lawson.
Witnesses: Edward Cole, Mathew Dunlap, Jas. Alexander.

ALEXANDER, JAMES. Seaman. Oct. 24, 1762. Jan. 3, 1763. M.464.

Sole legatee: Mother Anna, widow, of Ireland. Exec: Thomas Osborn (chief mate) and Jas. McCrea (seaman).
Witnesses: John Lawson, Edward Cole.

MERCHANT, JOHN. City of Philadelphia. Inn holder. Jan. 7, 1763. Feb. 1, 1763. M.465.
Children: Elizabeth, Philip, Anne, Hester and Sarah. Exec: John Pemberton (tallow chandler) and Enoch Flower (joyner) of Philadelphia.
Witnesses: James Grogin, Antony Pearson.

BATE, THOMAS. Gynead, Co. of Philadelphia. March 27, 1762. Feb. 5, 1763. M.466.
Legatees: Brother William (of Wales), niece Mary Bate; brother-in-law John Jones; nephews Joseph, William and Thomas Jones; niece Eliza Mee and her daughter; relation Samuel Mee; friend Moses Peters, Senr.; Mary (daughter of Joseph Jones). Exec: Nephew Joseph and sister Jane Jones.
Witnesses: Evan Ellis, Evan David.

WHARTON, MARY. City of Philadelphia. March 13, 1762. Feb. 9, 1763. M.467.
Legatees: Brother Joseph and his children, Thomas Senr., Samuel, Joseph, John, William, Charles, Isaac, Carpenter, Mary, Robert and Benjamin; James, Thomas Junr., John and Joseph (children of brother John Wharton); Hannah and Mary (children of nephew Thomas Wharton, Senr.); Rachel and Mary (daughters of brother John). Exec: Thomas Senr., Thomas Junr., and Rachel Wharton.
Witnesses: George Gray, Richard Smith.

MORGAN, EVAN. City of Philadelphia. Gentleman. Jan. 29, 1763. Feb. 14, 1763. M.469.
Children: Sarah (wife of Wm. Masters), Elizabeth and Ann. Sisters: Elizabeth Ross and Ann Morgan. Nieces: Margaret and Catherine Ross. Legatee: Elizabeth Page of Philadelphia. Exec: Brother-in-law John Ross and Jacob Duchee.
Witnesses: Benjamin Price, Stephen Cormick.

SUDOR, DAVID. Germantown, Co. of Philadelphia. Proved Feb. 14, 1763. M.471.

Son: Name not given. Exec: Wife Mary and John Johnson.
Witnesses testify that testator acknowledged said will, but died without affixing his signature thereto.
Witnesses: John Bowman, Jacob Reindollar, Herman Keisel.

HALL, WILLIAM. City of Philadelphia. Chapman or shop keeper. Feb. 10, 1763. Feb. 17, 1763. M.473.
Son: Thomas. Grandson: William. Exec: Wife Jane and Paul Miller (gardner) of Philadelphia.
Witnesses: Thomas Crosan, Thos. Carpenter, Wm. Gallagher.

ROBESON, RUDMAN. City of Philadelphia. Gentleman. Dec. 23, 1762. Feb. 21, 1763. M.474.
Legatees: Mother Magdalen; sister Elizabeth Vanderspiegle and her husband William; Uncle Peter Robeson and his sons Edward and Peter; Andrew son of said Peter; cousins Andrew (son of Thomas Yorke) and Israel (son of Israel Robeson); the Penna. Hospital: the Rev. Wm. Smith; negro George Hinegas.
Witnesses: Nicholas Weber, Geo. and Christian Waskey.

FASE, PHILIP. Co. of Bucks, Penna. Yeoman. Feb. 12, 1763. Feb. 23, 1763. M.476.
Children: Katharina, Philip and Eve Margaret. Exec: Wife Margaret, Herman Brill and George Songmaster.
Witnesses: Geo. Wagner, Adam Songmaster, John Jemison.

PETERS, GARRET. Montgomery, Co. of Philadelphia. Jan. 29, 1762. Feb. 25, 1763. M.477.
Wife: Margaret. Children: Moses, Hannah (Rees) and Mary (Barge). Newphew Henry (son of brother Henry Peters). Exec: Son Moses.
Witnesses: John Roberts, Evan Jones.

FRAELICK, JOHN. Co. of Philadelphia. Yeoman. Jan. 18, 1763. Feb. 16, 1763. M.479.
Children: Nicholas, Margaret, Mary and Catherine. Exec: Wife Catherine, son-in-law Christian Beck and Godfryd Deil.
Witnesses: Christian Yauch, Philip Wentzel, Christian Lehman.

BLACKWOOD, JOHN. City of Philadelphia. Inn holder. Dec. 7, 1762. March 2, 1763. M.481.

Children: Mary, Marmaduke, John, Ibison, Joseph, Atcheson and Sarah. Exec: Wife Jane and Wm.Carson (peruke maker). Witnesses: Daniel Ent, Nicholas Weber, Thomas Rose.

CUNRADS, HENRY. Upper Dublin, Co. of Philadelphia. 11 mo. 27, 1762. March 12, 1763. M.304.
Wife: Jane. Children: John, Catherine, Edward, Elizabeth, Alice, Henry and Abigail. Exec: Cornelius Cunrads and Chilion White. Witnesses: Peter and Nathaniel Cleaver, Jos. Lukens.

DOUGHERTY, DUDLEY. City of Philadelphia. Merchant. Dec. 20, 1762. March 13, 1763. M.486.
Daughter: Ann. Brother: Dennis Martin. Nephew: Patrick (son of Martin Dougherty). Exec: Wife Ann, brother Dennis and Jas. Byrne. Witnesses: Wm. Hussey, Patrick Farrell, John Reily.

STERLING, ROBERT. Parrish of Kingston, Island of Jamaica, Esquire. Nov. 16, 1763. April 7, 1764. M.487.
Proved at St. Iaago de la Vega, Jamaica. Legatees: His brothers and sisters (names of latter not given); putative daughter Charlotte; and Sarah Morris. Exec: Brothers, James (of Scotland), Archibald and William; cousin Patrick Sterling of the parish of St. James; Malcolm Laing, Wm. Gordon, Alexander Grant and Gilbert Mathison. Witnesses: Robt. Cooper, Lee Severin, Frank Sparre, Leeson Blackwood.

JENKINS, WILLIAM. Co. of Philadelphia. July 20, 1762. March 12, 1763. M.495.
Children: Joseph, Mary and John. Exec: Wife Lydia. Witnesses: Sarah Cadwaladar, Isaac Knight.

DIXON, JAMES. May 11, 1759. March 17, 1762. M.497.
Children: Robert, Mary and Sarah. Exec: Wife Elizabeth. Witnesses: Paul Isaac and Sarah Voto.

WAYNE, FRANCIS. Co. of Chester, Penna. Yeoman. Dec. 30, 1762. March 19, 1763. M.498.
Wife: Elizabeth. Children: Abraham, Michael, John, Humphrey, Hesther (wife of John Thomas), Elizabeth (Lyle) and Rebecca. Grandchildren: Mary, Sarah and Rebecca Gardner; Isaac and Jacob Wayne, (five children of daughter Rebecca, names not given); Martha

and Francis Lyle; Hannah Wayne. Brother-in-Law: Isaac Hughs. Exec: Michael and Abraham Wayne.
Witnesses: Robert Jones, Geo. Sutter, Thomas Turbett.
Codicil: Jan. 9, 1763.
Brother Isaac Wayne made Trustee.
Witnesses: Robt. Jones, Thomas Walter, Ann Rodgers.

ROBERTS, ANNE. Co. of Philadelphia. Single woman. Feb. 8, 1763. March 23, 1763. M.502.
Beneficiaries: Sisters Katherine and Margaret Sturges, Sarah and Mary Roberts; brothers John and Edward; nephew Edward Roberts; nieces Anne and Elizabeth Sturges. Exec: Brother-in-law Jonathan Sturgis.
Witnesses: William and John Johnston.

BERGENHOFF, JOHN. Co. of Philadelphia. Husbandman. Sept. 24, 1757. March 25, 1763. M.504.
Children: Margaret (Orner) and Nicholas. Grandchildren: William and John Bergenhoff. Exec: Wife Anna Katherine and Conrad Schultz.
Witnesses: Joseph Ingels, John Cunard, Patrick Menan.

MC DANIEL, HENRY. July 17, 1762. April 15, 1763. M.506.
Exec. and sole Legatee: Son Joseph.
Witnesses: Jno. Dunlap, Samuel Uppowen.

PETTY, JOHN. Co. of Philadelphia. Merchant. April 1, 1763. April 15, 1763. M.507.
Legatees: John and Samuel Petty of Great Britain; the overseers of the poor of Philadelphia; negro Hercules. Exec: Thomas Say and Jeremiah Warder.
Witnesses: John Biles, Robert Tuckniss, Peter Thomson.

EDWARDS, GEORGE. Co. of Philadelphia. Yeoman. March 28, 1763. April 15, 1763. M.508.
Children: George, William, Mary (Jones), Martha, Esther (Chapman), Jean (wife of Samuel Willis, blacksmith), Rebeckah, Agness and John. Exec: John Hufty, farmer, and Benjamin Hufty, sadler.
Witnesses: John Purnell, Thomas Stammers.

# INDEX

-C-

-G-

-K-

-L-

-O-

-S-

-T-

-U-



-V-

-W-

-Y-



-Z-

**Other books by F. Edward Wright:**

*Abstracts of Bucks County, Pennsylvania Wills, 1685-1785*

*Abstracts of Cumberland County, Pennsylvania Wills, 1750-1785*

*Abstracts of Cumberland County, Pennsylvania Wills, 1785-1825*

*Abstracts of Philadelphia County Wills, 1726-1747*

*Abstracts of Philadelphia County Wills, 1748-1763*

*Abstracts of Philadelphia County Wills, 1763-1784*

*Abstracts of Philadelphia County Wills, 1777-1790*

*Abstracts of Philadelphia County Wills, 1790-1802*

*Abstracts of Philadelphia County Wills, 1802-1809*

*Abstracts of Philadelphia County Wills, 1810-1815*

*Abstracts of Philadelphia County Wills, 1815-1819*

*Abstracts of Philadelphia County Wills, 1820-1825*

*Abstracts of Philadelphia County, Pennsylvania Wills, 1682-1726*

*Abstracts of South Central Pennsylvania Newspapers, Volume 1, 1785-1790*

*Abstracts of South Central Pennsylvania Newspapers, Volume 3, 1796-1800*

*Abstracts of the Newspapers of Georgetown and the Federal City, 1789-99*

*Abstracts of York County, Pennsylvania Wills, 1749-1819*

*Bucks County, Pennsylvania Church Records of the 17th and 18th Centuries*
*Volume 2: Quaker Records: Falls and Middletown Monthly Meetings*
Anna Miller Watring and F. Edward Wright

*Caroline County, Maryland Marriages, Births and Deaths, 1850-1880*

*Citizens of the Eastern Shore of Maryland, 1659-1750*

*Cumberland County, Pennsylvania Church Records of the 18th Century*

*Delaware Newspaper Abstracts, Volume 1: 1786-1795*

*Early Charles County, Maryland Settlers, 1658-1745*
Marlene Strawser Bates and F. Edward Wright

*Early Church Records of Alexandria City and Fairfax County, Virginia*
F. Edward Wright and Wesley E. Pippenger

*Early Church Records of New Castle County, Delaware, Volume 1, 1701-1800*

*Frederick County Militia in the War of 1812*
Sallie A. Mallick and F. Edward Wright

*Inhabitants of Baltimore County, 1692-1763*

*Land Records of Sussex County, Delaware, 1769-1782*

*Land Records of Sussex County, Delaware, 1782-1789*
Elaine Hastings Mason and F. Edward Wright

*Marriage Licenses of Washington, District of Columbia, 1811-1830*

*Marriages and Deaths from the Newspapers of Allegany and*
*Washington Counties, Maryland, 1820-1830*

*Marriages and Deaths from The York Recorder, 1821-1830*

*Marriages and Deaths in the Newspapers of Frederick and*
*Montgomery Counties, Maryland, 1820-1830*

*Marriages and Deaths in the Newspapers of Lancaster County, Pennsylvania, 1821-1830*

*Marriages and Deaths in the Newspapers of Lancaster County, Pennsylvania, 1831-1840*

*Marriages and Deaths of Cumberland County, [Pennsylvania], 1821-1830*

*Maryland Calendar of Wills Volume 9: 1744-1749*

*Maryland Calendar of Wills Volume 10: 1748-1753*

*Maryland Calendar of Wills Volume 11: 1753-1760*

*Maryland Calendar of Wills Volume 12: 1759-1764*

*Maryland Calendar of Wills Volume 13: 1764-1767*

*Maryland Calendar of Wills Volume 14: 1767-1772*

*Maryland Calendar of Wills Volume 15: 1772-1774*

*Maryland Calendar of Wills Volume 16: 1774-1777*

*Maryland Eastern Shore Newspaper Abstracts, Volume 1: 1790-1805*

*Maryland Eastern Shore Newspaper Abstracts, Volume 2: 1806-1812*

*Maryland Eastern Shore Newspaper Abstracts, Volume 3: 1813-1818*

*Maryland Eastern Shore Newspaper Abstracts, Volume 4: 1819-1824*

*Maryland Eastern Shore Newspaper Abstracts, Volume 5: Northern Counties, 1825-1829*
F. Edward Wright and Irma Harper

*Maryland Eastern Shore Newspaper Abstracts, Volume 6: Southern Counties, 1825-1829*

*Maryland Eastern Shore Newspaper Abstracts, Volume 7: Northern Counties, 1830-1834*
Irma Harper and F. Edward Wright

*Maryland Eastern Shore Newspaper Abstracts, Volume 8: Southern Counties, 1830-1834*

*Maryland Militia in the Revolutionary War*
S. Eugene Clements and F. Edward Wright

*Newspaper Abstracts of Allegany and Washington Counties, 1811-1815*

*Newspaper Abstracts of Cecil and Harford Counties, [Maryland], 1822-1830*

*Newspaper Abstracts of Frederick County, [Maryland], 1816-1819*

*Newspaper Abstracts of Frederick County, 1811-1815*

*Sketches of Maryland Eastern Shoremen*

*Tax List of Chester County, Pennsylvania 1768*

*Tax List of York County, Pennsylvania 1779*

*Washington County Church Records of the 18th Century, 1768-1800*

*Western Maryland Newspaper Abstracts, Volume 1: 1786-1798*

*Western Maryland Newspaper Abstracts, Volume 2: 1799-1805*

*Western Maryland Newspaper Abstracts, Volume 3: 1806-1810*

*Wills of Chester County, Pennsylvania, 1766-1778*

www.ingramcontent.com/pod-product-compliance
Ingram Content Group UK Ltd.
Pitfield, Milton Keynes, MK11 3LW, UK
UKHW020123290926
15471UKWH00003B/236

9 781585 490578